Management for Professionals

More information about this series at http://www.springer.com/series/10101

Wided Batat

The New Luxury Experience

Creating the Ultimate Customer Experience

 Springer

Wided Batat
B&C Consulting Group
Paris, France

ISSN 2192-8096   ISSN 2192-810X   (electronic)
Management for Professionals
ISBN 978-3-030-01670-8   ISBN 978-3-030-01671-5   (eBook)
https://doi.org/10.1007/978-3-030-01671-5

Library of Congress Control Number: 2018962965

This Springer imprint is published by the registered company Springer Nature Switzerland AG
The registered company address is: Gewerbestrasse 11, 6330 Cham, Switzerland

Praise for The New Luxury Experience...

"This book provides a holistic perspective on marketing of luxury brands, offering both useful practical advice as well as illustrating important cases."
-- Ravi Dhar, Director, Yale Center for Customer Insights, Yale University

"Wided Batat's book offers a fresh, insightful and comprehensive analysis of the concept of the consumer's experience with luxury whatever that may be. The Five experiential luxury strategies proposed by Wided highlight that luxury management should go above and beyond the design and branding of luxury goods and services. I also commend the consideration given to the younger generations' approach to luxury and to corporate social responsibility aspects. Luxury marketers should find this book very useful indeed."
-- Francesca Dall'Olmo Riley, Professor of Brand Management, Kingston Business School, UK

Preface

More than in any other sector, luxury consumption is a response to a search for emotions, pleasure, uniqueness, consideration, and greatest services. The luxury consumer wants to live experiences – not just buy luxury products or services. To meet the new demands of customers, this book offers a concrete vision of the new luxury experience and tools that will help to create a memorable and an ultimate luxury experience, both online and offline. How do we define a luxury experience? How can luxury houses design efficient, enjoyable, and memorable luxury experiences that differentiate them from their competitors? What are adequate strategies and tools? These are the questions that this book responds to, based on numerous industry examples, testimonials from luxury businesses, and mini-case studies.

This book is indeed the first to offer a concrete and analytical vision of the luxury experience and its offline and online implementation in various domains, such as luxury hotels and palaces, gastronomic restaurants, luxury retail, etc. The content offered in this book provides luxury businesses with a practical, contemporary, and multidisciplinary expertise that is useful to create a memorable luxury experience that is tailored to the emotional and functional needs of luxury customers. Using a theoretical and practical approach as well as expert opinions, figures, and illustrations of several examples of luxury brands, the reader can understand the theoretical foundation, the implementation process, and the emerging challenges related to the new experiential luxury marketing and its big five experiential luxury strategies that address the functional, emotional, hedonic, and relational needs of the new luxury consumer.

The first part of this book explores the evolution of luxury from object to experience and includes three principal chapters. In Chap. 1, I examine the idea of "luxury." Indeed, prior to defining the "luxury experience," there is first a need to explain what we mean by "luxury" and what are its origins, characteristics, and typologies. To do so, this chapter aims to trace back the rise of luxury and its shift from a traditional perspective related to conspicuous and distinctive luxury consumption to the emergence of the "luxury experience," a more emotional, sensory, and symbolic consumption of luxury. Chapter 1 takes a sociological perspective to explore people's motivations to purchase and consume luxury products and services. In sociology, luxury has been studied according to two main approaches: conspicuous (American approach) and distinctive (French approach). Existing definitions of luxury will be analyzed, and then a new definition of luxury will be offered. This chapter contributes to the field of luxury by offering an updated definition that incorporates the customer experience to explain the transition from traditional luxury marketing to the new experiential luxury marketing, which will be explained in Chap. 2.

In the second chapter, I analyze theories underpinning customer experience marketing by providing a cross-sectional analysis of diverse studies in human sciences and business disciplines that tackle the concept of "customer experience." Chapter 2 addresses the customer experience to answer the following questions: What do we know about what happens in the customer experience in luxury? How does customer experience transform luxury marketing? Does the customer experience allow luxury brands to differentiate their offers, retain their customers, and attract new ones?

I propose to start from the limits of traditional luxury marketing to better understand how luxury businesses can implement experiential luxury marketing and thus convert their experiential thinking into strategies, communication, staff training, digital strategies, and techniques of sales to distinguish themselves and develop a strong and sustainable competitive advantage.

Chapter 3 will focus on luxury brands and the necessity to introduce customer experience in order to keep up with evolving consumer behaviors and new luxury trends. Indeed, today's luxury consumers are becoming familiar with instant accessibility and will expect their luxury experiences to be personalized and emotional. Thus, luxury brands need to better understand their customers and emerging social trends in order to offer the luxury experiences consumers really want through meaningful messages that resonate through different products and marketplaces. In this chapter, I explore the key changes in consumer behaviors and the new luxury trends that affect customer experience and can help luxury businesses design suitable experiences by taking into account both tangibles (e.g., the need for high-quality products, heritage, and ancestral know-how) and intangible (e.g., emotional needs) aspects of luxury.

The second part of this book explores, throughout five chapters, the big five strategies luxury businesses should implement to design the ultimate luxury experience. In Chapter 4, I present the first strategy: capturing luxury customer values. This strategy is critical for luxury brands since the perception of luxury value is essential to the enjoyment and the satisfaction of consumers and is, consequently, of huge significance to luxury brands. The objective of this chapter is to examine consumer value as a relevant component that luxury houses should integrate into their strategies and communication campaigns. In fact, one of the big five strategies used to attract consumers and connect with them is based on capturing, sharing, and connecting with the values of their luxury consumers – if we assume that luxury goods (products and services) are also bought for their symbolism and perceived values.

In Chap. 5, I introduce the second luxury experience strategy based on the idea of the experiential branding of luxury. Luxury businesses should use this strategy to create an emotional luxury experience with a strong bond connecting the customer to the luxury brand. Instead of using brand promotion as in the 4Ps of the traditional marketing mix, the emphasis on the cultural meanings behind a luxury brand provides a necessary complement to promotional strategies by including a focus on the significances that are shaped by specific cultural settings in order to design suitable and powerful luxury experiences that are meaningful to consumers. Then, Chap. 6 will focus on the third luxury experience strategy: experiential setting design. This chapter explains the way luxury businesses can design their experiential settings by emphasizing the phygital aspect of the experiences which will guarantee the continuum between physical place and digital space. By designing experiential settings, luxury businesses will be able to create a memorable and rewarding luxury experience that makes sense and allows the luxury brand to communicate its DNA throughout the phygital experiential journey of the customer.

Chapter 7 introduces the fourth luxury experience strategy related to the human dimension in luxury: luxury staff training. Although the human value dimension guarantees a certain quality of service, customer satisfaction, and thus emphasizes the coherence in the experience, efficiently training luxury employees is often approached in a very narrow way by luxury companies. This chapter examines another strategy related to the importance of empathic training of luxury staff to provide the customer with the ultimate luxury experience that is both efficient and touching. Chapter 8, the last luxury experience strategy in part two of this book, introduces the strategy: consumer initiation to luxury. In this chapter, I introduce consumer education and consumer initiation to luxury as one of the big five strategies luxury companies should implement to empower their customers and make sure they will better enjoy their luxury experiences. I explain in this chapter the educational policies and programs luxury houses can implement to educate their customers and help them develop skills, know themselves, and enjoy novelty for a better appreciation of their luxury experiences with the brand.

The third part of this book, which relates to the future challenges facing luxury experience offerings, includes three main chapters. In Chap. 9, I introduce the first challenge related to the necessity of using alternative market research tools to understanding luxury experiences online and offline. This chapter introduces experiential and e-experiential research methods as an alternative to studying luxury experiences. Chapter 10 focuses on a second challenge that questions the way millennials and post-millennials are reshaping luxury. Indeed, millennials and post-millennials are particularly strategic targets for the luxury industry and its services. Not only does this challenge represent a significant weight for luxury, but it is also a deeply globalized issue, which is a major asset for international luxury brands. This chapter addresses the following questions: What are the expectations of millennials and post-millennials in relation to their consumption of luxury goods? What are their values, and is there possible overlapping with those values embodied by luxury brands? Do youth and luxury really need each other, and if so, what are their mutual contributions? Which luxury brands are consciously seeking to speak to this specific generation, and how do they do it? Finally, in Chap. 11, I will conclude by addressing the third challenge linked to the compatibility of luxury experiences with sustainable development and corporate social responsibility (CSR). Indeed, where sustainable development often advocates sobriety and simplicity, luxury, conversely, reflects an image of abundance and complexity. In this chapter, I explore the sustainable practices of luxury houses and the CSR strategies they can implement to create sustainable and engaged luxury experiences.

In this book, I have combined my professional expertise, my research, and prior works on the customer experience topic related to the field of luxury to introduce a new framework based on the idea of the big five strategies luxury businesses should take into account when creating and designing experiential offerings. These offerings guarantee a sustainable competitive advantage because the ultimate phygital luxury experience created (offline and online) cannot be replicated by others. This book provides an extensive review of the existing knowledge in this field as well as examples of luxury brands, and tools, that I hope will help readers, luxury businesses, researchers, students, and scholars gain a better appreciation of how we can create an ultimate and unique luxury experience and how the luxury experience can be implemented using the big five strategies in different luxury fields. Enjoy your luxury reading experience!

Paris, France   Wided Batat

Contents

Author Biography

 **Wided Batat** is a marketing professor and an internationally renowned expert and speaker on experiential and digital marketing specialized in the fields of retail, luxury, food, well-being, youth cultures, generation Z&Y, millennials and post-millennials, and tourism. She has published dozens of books in English and French and articles in top-tier academic journals that have received several awards. Professor Batat introduced an innovative and disruptive approach to global and digital customer experience by providing a strategic framework of the customer experience offline and online and the new experiential marketing mix (7Es). Entrepreneur, Professor Batat is also a bilingual (French and English) international professional trainer and the founder of B&C Consulting Group, an innovative market research and consumer insights company specialized in global and digital customer experience design, buying behavior, and consumer trends. Follow her on LinkedIn and Twitter.

List of Figures

List of Tables

List of Mini-cases

List of Testimonials

Part I

The Evolution of Luxury: From Object to Experience

Luxury, Back to Origins

1

Prior to defining the "luxury experience," we first need to explain what we mean by "luxury" and what are its origins, characteristics, and typologies. In this chapter, I'll trace back the rise of luxury and its shift from a traditional perspective grounded in the logic of conspicuous and distinctive luxury consumption to the emergence of the "luxury experience," a more emotional, sensory, and symbolic consumption of luxury. The objective of this chapter is, first of all, to explore the existing definitions of luxury by providing a summary of relevant aspects that should be retained throughout the analysis of several books and studies on luxury marketing. I'll then offer a new definition of "luxury," which is more in tune with the customer experience and today's customer perception and practice of luxury.

This chapter takes a multidisciplinary perspective on authors, particularly in sociology, who focused on luxury and the way they define luxury consumption and consumers' motivations to purchase and consume luxury products and services. In sociology, luxury has been studied according to two main approaches: conspicuous (American approach) and distinctive (French approach). These two approaches are often at the heart of the motivations that drive individuals to buy and consume luxury brands and goods (products and services). These two perspectives are embedded within two cultural settings, French and American, in which the definition of luxury is shaped and which can help luxury brand managers understand the different motivations of luxury consumption.

1.1 French and American Perspectives on Luxury

This section introduces the French and American perspectives through two major theories: (1) the theory of leisure class or "conspicuous consumption" introduced by the American anthropologist Thorstein Veblen in the United States in 1899 and (2) the "distinction theory" of the sociologist Pierre Bourdieu published later in France in 1979. These two theories have, in fact, dominated studies on the consumption of

© Springer Nature Switzerland AG 2019
W. Batat, *The New Luxury Experience*, Management for Professionals,
https://doi.org/10.1007/978-3-030-01671-5_1

luxury in many disciplines (e.g., sociology, history, psychology, economics, etc.) which then contributed to the study of luxury in the marketing and consumer behavior field.

1.1.1   Conspicuous Luxury

The "conspicuous consumption" theory of the anthropologist Thorstein Veblen has contributed much to the understanding of the characteristics of the consumption of luxury items and brands. Veblen states that the motivation of the individual to purchase luxury items is to define a social status which should be recognized by all the other social actors belonging to the same social sphere. Throughout understanding luxury consumption practices within the old American aristocracy to the adoption of luxury and its codes by new emerging social classes, such as the bourgeoisie and new rich (e.g., wealthy traders from the provinces), Veblen identified the traits related to the consumption of luxury within these different social classes. These luxury traits can be summarized as follows:

- In the Roman times, wealth preceded power, and abundance indicated the level of influence and power. Money reflected strength and power, so people had to show that they have money by exhibiting their rare and valuable objects.
- In the imperial society, competition between politicians generates ostentation, which provokes the pleasure of being envied and, consequently, contributes to belittling envious people. The gift of luxurious presents, although it does not reflect one's real financial situation, is a common motto among politicians. The main purpose of this practice, although it may harm the donor, is the assurance and the gain of a high social status. This practice has also been observed among aristocrats who ruin themselves by living beyond their means or by offering valuable gifts in order to maintain their social position.
- Unlike aristocrats, who may struggle to keep their rank in society, the wealthy, new bourgeois has a more rational and realistic approach to luxury consumption and its contribution to his/her social status. The bourgeoisie also views such lavish practices as "wasteful."

Veblen has also identified other forms of waste: "conspicuous/visible leisure," which consists of dedicating time to unproductive tasks such as reading, learning dead languages (e.g., Latin), music, etc. The conspicuous consumption practices and the desire to show one's wealth can also be expressed through activities that are not related to productive work. The United States of the 1920s is an iconic era that reflects in a very obvious manner conspicuous consumption practices proudly displayed by a certain group of wealthy American people. For example, F. Scott Fitzgerald's novel *The Great Gatsby*, as adapted for the big screen, perfectly portrays the conspicuous lifestyle of the rich new Americans by examining the life of a young millionaire "Gatsby" born from a modest background. The conspicuous lifestyle of this rich young man was mainly illustrated by his luxurious and extravagant receptions to which were invited the notables of the city. This allowed the young, rich man to generate for himself a "legitimate" and "recognized" image of wealth and, consequently, seduce a young woman belonging to the aristocratic American society.

These kinds of practices did not disappear; instead they still persist in our contemporary consumer societies in which the middle-upper classes, whether they are Western, Eastern, or from other cultures, are often led to develop and adopt conspicuous consumption lifestyles for several reasons, such as social anxiety, the desire to rise in social status, the search for new consumer experiences, self-esteem enhancement, etc. These examples highlight the *evolutionary factors* (according to the era) and *changing* aspects (following social motivations and cultural settings) of the conspicuous consumption of luxury. This type of consumption can be defined by drawing on the work of the sociologist Pierre Bourdieu and his concept of "capital" disseminated in marketing and consumer studies. Table 1.1 summarizes the different types of conspicuous consumption of luxury classified according to four dimensions of the individual's capital, cultural, social, economic, and symbolic, as well as a new dimension I have added, which is very important for studying luxury experiences: "emotional capital."

As shown in Table 1.1, we can assume that the conspicuous consumption of luxury has a strong link with an individual's emotions and symbolism as well as the meanings individuals assign to their luxury consumption practices, which are anchored within a particular cultural setting and are shaped by certain social norms and codes.

Following Veblen's definition, the conspicuous consumption of luxury is not only related to the usefulness of the objects and the types of goods consumed; it is also considered according to its orientation and the motivations of the individuals to

Table 1.1 Five typologies of conspicuous luxury

Type	Objective	Consumption sphere	Example
Economic conspicuous luxury	The goal of luxury is to show economic power, a high standard of living, and wealth	Exterior sphere	Luxury car, luxury houses, etc.
Social conspicuous luxury	The goal is to show social success and high social status	Exterior sphere	Luxury leisure activities, travel, etc.
Cultural conspicuous luxury	The goal is to communicate values, social and individual identity, and belonging to a certain consumer culture	Exterior and interior/private sphere	Luxury clothing, accessories, etc.
Symbolic conspicuous luxury	Self-oriented and serves to attribute meaning to luxury consumption	Interior/private sphere	Wine, art and master paintings, vintage cars, etc.
Emotional conspicuous luxury	It is a consumption to fill emotional, social, intellectual gaps, etc.	Interior/private sphere	Luxury spa and wellness, luxury prostitution, etc.

purchase and buy luxury goods (products and services). Veblen emphasizes the idea that the individual does not consume in order to merely satisfy a tangible need. His/her main expectation is not only related to the utility aspect of the good or service consumed, but it is also related to how individuals *consume in order to defend their social status in the society and preserve their honor.* Thus, conspicuous luxury operates by sending tacit social signs as well as explicit messages, visible or invisible, directly or indirectly, to other social actors who can decode them by referring to luxury objects and lifestyles displayed by individuals. The four components of conspicuous consumption of luxury, visible, symbolic, identity, and social, are all related to each other, function in an uninterrupted interaction, and are connected to the evolution of consumption experiences throughout time and within different cultural settings (Fig. 1.1).

The four key elements exposed in Fig. 1.1, namely, visibility, symbolism, identity, and social belonging are explained in the next section.

- *Visible luxury.* It is an integral part of the conspicuous luxury consumption that allows individuals to display and communicate their wealth and social status in order to attract and retain the esteem and the consideration of others. To achieve this objective, individuals display luxury items and brands that encompass suitable social meanings to communicate their values. These values can be decoded by other social actors by focusing on three main aspects that make luxury visible:
  - The desire to express one's identity;
  - Its recognition by others;
  - A high visibility of the good, in other words *worn to be seen.*

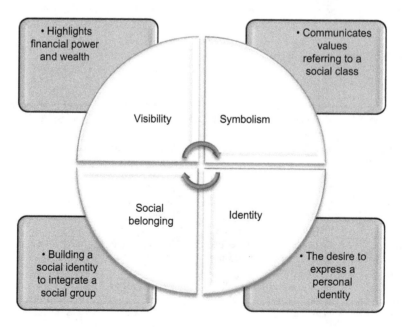

Fig. 1.1 The components of conspicuous consumption

Veblen argues that the purchase of luxury goods allows individuals to highlight their financial power and wealth. Furthermore, excessive, outrageous, and socially unacceptable visible behaviors may be associated with the desire to make luxury not only visible but also *transgressive* (e.g., lighting cigars by burning $100 bills or Instagram's #Rich Kids of Beverley Hills).

Mini-case 1.1

Visible luxury in the digital age: When rich young people show off on Instagram

In the digital age, visible luxury is expressed without complex or shame on social media where it is also shared and commented on by others. Tumblr's #rich kids of Instagram is a perfect illustration of the expression of "uninhibited luxury" in today's contemporary and digital Western societies (e.g., #rich kids of Beverly Hills, #rich kids of France) or even Eastern consumer societies (#rich kids of Teheran). In these online communities, the rule is that luxury should be displayed and obviously seen and noticed by others.

This conscious and desired exhibition of luxury brands and items speaks to the desire of these wealthy young people to express their identity, to be recognized by others, and to make visible their wealthy status by displaying luxury in an artistic, creative, ostentatious, and sometimes provocative manner.

The hashtag #rich kids of Instagram is a combination of visible and obvious clichés regarding wealthy and materialistic, spoiled young people that are posted on the social media site Instagram where the golden youth of the world shares its luxurious everyday life. On vacation, partying on a yacht with friends, or unveiling their new luxury watches, these young people, who have always known this luxurious environment, assume and share external signs of wealth in a logic of competition and provocation. On Tumblr, one can notice there is a lot of opulence that shows young people's favorite luxury brands, luxury leisure habits, ability to travel by private jet, etc.

Therefore, the visibility of luxury can be explained by focusing on three main levels: intimate luxury, open internal luxury, and external luxury (Table 1.2). These levels are closely related to individuals' social spheres and the kind of luxury good they consume.

- **Symbolic luxury**. The symbolism of conspicuous luxury refers to luxury goods that have a symbolic meaning anchored within a particular social context or within a certain brand community. Thus, luxury goods go beyond a simple utilitarian logic and are considered in these communities as an extension of the individual's personal and social identity by displaying conspicuous but meaningful behaviors and attitudes toward luxury through:

  - A conspicuous consumption of luxury used by individuals to convey a set of signs and values referring to a style of consumption linked to a higher social class.

Table 1.2 Three dimensions of visible luxury

Dimension	Characteristic
Intimate sphere	Hidden luxury is not accessible to external actors and, therefore, cannot be considered conspicuous consumption. Consumer goods are part of the intimate space that the possessor chooses to share or not to share with people according to various motivations
Open internal sphere	It refers to the social and family environment. This can include such things as decorating personal, interior spaces with works of art and paintings that are exposed but not used
External sphere	Refers to all the external signs of ostentatious/conspicuous consumption (e.g., accessories and luxury cars that convey a wealthy image, a high social position, and prosperity)

- The search for social symbols in luxury allows consumers to differentiate themselves and affirm their unique identity while maintaining a close relation to a given social group.
- The purchase of luxury products is driven by the appropriation of symbols desired by the individual to satisfy his/her needs of social belonging to a reference group that displays similar values and lifestyle.
- In luxury consumption, in which the display of conspicuous consumption is obvious, we can name two sectors: fashion and automotive. In these sectors, many symbolic reasons can encourage the consumer to buy a particular luxury car or a luxury brand outfit.

Furthermore, consumers can use luxury goods for a double purpose: (1) in order to convey a message to their reference group (the group they belong to) or to their aspiration group (the social group they would like to join thanks to the consumption of similar luxury goods and brands) and (2) in order to build a social identity (e.g., "me" as seen by others when I wear these luxury clothes or when I drive this luxury car). Identity construction and social belonging created by consuming luxury are, therefore, two critical factors that contribute to improving the individual's well-being at the personal, relational, and social level.

Mini-case 1.2

Rolex, a symbolic and social expression of one's identity

Beyond the functional dimension and the ancestral know-how of the Haute Horlogerie brand, the Rolex watch meets the expectations of consumers who are looking for both symbolic and social dimensions. This type of motivation is particularly characteristic of the luxury watchmaking industry in which statutory consumption is an integral part of Rolex's identity that seeks to satisfy symbolic needs beyond functional aspects and the know-how of the watch brand.

(continued)

Mini-case 1.2 (continued)

Customers who buy a Rolex watch would then seek psychological compensation for unsatisfied symbolic and social needs. The purchase of a Rolex watch is therefore a dream and a symbolic projection in an aspirational world, in other words, the aspiration that is related to the universe of the Rolex brand, the history of the house, its heritage, its values, its reputation, or even its prestige.

In contrast to the functional motivation (e.g., the quality of the watch or the technology used), the brand (Rolex) becomes a priority over the product (watch), and it is especially its capacity to embody the concept of "ideal self" of the consumer which will motivate the decision of purchase and especially the adhesion to the universe of the brand.

- **Identity**. Personal identity is unique and reflects the real "me" that includes all the elements that belong to it, such as personality, lived experiences, and attitudes. This personal identity, although unique, is composed of several dimensions:
  - "Spiritual self" or self-awareness;
  - "Social self" referring to the identity of the individual as seen by others;
  - "Physical self" including hair color, eyes, size, etc.

The consumption of luxury goods can, therefore, affect one or all of these three "me's." For example, by displaying luxury brands, individuals hope to gain recognition and legitimacy at the level of their "social self," which is important in the conspicuous consumption of luxury since it signifies the way one is perceived by others who can decode his/her acts of consumption that are often associated with one's personality. In this perspective, the consumer attempts to buy luxury goods and brands that convey an image of him/herself and allow him/her to connect with his/her reference group or strengthen his/her position as well as his/her differentiation among his/her own social group.

Mini-case 1.3

"Vegan-luxury" identity: Stella McCartney to build a committed, modern, and responsible identity

Stella McCartney is a vegan and eco-friendly luxury brand and company. The brand claims a responsible, honest, and committed identity and federates around itself consumers who define themselves and perceive themselves as such.

(continued)

Mini-case 1.3 (continued)

The differentiation of the brand vis-à-vis its competitors lies in its commitment and fight against animal abuse in order to meet the needs of fashion while being in tune with a consumer who is aware of the impact that his/her luxury consumption has on the environment.

This committed luxury consumer defines him/herself as unique in relation to his/her environmental values and principles. He/she buys luxury brands that respect his/her ideology. In addition to its commitment, the luxury brand Stella McCartney also works to develop innovations that replace animal raw materials by using similar products of non-animal origin, guaranteeing modernism, comfort, and aesthetics without guilt or shame.

On its website, the brand also displays its identity, its philosophy, and its vision of luxury through an engaged discourse, "Our Sustainable Commitment," which focuses on three main aspects: responsibility, honesty, and modernism.

- **Social belonging**. The conspicuous consumption of luxury allows individuals to identify with certain social groups. Norms in social groups can influence the conspicuous consumption of individuals. Indeed, the purchase of a luxury good (product and service) should obey the dominant values and meanings in the social group individuals belong to. Thus, the social group is as important as the symbolism of the conspicuous consumption of luxury. Therefore, if a luxury brand would like its products to be adopted by consumers, it should make them stand out or assimilate them according to the symbols and codes of the consumption culture within a particular social group.

Mini-case 1.4

Porsche GTS community and the art of belonging to the Porschists community

The German sports car brand Porsche adopts a strategy focused on the relationship with its customers through the launch of a community of Porschists who meet each other to discuss the brand's models as well as the social and sporting activities around luxury sports cars. By launching its GTS models (Grand Touring Sports), Porsche wanted to show to its current and potential customers that its cars were made for beautiful roads, with elegance, and sportiness.

The Porsche GTS app was launched by the brand to federate its customers around its values. If the Community App is for Porsche customers, it can easily be employed by many other users for its usefulness. The app allows

(continued)

Mini-case 1.4 (continued)

Porschists to discover the most beautiful GTS roads all over the world. The system is based on Google Maps. One can zoom in on a region as well as choose the roads and consult the user's appreciation. Porsche's communication through this app is focused on discovering the pleasure of driving on the most beautiful roads.

Furthermore, Porschists can help enrich the app by creating Porsche courses and sharing their favorite roads with other GTS enthusiasts. The objective of Porsche is to connect the Porschists community and enhance the exchange between its members who can feel free to propose and share beautiful roads.

1.1.2 Distinctive Luxury

The consumption of luxury and the motivations behind it can be explained by the theory of distinction that the French sociologist Pierre Bourdieu introduced in 1979. Although this theory is based on certain principles of Veblen's approach to conspicuous consumption, Bourdieu does not relate directly to the theory of the leisure class. In the Bourdieusian perceptive, the consumption of luxury is seen as a means that allows individuals to distinguish themselves from the massive trend of consumption prevalent in the society. In the theory of distinction, Bourdieu explains that the upper classes that are trying to distinguish themselves construct and affirm an identity of their own. Luxury goods (products and services) are transformed into symbols of power that convey their specific culture and communicate their high social status.

For example, the codes and sociocultural norms of brands, such as Dior, Chanel, or Yves Saint Laurent, are defined according to the brand identity DNA and are part of different luxury cultures whose codes are aimed at different profiles of women. While the codes that Chanel wishes to communicate to its female clients refer to the elegance of women who are considered sophisticated seductresses and who like to be noticed, for Yves Saint Laurent, the codes are rather related to a profile of a woman who wants to be fatal, independent, inaccessible, and in competition with men. Table 1.3 highlights the distinction between the codes of two luxury brand cultures: Dior and Chanel.

The consumption of luxury, therefore, reflects an important social function. It allows the establishment of connections and relationships with other social actors belonging to reference groups. In this case, the conspicuous and distinctive consumption of luxury guides the preferences and choices of luxury goods and brands consumed and exhibited in the public sphere. Therefore, the consumption of visible and identifiable luxury brands contribute to the affirmation of one's identity and social status. In the Bourdieusian perspective, to be distinctive, luxury should be

Table 1.3 Two distinctive luxury cultures: Dior vs. Chanel

Elements of differentiation	Dior	Chanel
Profile of the female target	Respect for tradition, insolence, and daring The idea of a flower-woman	Elegance and simplicity The idea of style that does not go out of time
Values	Refinement, energy, and madness	Modernity, freedom of the woman, and perfection
Iconic products	Perfume J'adore, Lady Dior bag, Dior Addict Lipstick	Chanel perfume N°5, Chanel suite, the little black dress "La Petite Robe Noir"
Codes	Bright colors, prints, and flowers	Black and white, pearls, quilted materials
Artistic director	Maria Grazia Chiuri	Karl Lagerfeld
Ambassadors related to the universe of the brand	Nathalie Portman, Monica Bellucci, Sharon Stone, etc.	Emma Watson, Marilyn Monroe, Lilly-Rose Depp, etc.

inaccessible, exclusive, rare, and new. If luxury becomes widely diffused, it loses its distinctive value and becomes commonplace, mundane, and trivialized. Therefore, luxury brands should find a balance between diffusion and banalization of luxury by remaining attentive to the extension of the brand's domain and its associations with other consumer goods and brands.

Mini-case 1.5

Pierre Cardin, from exclusive luxury to mundane brand

Pierre Cardin is one of the luxury fashion brands that have become commonplace because of a massive democratization generated by the over-selling of the designer's name. Today, the brand is associated with a wide variety of products that do not necessarily have a link with the brand's universe and DNA (e.g., Cardin chocolate sold in supermarkets). Thus, by popularizing its name in various products, the Pierre Cardin brand has lost its luxury value and has become commonplace.

The distinct theory of the consumption of luxury highlights the importance of status and social life that are structured around codes, symbols, and negotiation strategies. Every consumer plays a specific social role by consuming certain types of luxury goods and brands to affirm his/her social status while differentiating his/her identity. Through the consumption of certain luxury brands, the consumer makes a representation of him/herself and expresses his/her values. Thus, the two theories refering to a French perspective (distinctive luxury) and an American perspective (conspicuous luxury) are very complementary and provide a profound comprehension of the social and symbolic dimensions associated with the consumption of luxury and the motivation behind it. This idea supports my proposal for a redefinition of luxury, which is at the heart of this book and which refers to luxury as a *personal experience* that offers a major focus on the intangible dimensions of luxury beyond the functional aspects and incorporates symbolic, social, ideological, subjective, and emotional dimensions. Thus, my definition highlights the conceptualization of luxury in marketing using an experiential approach that takes into account different perceptions and applies a bottom-up approach of what luxury means from a consumer's perspective. In the next section, I explain the multinational aspect of luxury, explore its multiple approaches, and offer a new accurate definition that can be useful for luxury professionals and academia.

1.2   Redefining Luxury Through Seven Main Perspectives

In this section, I explore the different definitions given to luxury by authors in the marketing field. By analyzing prior studies that dealt with luxury consumption, I noticed that defining luxury, its sector, and its categories in a precise way is not a very easy task because it is viewed as a sector in which luxury can be defined according to several approaches: by price, quality, exclusivity, and regulations, as well as by economic and social market actors. These approaches make it almost impossible to define luxury. For this reason, I attempt in this section to redefine luxury by approaching it from a global standpoint, bringing together different perspectives.

Most studies analyzing the luxury sector highlight the difficulty of defining luxury and its typologies. Existing definitions are far from convincing and are limited to certain types of practices, goods, or luxury brands. Definitions also vary among luxury players. For example, Karl Lagerfeld defines luxury in a very subjective way "my greatest luxury is not having to justify myself to anyone" and in another definition "luxury is the freedom of mind, independence, in short the politically incorrect" or as stated by Coco Chanel "luxury is not the opposite of poverty but that of vulgarity." If we seek a more exhaustive definition of luxury, we can find it in dictionaries that define luxury as a lifestyle characterized by large expenditures devoted to the acquisition of unnecessary goods, for a taste of the world's ostentation and greater well-being.

In marketing, Kapferer and Bastien explained the difficulty related to the definition of luxury. They evoke a definitional blur of luxury, which in some studies is considered as a "category" and in others as a "field of application" (sector of activity). The two authors associated the notion of the brand with that of luxury to propose an updated definition of luxury: "the concept of luxury is not a category in the absolute, but a relative set that cannot be dissociated from the political and social structure of the century to which it belongs" (2015:53). By drawing on this definition, I can say luxury is in each of us. It is produced by and for the individuals who practice it. What is luxury for some is commonplace for others. The same brands can be perceived as luxurious or not according to how they are defined, perceived, and consumed by those who wear them. On the other hand, if a consumer is asked what luxury means for him/her, a variety of responses can be expected from the same individual depending on how his/her lifestyle changes.

However, luxury has often been defined in terms of a single chosen perspective that makes the concept ambiguous and non-operational from a managerial standpoint. To propose a new definition that is both global and operational, I offer an analytical work that highlights seven main perspectives according to which luxury can be defined: institutional, organizational, academic, media, craftsmanship, consumer, and historic and cultural (Fig. 1.2). These perspectives are explained in the next section.

Following the identification of these seven perspectives, it seems important to propose a new definition of luxury based on the perspective chosen to define luxury.

A New Definition of Luxury
Luxury is both evolving and multidimensional. It gathers several meanings that the individual assigns to it according to the norms and codes of his/her own consumption culture. These meanings evolve with time as well as with social and individual changes. Luxury is also closely tied to the culture and practices of the group in which it emerges, shapes, and develops. Therefore, luxury is in all of us. It is produced by and for the individuals and professionals, institutions as well as by political and social actors who practice it. What is luxury for some is, therefore, mundane for others. Thus, the definition of luxury depends on the chosen perspective that must be identified beforehand.

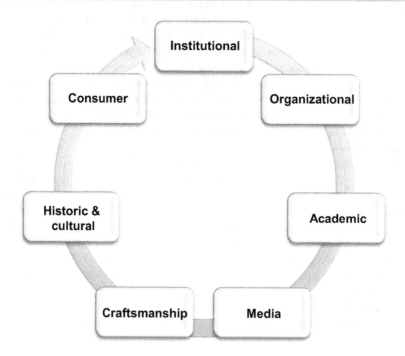

Fig. 1.2 Seven main perspectives of luxury

1.2.1 Institutional Perspective: How Does Regulation Define Luxury?

In the institutional perspective, public organizations define luxury according to economic and social criteria. For example, in France, the Office of the Economic and Social Council commissioned in 2007 a study on luxury, the production of goods and rendering of services in the luxury sector. This study was commended to the section of productive activities, research, and technology with the main objective of delivering recommendations aimed at sustaining employment and training, identifying all the luxury actors in their diversity, and ensuring the transmission of the French know-how in the luxury sector.

To meet these objectives, the committee was required to look into the question of the definition of blur, namely, what luxury is and what it is not, prior to the selection of luxury market actors to study. In fact, the conclusions of the previous study on luxury carried out in 1996 by the Economic and Social Council underscored the difficulty of precisely defining the perimeter of a multiform sector, such as luxury. While the economic delimitation of luxury is difficult to grasp, the French administrative regulations have solved this problem by proposing a definition based on the logic of "activity categorization." In France, the luxury sector has always been strictly regulated since the decree of January 29, 1945, which distinguishes luxury from other segments of the same activity. The decree defines 17 activities related to luxury that include all industries, craftsmanship, and creative activities, ranging from art, floral art, and leather to music publishing and throughout fashion as well as jewelry.

In the report of the 2007 study, the Office of the Economic and Social Council identified the criteria differentiating luxury from premium by adapting the components of marketing mix to luxury. In addition to these criteria, the committee members who worked on this study were able to identify a very important complementary dimension, namely, the link between *tradition* and *innovation*.

1.2.2 Organizational Perspective: Luxury Defined by the Industry

Luxury groups and industries believe that the definition of luxury should keep its specificity unclear. In doing so, the definition of luxury is considered part of the responsibility of advertising and merchandising departments that deal with the design of luxury based on targets and markets. For example, the groups LVMH and Kering assert that this definitional approach is the only effective approach since it allows several products and brands, which sometimes do not have similar characteristics, to be grouped under the same "luxury" category. The role of advertising and merchandising is, therefore, to convince consumers that these products and brands belong to the field of luxury.

For this reason, luxury groups and businesses are implementing various techniques, such as storytelling and dream marketing, to define luxury and build a luxurious universe that brings together goods of various origins, ranging from prestigious and expensive products (e.g., Sonia Rykiel outfits) to goods identified under the same luxury brand (e.g., Sonia Rykiel bath towels). This strategy is often complemented by the implementation of a planned obsolescence to arouse desire and encourage the consumer to renew his/her purchase. Thus, the popularization of brand names has reached its peak with the declination of several major luxury brands that formerly embodied a field of expertise.

1.2.3   Academic Perspective on Luxury

Most disciplines in the humanities and social sciences, ranging from philosophy and sociology to economics and marketing, have all studied luxury. Each discipline approaches it according to perspectives and paradigms that are relevant to its field (e.g., defining luxury by the price in economics, luxury as social representations in sociology, etc.). In sociology, the question of the definition of luxury has been studied according to two logics: conspicuous and distinctive. Furthermore, luxury in the social sciences has always been linked to another concept: the "taste" of social elites. For sociologists, luxury goods are elite consumer products that highlight their character in terms of taste and social organization.

Sociology defines luxury goods as a collection of all expensive products reserved for social elites. This definition has some shortcomings, as luxury goods may also be used by other classes in search of social meanings. Therefore, how can the question of the definition of luxury be asked? To answer this question, we should explore the concept of "taste" in the adoption of luxury goods (products and services) and social representations. Although individuals say they like luxury goods, this love is a pretext that allows them to achieve social goals in terms of social elevation, recognition, differentiation/distinction, identity building, socialization, belonging, etc.

However, while sociology emphasizes the link between "taste" and "luxury" to underline the dynamic of social representations that lead to imitation and differentiation, in economics, luxury has been defined in a very pragmatic way, according to the price of goods (products and services). The economic approach to luxury is based on the principle of price elasticity and demand. It defines luxury according to a segmentation of the market in three segments differentiating luxury from other sectors: *inferior goods*, *goods of necessity*, and *luxury goods*. This categorization, although practical and easy to apply, raises criticisms related to its reductive nature.

In marketing, existing studies go beyond the economic approach, beyond the contributions of social sciences to define luxury and its dimensions. From this perspective, marketing authors have attempted to define luxury through the establishment of a categorization of all luxury goods (products and services). Table 1.4 summarizes the different definitions and categories of luxury identified by the main authors in marketing.

Table 1.4 Luxury categorizations in marketing

Author	Classification criteria	Type of categories
Bearden and Etzel (1982)	Need Consumption sphere	Public goods Private assets Luxury consumed in public sphere Luxury consumed in private sphere
Castera et al. (2003)	Waste vs. dream	Luxury as waste is found in the price difference between a product that offers the same functionality and is considered wasteful A dream luxury refers to image and representation related to luxury. Luxury brands are linked to a dream world
Alleérès (2003)	Accessibility	The inaccessible luxury targets the very well-off class This is the domain of the most valuable brands and products. The clientele is distinctive and is sensitive to perfection, rarity, originality, and prestige. This luxury brings together reference products The intermediate luxury: a declension of famous brands in limited series. The target is sensitive to the quality and prestige of brands The luxury accessible through the large series of declensions of luxury brands. Less affluent customers are sensitive to content and value for money
Dubois and Duquesne (1993) Dubois and Paternault (1993)	Product prices	Accessible and cheap luxury: a bottle of champagne over $20, a bottle of perfume or glasses of a luxury brand, etc. Exceptional luxury includes luxury clothes over $1,500, diamonds, etc.
Castarède (2003)	Hybrid criteria according to the purpose and profile of the target	The Superluxe is accessible to a select few (e.g., haute couture, luxury watchmaking, fine jeweler, rare dishes, yachts, automobiles, etc.) The luxury of social or economic valorization (e.g., scarves, ready-to-wear, luggage, pens, watches, etc.) The luxury of sensations and pleasures (e.g., perfumes, hobbies, gastronomy, etc.)
Kapferer and Bastien (2015)	Dream, seduction, and realism	Dream luxury is positioning out of time and not aiming at social elevation Premium properties linked to realism with a positioning according to the quality/price ratio Fashion is linked to seduction

1.2.4 Media Perspective on Luxury

The luxury and fashion media have also contributed to the definition of luxury and its related items. Some luxury online magazines define luxury as a dream generated by various elements of the luxury universe, such as atmosphere, materials, architecture, products, attitudes, and employees' elegance. The definitions given by the media go far beyond the main component, which is commerce and sales, by underscoring the existence of a universe of desire, pleasure, identification, image, serenity, and elegance. From a media perspective, luxury can also be referred to as refinement, high prices, dreams, preciousness, and celebrity – aspects that are part of extraordinary moments and things that individuals can engage in to please, seduce, and have fun.

Mini-case 1.6

Luxury according to fashion and luxury magazines

According to media and magazines specializing in fashion and luxury, luxury is defined as a form of emancipation, an ability to choose and enjoy one's choices. Luxury is also related to product features, for example, a lipstick case that does not scratch. It is the comfort of what one wears and its fluidity of use. It is at the same time soft, modern, and tactile. Luxury is what makes everything possible: sweetness, pleasure, and protection. Yet, luxury also goes beyond the product. More than a representation through an object, true luxury is an experience.

Luxury is an emotion, something that has no rational sense that is felt before defining itself. In the 1980s and 1990s, luxury was defined by the possession. Nowadays, luxury is linked to the feeling of fullness that it provides. Luxury can also be linked to rare moments that one can spend with his/her family, for example. Therefore, things become luxurious only from the moment when we can, at the end of the day, do without it. Thus, luxury is in everyone and in every single moment.

1.2.5 Craftsmanship Perspective on Luxury

The craftsmanship perspective has a definition of luxury that is rooted in the ground of its application. For example, in France, becoming an artisan, it is necessary that the profession should be listed in the official ranking of craftsmanship established by the local administration. This list includes various trades, ranging from a taxi driver and plumber, who are both artisans, to luxury craftsmanship, such as a leather tanner. Faced with this divergence of professions, "Artisanat, the first company in France," has created another category-appellation to distinguish the best artisans, those, who by their search for excellence, are naturally between art and crafts, distinguished from other professions that do not require know-how, tradition, and excellence, such as electrician.

The best artisans are classified and ranked in the "Artisanat" list and are part of a very small recognized group of people who collaborate with luxury brands, have superior quality products, target a wealthy clientele, and practice high prices that are justified by an expertise that is sometimes ancestral. This distinction enhances the interest of luxury businesses for this group because of its creative potential and the stories related to its artisanal craftsmanship. In the common unconscious, craftsmanship is inseparable from luxury in the minds of consumers. This association, created by marketing and communication messages, contributes to the emergence of a confusion in the definition of luxury from the point-of-view of craftsmen and artisans, who are often subject to pressure from luxury groups (e.g., speed, high prices excluding potential customers, etc.). The divergence between luxury groups and craft suppliers is reflected in a definition of luxury according to the perspective of artisans and the way they define luxury, which highlights a strong link with the following aspects:

- High quality of the goods;
- Ancestral manufacturing methods;
- Transmission of know-how;
- Satisfaction and proximity with customers;
- Accessible prices defined by the quality of the product and its rarity.

1.2.6 Historic and Cultural Perspectives: Does Luxury Have a Culture and a History?

Cultural diversity and the democratization of access to luxury, especially in emerging countries and among the new rich, generate a great diversity in the definition of what luxury is. Luxury brands are facing this growing cultural diversity of their customers by adapting their products and services as well as their communication to each cultural context and group. The luxury consumption observed in each context is anchored in the local culture as well as in the history of luxury, its emergence, and advances within each cultural setting. Drawing on the work of the historian Jean Castadère (2007), who defines the history of luxury, I offer, in Fig. 1.3, a classification of the cultural and historical evolution of luxury over four centuries, from its emergence to the present.

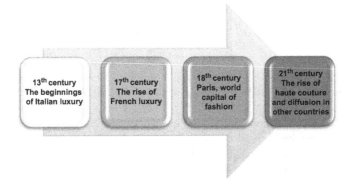

Fig. 1.3 Luxury development in history

The cultural and historical evolution of luxury means luxury brands will have to face major challenges in the future in terms of being able to establish a balance between their historical customers (e.g., French, North American, European, etc.) and their new customers (e.g., Chinese, Russian, Indian, African, etc.), whose discovery, adoption, and acculturation of luxury is very recent. Following this perspective, the definition of luxury is, therefore, primarily cultural: the French definition of luxury is not similar to North American luxury and even very different when compared to Chinese, Russian, or Arab luxury.

Mini-case 1.7

Amouage, a luxury perfume with the essence of Arab culture

Amouage is a luxury perfume company founded in 1983 in the Sultanate of Oman at the request of Sultan Qabus Ibn Saïd who wanted to publicize the Arab tradition of luxury perfumes worldwide. The first perfume was designed in 1984 by Guy Robert, a perfumer from Grasse (French perfume town). As for the packaging and the bottle, it is Asprey, a London brand of luxury goods that have been commissioned to design bottles made of semi-precious stones, silver, gold, etc. Amouage aimed to create the first Omani luxury fragrance brand by integrating both historical and cultural dimensions of the Arab culture.

Oman has been a land of perfumes for thousands of years, and the scent is rooted in its culture and the traditions of its people. By reconnecting with its traditional know-how rooted in the culture and history of Oman, Amouage has incorporated this intangible heritage into a process of development characterized by creativity and originality that position the brand in a very strong way on the international market.

The brand has also thought to protect its know-how as well as its aesthetic creativity through the intellectual property or patent to continue to disseminate its exclusive products representing a culture, a history, a know-how, and also Arab traditions around the world.

If we consider a cultural perspective, other cultures have other stories and traditions. For instance, French luxury has its origins in the habits of the ancient families of aristocracy and high society. In France, luxury is not only the symbol of social success, but also of refinement and the love of what is "beautiful" and "refined." French luxury combines tradition, craftsmanship, and elegance and is considered a major pillar of the national economy. It has an international reputation differentiating it from other countries, its own know-how, and its luxury goods and brands that make its reputation.

> **Mini-case 1.8**
>
> **French luxury, a source of inspiration at the international level**
>
> French luxury is a reference on the international scene and has served as an example for many countries that have embarked on the adventure of luxury. For example, the beginnings of watchmaking and haute-horlogerie in Switzerland or Italy and its luxury positioning by its leather and haute couture lines. According to the Deloitte global study "Powers of Luxury Goods" published in June 2015, French luxury brands are in the lead. In the study, global luxury players were ranked according to their turnover in 2013. It has been established by selecting four main activities of the luxury industry:
>
> - Bags and accessories;
> - Designer clothes (ready-to-wear);
> - Jewelry and watchmaking;
> - Perfumes and cosmetics.
>
> The ranking of the study has once again placed the French group LVMH as the number one world luxury leader in the top 100, with sales reaching 21.7 billion euros in 2013. The second place was attributed to the Swiss group Richemont, which owns the Cartier watch and jewelry house, Van Cleef & Arpels; Montblanc follows in the ranking with a turnover of 13.4 billion dollars. The US cosmetics group Estée Lauder was ranked third with $10.9 billion in sales in 2013.
>
> *Source: Deloitte study "Powers of Luxury Goods" at http://www2.deloitte. com/en/en/pages/consumer-business/articles/global-powers-of-luxury- goods-2015.html accessed 5 September 2017*

Furthermore, Dubois and Laurent (1996) compared cultural perceptions of luxury in several countries. A selection of different cultural definitions of luxury based on consumer perceptions is provided in Table 1.5.

Table 1.5   Cultural perceptions of luxury

France, Australia, and Poland	Denmark, Norway, and the Netherlands	Spain, Portugal, Italy, and Hong Kong
Perception of luxury as elitist	A democratic vision of luxury	A feeling of distance toward luxury

1.2.7   A Consumer Perspective on Luxury

The definition of luxury depends upon consumers' perception of what they consider to be luxury goods. These perceptions are related to consumer profiles and attitudes toward luxury. Marketing authors Dubois et al. (2001) identified four main consumers perceptions of luxury goods:

- Consumers who perceive luxury as an excessive conspicuous consumption practice because of the high price, which they find indecent and immoral.
- Consumers who equate luxury with a dream and a universe of inaccessible comfort. It is a world to which they do not belong but which is sometimes part of the dream.
- Consumers who associate dimensions, such as passion, fascination, dream, fanaticism, joy, deep love, and sensitivity to luxury.
- Consumers who consider that luxury products are an extension of oneself in relation to the personal and social identity of the individual.

Other authors in marketing, such as Vigneron and Johnson (2004), proposed a conceptualization of luxury from the point-of-view of the consumer by constructing a measurement scale composed of five key dimensions: hedonic, self-extended, perceived quality, rarity, and the conspicuous dimension of luxury. For each consumer profile, there is, therefore, a specific attitude toward luxury and its conceptualization that is adapted to each type of consumer.

Consumer attitudes toward luxury consumption have often been the subject of several marketing studies. Authors identified numerous consumer profiles that can be explained according to the typologies proposed by Dubois and Laurent (1996). These typologies are relevant because they make the connection between the consumer's profile and his/her own definition of luxury. Table 1.6 summarizes the different conceptualizations of luxury according to consumers' profiles.

Table 1.6 Luxury definitions according to consumers' profiles

Elite luxury	Open luxury	Rejected luxury	Far luxury
• Favorable attitude toward luxury • People in this category love luxury and find it enjoyable • They favor the visit of selective sales outlets • For these individuals, the products should be expensive, qualitative, and limited	• No elitist attitude toward luxury • For these consumers, luxury is enjoyable • In the open vision, luxury does not refer to a single social sphere or a minority	• These individuals reject luxury for what it represents (elitism) • They have a negative attitude toward luxury • They consider luxury as useless • They think that luxury can be democratized and affordable by a majority of people • The majority think that few people have luxury items and one should be snobbish to buy it	• This profile is far from luxury but is not hostile to the idea of luxury • The vision of luxury is quite elitist • They find luxury goods expensive for what it is but nice to own • The majority says never buy luxury goods • Their experience with luxury is very limited

1.3   From Conspicuous and Distinctive to Experiential Luxury

The entry into an era where the individual is more self-centered and the focus on his/her well-being has shifted luxury from conspicuous and distinctive motivations for luxury consumption to a more experiential consumption in which emotions are central in the consumption and purchase of luxury goods. The consumer no longer seeks to distinguish him/herself or to belong to a reference group by consuming luxury goods; he/she now aspires to live unforgettable and touchable experiences. Several factors can explain this transition that has contributed to the rise of an experiential and emotional luxury. Figure 1.4 presents this transition and the main related factors.

Experience is at the heart of the new luxury marketing and goes beyond the proposal of the implementation of the 4Ps (product, price, place, and promotion) of the marketing mix model in the field of luxury. The customer experience has become a trending theme among professionals who are accustomed to implementing it through the use of sensory marketing, which reduces its strategic and creative scope. Indeed, consumers are moving from a logic that focused solely on luxury brands and on their products to something that values the consumer, makes him/her live unforgettable experiences, and generates strong emotions. A good and positive experience with the brand has the power to retain and bring back the customer thanks to an indelible link with the brand. However, the customer experience varies according to the area of consumption.

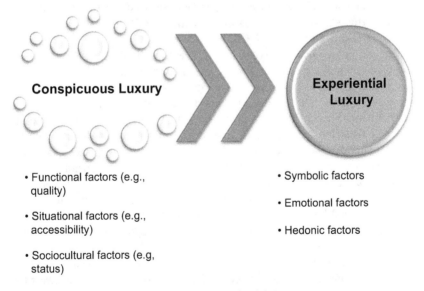

Conspicuous Luxury

Experiential Luxury

- Functional factors (e.g., quality)

- Situational factors (e.g., accessibility)

- Sociocultural factors (e.g, status)

- Symbolic factors

- Emotional factors

- Hedonic factors

Fig. 1.4 Luxury transition from conspicuous to experiential

Some areas are, by definition, experiential, such as tourism, while others are rather functional, like shops and outlets. In the luxury field, we can classify the luxury experience according to two experiential levels: high and moderate experiential fields. Two examples, tourism and hospitality (hotels and restaurants) and the retail sector, will serve as illustrations for describing the types of luxury experiences encountered in a high and moderate experiential setting.

1.3.1 Highly Luxury Experiential Settings

Among the luxury domains where the customer experience is a central component of the offer, luxury tourism and hospitality (e.g., luxury hotels, gourmet restaurants) is a sector where services are, by their nature, highly experiential. For example, we do not consume a destination or hotel; we live an experience that includes all the market actors and external factors, which are an integral part of the offer: hotel, VIP transport, restaurant, etc. In gourmet restaurants, theming, the WOW effect, story-telling, craftsmanship, service, and social connections should all be aligned to provide guests with a memorable, enjoyable, and satisfying gastronomic dining experience that is both functional (e.g., quality of the product, creativity of the chef, etc.) and emotional (e.g., interaction with the waiters and with other customers, the ambiance, etc.).

Mini-case 1.9

The experience of the gourmet gastronomic restaurant: Should we include the standard of "customer experience" in referencing the Michelin Guide and Relais & Châteaux?

Integrating the customer experience into referencing the Michelin Guide is essential in highly experiential luxury settings, such as gastronomic Michelin star restaurants. In gastronomic restaurants, the idea is to live emotional, creative, innovative, and surprising experiences through the discovery of Michelin star chefs. Therefore, institutions such as the Michelin Guide and Relais & Châteaux should rethink their evaluation criteria for highly experiential luxury domains, such as restaurants, luxury hotels, and palaces. Beyond the quality of service, which is critical in the luxury sector, the customer experience should be taken into account when establishing the annual referencing and assigning the Michelin stars to restaurants and Relais & Châteaux labels to distinguished hotels. Indeed, the pleasures of the table and hotel experiences are rich experiences, conditioned by the perception and the emotional aspects of each individual.

This subjective dimension of the experience requires a deep analysis of the dimensions connected to customer experience to provide concrete answers to professionals in the luxury hotel and restaurant sector in order to best meet the

(continued)

Mini-case 1.9 (continued)

functional, as well as the emotional, needs of their customers by identifying the elements that contribute to providing customers with the ultimate restaurant or hotel experience.

Depending on the level of experience of each customer, for example, low (beginner), average (curious), and high (initiated), the appreciation of the gastronomic and luxury hotel experience is completely different. Unlike a curious customer (average), who is seduced while being delighted, an experienced customer (high level/initiated), accustomed to the universe of Michelin star restaurants and luxury hotels, will be demanding and will focus on the smallest details.

- **High experiences in Michelin star restaurants**. These highly luxurious, gastronomic-experiential settings can enchant customers and should offer them, beyond quality and creativity, two main elements: authenticity and stories. An experience in a Michelin star restaurant is not only related to the quality of products and the know-how of chefs in the kitchen; it also includes the physical place, the service, the overall atmosphere, the tableware, as well as the chef who expresses him/herself through his/her creative cooking. The experience of the haute cuisine is, therefore, a set composed of several elements that all together create balance and offer consumers the ultimate experience. Furthermore, location and the history of the restaurant are other two important elements that should be emphasized when offering a gastronomic experience, but above all, if they are without excellent service and feature ordinary menus, then the experience is interpreted as empty and without any meaning for customers.

Thus, the experience of the restaurant should match the expectations of customers and what they like. A historical restaurant with an ancestral heritage should then translate the history of the place in the dishes and throughout the menus. The history of the place can position the restaurant as a unique place that offers a unique experience to its clients. In fact, other restaurants can copy the concept, the cuisine, and the décor; however, they cannot reproduce the same atmosphere, experience, or history of the restaurant which makes it distinctive. Therefore, the experience of the place and the storytelling go beyond the quality of the cuisine since it is connected to a certain local culture. When people book in a gastronomic restaurant, they would expect mystery through the discovery of each stage of their journey at the reception, the valet, the service, the meal, the interaction with the chef, etc.

Another important factor in helping customers immerse themselves in an extraordinary culinary experience is the service, which should include two main aspects: professionalism and kindness. Staff training that helps them to develop kindness toward clients is also a critical element in the appreciation of the gastronomic experience. Employees should be generous, have human qualities, and enjoy sharing.

Even if they are not technically and professionally excellent, they can still be trained; however, they should, nonetheless, possess the elementary values that make clients feel unique and pampered. It is also necessary to be kind to customers who make efforts, including young people. Gastronomic restaurants should not trivialize them, especially when they experience for the first time this luxury domain. They can feel intimidated and thus need more attention, assistance, and sympathy.

Indeed, employees should guide and assist customers in their gastronomic journey by adapting their menus and the service to the food culture of their clients. For example, Chinese customers experiencing French restaurants for the first time are gradually discovering foreign cuisine and might not always be receptive and enchanted by the taste of food and drinks. In this case, they would expect more attention and assistance from the staff to accompany them in their discovery of dishes and wines by explaining the ingredients and speaking their language, and if the meal does not suit them, the chef should propose an alternative to please and surprise them.

- **High experiences in luxury hotels.** Luxury hotels should offer a hotel experience by implementing a 360° experiential protocol that starts from top managers to room service staff. The difference between luxury hotel experiences and other hotel experiences is related to the hotel itself, its location, history, as well as the staff that makes up the reputation of the hotel. Each employee is, in a way, viewed as an ambassador of the hotel's identity. He/she embodies his/her everyday life through his/her attitudes, his/her words, his/her passion for the job, and his/her interactions with guests.

The staff should be proud to belong to the hotel. This can be reflected in their behaviors and attitudes. When employees, who are in contact with customers, feel good and proud, they can please the guests as well as have more fun in serving and enchanting the clientele, who will immediately notice it. In order to create this atmosphere, luxury hotels should be able to recruit managers who are passionate and will also recruit people like them, who can not only serve the client perfectly but also know how to anticipate his/her needs, build a good relationship with him/her so that he/she feels at home, call him/her by name, etc. All these elements reflect the way luxury hotels customize the exchange with their customers in a very high and demanding experiential setting. Thus, customer experience is a very important element and should be initiated as soon as the client arrives through a personalized welcome from the top manager or a member on behalf of the hotel manager to show that all customers are important, whether they come for one night or more. Indeed, the hotel experience, through a personalized hosting protocol, responds to new customer needs that go beyond service by expressing emotional expectations, warmth, and proximity.

Emphasizing customer experience in a highly experiential setting, such as a luxury hotel, can be accomplished by focusing on several aspects and details such as keeping the kitchen of the hotel restaurant open so that the chef can interact with clients who can enjoy the kitchen atmosphere. In order to offer a successful and satisfying luxury hotel experience, managers should collaborate with the staff and train them to develop their engagement, anticipation, and responsiveness. Therefore, it is obvious that in the field of luxury tourism and hospitality, tourism stakeholders should rely on the customer experience in order to be competitive, emphasize their differences, and offer their customers authentic, exceptional, unique, magical, emotional, and, above all, memorable experiences, bringing together several aspects and involving several actors in 360°, ranging from the hotel's management to the catering – even to the room cleaning service. For luxury services, the concierge is also an essential area of experience where the offer often exceeds the practical aspect of the service in order to meet the most unusual expectations from luxury customers.

1.3.2 Moderate Luxury Experiential Settings

Moderate luxury experiential settings include domains such as retail where the customers do not stay for a long time like in a hotel or a restaurant. The customer experience in the retail sector is then moderate and can be expressed through several forms: a hyper-customization of the service facilitated by customer relationship management (CRM) and digital tools, a streamlined customer journey, offer staging, and experience theming. Table 1.7 presents the characteristics and types of these four retail experiences.

Table 1.7 Types of customer experience in luxury retail

Hyper-personalized customer experience	It is an experience centered on a hyper-personalized service according to the profiles of the customers. The processing of data from CRM tools allows contextualization and customization of the offer. The level of customization depends on the customer and the purpose of the luxury brand
Fluid customer experience	A fluid in-store experience refers to instant customer support as soon as he/she enters the store. Mobile digital devices and qualified, customer-oriented staff can make the experiential journey enjoyable and efficient
Immersive customer experience	Delivering an immersive experience requires the implementation of experiential storytelling. It is the creativity and the universe of the brand that are put at the center of the experiential offer, be it off- or online
Digital customer experience	The digital customer experience is related to the incorporation of technology and connected objects into the in-store and retail offering. Screens, holograms, video projections, augmented reality, or robots are all digital devices and tools that can be incorporated to offer a pleasant digital customer experience

Mini-case 1.10

The three pillars of Roche Bobois luxury furniture retail experience: Creativity, quality, and diversity

The French luxury furniture brand offers to its clients a unique retail experience that is rooted in its history and the philosophy of the brand. While it is difficult to summarize in a very succinct way what a brand's DNA is, it can be broken down into three founding pillars of Roche Bobois: creativity, quality, and diversity. These three pillars of the offer are certainly key elements of the success and uniqueness of Roche Bobois in France and around the world. Furthermore, the three pillars are all at the heart of the retail experience and customer satisfaction.

First, creativity is expressed through collaborations of the brand with designers and big names in the world of fashion, such as Christian Lacroix, Missoni, or Jean Paul Gaultier. For Roche Bobois, creativity is a key element and is considered the starting point of all the company's actions and reflections. Creativity begins with a function (a piece of furniture, it is made to live with) and the mission of Roche Bobois is to aestheticize this function. Unlike some prestigious furniture brands and decoration that sometimes consider design as an exercise of style, Roche Bobois always tries to make it accessible and designed to fit into a consumer's everyday life, hence the idea is to "aestheticize a function."

The second pillar of Roche Bobois is its DNA, which reflects the quality and the attention paid to specific details. The products are made in Europe and are manufactured in semi-industrial or semi-artisan factories. This manufacturing process allows the French furniture brand to go further, especially in product customization. Today, the customer can indulge in personalization as the brand tries to respond as closely as possible to the customer's wishes thanks to its short circuits and its proximity with European manufacturers. At the level of customization, the brand can go very far, but it refuses to denature the idea of the designer. Overall, there is a very wide range of possibilities. For example, the customer has hundreds of possible combinations between the different configurations and coatings that are offered.

The third pillar is that of the diversity of its offer, which ranges from very design-specific pieces to more accessible contemporary collections as well as the collection of "new classics" that revisits French styles from the eighteenth to the twentieth century but with a real contribution of modernity.

Consumer perception and the experience of Roche Bobois. If the positioning of the luxury furniture brand in France is resolutely upscale, at the international level, it borders on luxury. This is particularly the case in the United States, China, the Middle East, and many other countries. This luxury

(continued)

Mini-case 1.10 (continued)

positioning is supported by Roche Bobois' baseline "French Art of Living" and is expressed by the originality of its creations, the way they are displayed in its stores, or by the architecture of the showrooms. The brand's connections and collaborations with fashion and arts also contribute to its ambition to express the codes of an exclusive and international brand.

Roche Bobois has invested a lot in partnerships and sponsoring cultural events, such as the Pavilion France at the Universal Exhibition in Milan and the Jean Nouvel exhibition at the Musée des Arts Décoratifs in Paris. Roche Bobois has also sponsored organization of events in collaboration with artists, photo exhibitions in its showrooms, and many other events. All these initiatives give even more content and meaning to the "French Art of Living" that the brand claims. The notion of luxury that it conveys is that of an accessible luxury and not of a remote and arrogant luxury. Roche Bobois strives to create affinity and closeness with its customers by focusing on the consumer's emotion and affect rather than that of the intellect.

Furthermore, the staff expresses a real feeling of belonging as well as a loyalty and a very strong pride in the brand. It is a company that remains predominantly family, which is fully felt by the staff, through the homelike feel the company fosters. At Roche Bobois, there is a good spirit and employees work on pleasant projects. There is also very little turnover in the workforce, which shows the commitment of employees to Roche Bobois. The staff is also trained to provide a pleasant and satisfying customer experience. Roche Bobois has its own internal sales school. A number of courses are developed and delivered by in-house experts to all French and international teams, in Paris, or through local relays. Trainers are familiar with the brand, its history, customers, ambitions, and challenges.

Training is obviously a key factor here. Selling furniture and decoration is a very complex business because the customer, before entering the furniture store, is a bit insecure and in doubt. This is a very involved purchase, which costs a certain price that brings into play the social status and intimacy of the customer's home. There is also the fear of the lack of taste. For Roche Bobois, it is, therefore, important to reassure and comfort its customers. Reinsurance is a determining factor in the furniture sales process, and the role of the seller is an integral part of this process. The person selling should be able to reassure, explain, but also initiate an educational approach to enlighten the customer on the origin of the products, their manufacturing technique, etc. Besides, sellers should be able to explain the product, its history, its design, its inspiration, or the vision of its designer. This pedagogy is also expressed in stores through merchandising and videos on the manufacture of furniture.

(continued)

Mini-case 1.10 (continued)

Roche Bobois conveys the discourse of excellence to its staff to ensure the quality of the customer experience. Excellence is a permanent pursuit for a luxury furniture brand that claims, "Retail is detail," referring to the fact that every detail is important. The sale of furniture is a binary approach: it is accomplished, or it isn't. It may not be accomplished because of micro-details even if all the work of creation, quality, presentation, and advertising is properly done upstream. An unfortunate or neglected detail can quickly make the soufflé fall. Roche Bobois, therefore, cultivates this requirement for excellence at every link in the chain. The brand regularly renews store concepts, advertising campaigns, and collections. Its stores are increasingly digitalized with the use of tools and 3D software. The Roche Bobois website has a planner accessible to Internet users, a configurator, and, in store, the sellers can use tools that are much more sophisticated and powerful. All of this contributes to this quest for excellence, which must be lived by all the customers, wherever they are in the world and whatever the importance of their project.

The Roche Bobois luxury retail experience. Customers who come to Roche Bobois expect a unique experience, and the French furniture brand makes sure that they receive a unique experience and that it is consistent with the image of the brand as expressed in its communications. The company has a big network that includes a diversity of 250 stores in the world, some in ownership (one hundred) and the others in franchise, a presence in more than 50 countries. The shopping experience can be lived differently. Thus, the daily requirement is to constantly raise the level of the customer experience. In order to do so, the brand developed a training course on "luxury attitude," designed to find the codes and spirit of luxury brands at Roche Bobois.

In its stores, the brand offers a sensory experience in which the emotion is created and amplified by the display, by the presentation of the collections, or by the architecture of the store. The customer experience is very important, especially when customers are in less exclusive locations, such as extramural shopping areas. In these areas, Roche Bobois works on the architecture of the facades (they should be graphic and spectacular) and the staging inside the store. Once the customer has crossed the threshold of the store, he/she should forget the external environment of a commercial mall to delve into a world of creativity and elegance. The circulation of customers, the sequence of moods, the highlighting of materials, colors, olfactory marketing, and the musical atmosphere are all an integral part of the Roche Bobois customer experience.

To better understand the reality of the customer experience in store, Roche Bobois regularly organizes mystery shoppers' surveys at a rate of three to four visits per store, per year. The data analyzed highlight areas for improvement. These data allow the brand downstream to guide training on the identified

(continued)

1.4 Summary

Sociologists studied luxury according to two main approaches: conspicuous and statutory consumption and distinctive luxury consumption. These two theories dominated studies in various disciplines, including luxury marketing. In this chapter, we proposed a new, multi-perspective definition that brings together seven main perspectives: institutional, organizational, academic, media, craftsmanship, historic and cultural, and consumer. Therefore, the shift from motivators, such as conspicuous and distinctive, to more experiential motivations for luxury consumption can be explained by intangible drivers: emotional, symbolic, and ideological aspects related to luxury consumption.

Yet, in the case of luxury experience (high and moderate) design and management, the marketing mix applied to luxury has proven to be inadequate, or even counterproductive, in the creation of emotions that allow the customer to experience a positive and memorable experience. Therefore, certain questions arise: How to define the customer experience in luxury and how to apply it? Why continue to buy luxury products and brands that offer no positive and rewarding experiences? What kind of customer experience should luxury houses offer if faced with the possibility of an uberization of luxury? What is the true price of the luxury experience? These questions will be explored in Chap. 2.

The New Experiential Luxury Marketing Model

2

The new definition of luxury provided in the previous chapter highlights the transition from the traditional "luxury marketing" that refers to conspicuous and material aspects of luxury consumption to a more experiential perspective on luxury through the introduction of a new framework: "experiential luxury marketing." This chapter provides a cross-sectional analysis of various studies that have addressed the customer experience to answer the following questions: What do we mean by customer experience? What do we know about what happens in the customer experience in luxury? Does the customer experience allow luxury brands to differentiate their offers, retain their customers, and attract new ones?

The objective of this chapter is to question the notion of "experience" and its application in luxury marketing through the customer experience from different perspectives. I propose to start from the limits of traditional luxury marketing to better understand how luxury houses can convert the experiential mind-set into strategies, communication, and techniques of sales to differentiate themselves and develop a strong competitive advantage.

2.1 How Does Customer Experience Transform Luxury Marketing?

The aim of this section is to question the concept of "customer experience" and its application in luxury marketing. Indeed, luxury brands should rethink their marketing and communication strategies by shifting the focus from traditional to experiential luxury marketing. In the luxury sector, customer experience responds to two major issues: (1) the change in customer behavior and (2) the advent of a new consumer who has emotional needs that go beyond the simple functional benefit. Furthermore, customer experience has become an obvious subject in today's businesses, but it is often confused with other concepts such as customer relationship

© Springer Nature Switzerland AG 2019
W. Batat, *The New Luxury Experience*, Management for Professionals,
https://doi.org/10.1007/978-3-030-01671-5_2

management, relational marketing, or sensory marketing. There is, thus, a need to clarify the concept of customer experience before examining its implementation in the field of luxury consumption.

2.1.1   What Does Customer Experience Mean?

The concept of "experience" can be defined as the acquisition, whether deliberate or not, of the understanding of human beings and things through their practices in the real world and thus its contribution to the development of knowledge. An analysis of a broad review of the works showed that the "experience" concept is not obviously related to one specific field or discipline. Works on experience are part of an extensive variety of scientific disciplines, including philosophy (e.g., Reed 1996; Dewey 1964), sociology (e.g., Bourdieu 1979), marketing management (e.g., Pine and Gilmore 1999), consumer research (e.g., Schmitt 1999; Holbrook and Hirschman 1982), and design sciences (e.g., Sleeswijk-Visser 2009). These different disciplines attribute diverse definitions and conceptualizations to the concept of experience, and thus the definition of customer experience in marketing and consumer research may well benefit from the valuable input provided by other disciplines.

- For instance, philosophers and psychologists argue that experiences are private events that happen in reply to certain stimuli (e.g., Husserl 1931; Brentano 1973). They are often not only self-produced but also induced. In philosophy, experience is seen as an ambivalent ideological notion. The concept of experience has also been highlighted in sociological studies through the analysis of the "place of lived experience," which is anchored in a specific sociocultural context and linked to a process of formation of social representations. In sociology, authors focus on the "sociocultural experience," which is associated with the lived dimension in a social and cultural context where individuals have relationships with other social actors, institutions, marketplaces, family members, other stakeholders, and elements of their immediate environment.

  In anthropology, experience has been approached from the angle of "experimentalism," a term introduced by John Dewey in 1964 who states that the control of ideas is made by experiments, by the development of a successful experimental plan, and by testing hypotheses through conducting empirical fieldwork. Therefore, Dewey contributed to the definition of experience by highlighting its individual, symbolic, and cultural dimensions. The contribution of anthropology to the definition of experience underlines the important roles of meanings and symbolism that are anchored in the culture to which individuals belong.

- Later on, the concept of customer experience developed in marketing and consumer behavior studies addresses the relationship with the customer in terms of the consumer's lived experience that changes and evolves throughout his/her purchase and/or consumption journey (before, during, and after). The idea of experience journey goes beyond the need to understand buyer's journey, as the customer experience design encompasses sociocultural and other macro, meso, and micro factors that are directly or indirectly related to the way consumers live and evolve through their experiences. These factors can affect the whole customer experience and the connection with the brand, either in a positive or in a negative way, and thus have an impact on sales, customer satisfaction and loyalty, brand reputation and image, and so forth. The two journeys (purchasing and experiential) are different but remain very complementary and important for designing a successful luxury experience.

The rise of customer experience as an element in marketing can be explained by the shift in thinking related to the transition from a product-centric logic to an experiential logic that underlines the determining role of customer experience and its legitimacy in both academia and business. Indeed, for marketing scholars and companies, a customer experience framework is holistic by nature and is likely to link a set of variables (e.g., functional, emotional, environmental, cultural, etc.) whose analysis is most often conducted separately.

- The notion of "customer experience" first emerged in marketing in 1982 following the publication of the seminal article "The experiential aspects of consumption: consumer fantasies, feelings, and fun" published by two pioneering marketing scholars, Holbrook and Hirschman. Since this publication, the concept of experience has been integrated into the field of economics in the book *The Experience Economy* published by Pine and Gilmore in 1999, whose contributions become a central pillar of the foundation of the economy in the current context. According to Lemon and Verhoef (2016), the origins of customer experience can be traced back to the 1960s, when the first influential theories on marketing and consumer behavior were established and disseminated, particularly the work of Philip Kotler (1986) as well as John Howard and Jagdish Sheth (1969).
- The different definitions of customer experience emphasize the importance of aspects such as "subjectivity," "intangibility," and "symbolism," which are viewed as an integral part of the purchasing and consumption process. Consumption is, thus, no longer limited to functional benefits customers may be looking for, but it is also an "experience" in which the consumer can be involved and immersed. Luxury businesses and brands need to rethink their strategies by evolving their traditional luxury marketing tools to better understand the whole customer experience. Indeed, today's luxury customers are increasingly seeking immersion in diverse and varied experiences in order to seek out multiple new meanings to give to their life. For luxury brands, this change is accompanied by the implementation of new management tools. It is, therefore, no longer managing the relationship with the customer but rather managing the customer experience. The major purpose of experience management tools is to involve the customer in a pleasurable luxury experience designed by the company to offer him/her the possibility of living it in "full or semi-integral immersion" in interaction (in the marketplace) or not with the company (at home).

2.1.2 The Contribution of Customer Experience to Luxury

Why are we talking about customer experience in luxury? The excellence and quality of the product are no longer sufficient in the current context. Luxury brands should offer, in addition to exceptional know-how, a unique and rewarding customer experience. Indeed, there are still luxury houses that have a very average reputation or negative customer experience, arrogance, trivialization, and loss of value. However, a banal treatment and experience when we buy the exceptional is a disaster. All luxury brands have not yet succeeded, in stores and on the net, to value the consumer. But, beware; new competitors and pure players are arriving in addition to the rise of secondhand shopping and luxury item rentals.

According to the report of the Luxury and Creation Centre (www.centreduluxe. com) published in February 2016, the luxury experience today represents more than half of the global luxury market (55% in 2011) and is growing 50% faster than that of luxury goods. However, the report explains that the development of luxury experiences is difficult to understand because it results from very different behaviors highlighting the generational gap between baby boomers for whom experience is now added to the possession of physical objects and millennials and post-millennials who tend to replace possessions. In addition to the advent of these new young consumers with changing and paradoxical behaviors, other factors (see Chap. 3) related to the evolution of luxury may explain why, in this book, we are examining the customer experience in the luxury field.

Therefore, the experiential logic suggests that in comparison with traditional luxury marketing, the components should be reexamined in light of the concept of customer experience by focusing not only on functional stimuli but also on emotional ones. The main difference between traditional and experiential marketing is the "purpose of consumption." The perceived consumption goal, as each consumer would define it according to his/her own perspective, goes beyond the "maximization of the utility value" related to luxury goods in search of the "maximization of lived experience," which incorporates not only functional criteria (e.g., quality, price, etc.) but also symbolic, emotional, relational, and aesthetic criteria (e.g., brand is perceived as an extension of one's identity, well-being, social capital, etc.).

Consumers will then seek to maximize their emotional benefits and evaluate their luxury experience from the "pleasure" they will derive from it. In this perspective, luxury brands should no longer measure customer experience through customer satisfaction but more through the intensity of both the memory and pleasure customer luxury experience will generate. It is therefore important for luxury businesses to set up a new strategy that relies on experiential marketing tools to create and stimulate customer experience in the luxury field. Furthermore, luxury brands should assist their clients in creating their own luxury experiences. To do so, Pine and Gilmore (1998) propose five main factors of experiential marketing that companies have to take into account in the conception of the "experiential offer" to manage customer experience. Figure 2.1 introduces the five factors for customer experience management.

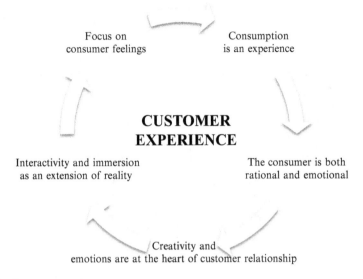

Focus on
consumer feelings

Consumption
is an experience

**CUSTOMER
EXPERIENCE**

Interactivity and immersion
as an extension of reality

The consumer is both
rational and emotional

Creativity and
emotions are at the heart of customer relationship

Fig. 2.1 Customer experience management

In the experiential perspective, it is assumed that luxury brands have evolved from a status of producer of goods and, then, of services into the new role of "producer of experiences." Experience is thus seen as a strong competitive advantage that allows the company to differentiate its offers and to establish a solid relationship with its customers. From this perspective, the memorability of the luxury experience is a key factor of success that is linked to consumer loyalty and positive word of mouth.

Offering luxury experiences also highlights the determining role of emotions in assessing or valuing the experience of consumers for whom it is no longer simply a question of consuming a luxury good but of experiencing consumption in interaction with the luxury brand and other market actors. Experiential luxury marketing, based on the logic of customer experience management, is therefore a winning strategy for luxury houses, as it provides a global vision of the different factors that traditional luxury marketing does not acknowledge, as shown in Fig. 2.2.

2.2   The Foundations of Experiential Luxury Marketing

In this section, I start with the limits of the traditional approach to luxury marketing and introduce a new framework: experiential luxury marketing. The main focus of this new framework is to allow luxury brands and retailers to better understand the meaning of customer experiences in the field of luxury goods and services and their importance in differentiating and enriching the offer targeting different luxury consumer profiles.

Luxury product	Luxury experience
Objective of the strategy is to improve the functional attributes and the material benefits of the unique know-how of the luxury product/service	Objective of the strategy is to improve consumers' consumption and purchase experiences of luxury goods (before, during, and after)
Define products and services tailored to different profiles of luxury consumers	The competitive advantage lies in the consumer's lived experience and the emotions that flow from it.
Consumers are considered rational decision-makers interested in the functional dimension and the unique know-how of the luxury brand	Consumers also have, in addition to functional needs, relational, emotional, ideological, cultural, symbolic, and experiential needs
Use of methods and analytical tools of classic luxury marketing that are quantitative and textual (questionnaires, focus groups, etc.)	Examine the tangible and intangible expectations of consumers in their luxury consumer cultures using innovative, immersive, and experiential marketing methods

Fig. 2.2 The shift from luxury product to luxury experience

The experiential luxury marketing philosophy is based on the idea of building a competitive advantage for luxury brands and retailers that goes beyond the goal of the traditional luxury marketing model. Thus, experiential luxury marketing is built on meeting the tangible and functional needs of consumers by integrating the customer experience and its functional, emotional, and symbolic dimensions anchored in the context of a consumer culture in which luxury is defined according to specific standards following subjective logics. Experiential luxury marketing thus contributes to enhancing the attractiveness of a luxury brand in a sustainable way, as it helps to meet both implicit and explicit needs of consumers in different luxury consumption cultures and subcultures.

Unlike traditional luxury marketing, experiential luxury marketing is based on an "experiential segmentation" of markets that is related to the way consumers define, in their own words, luxury (see Chap. 1). Furthermore, experiential luxury marketing incorporates two main ideas in the creation and the design of the offer targeting different segments:

- The purchase of luxury goods or brands should be experienced as a social, cultural, human, relational, hedonic, and emotional experience in line with the values and standards of the luxury customers.
- Consumers of luxury goods not only buy luxury brands, but they also produce meanings that emerge within the different luxury experiences lived in stores, at home, and also online.

In experiential luxury marketing, brands should not only meet the functional needs of their customers, but they should also include the following elements:

- Feelings of comfort;
- Positive and pleasant emotions;

- A sense of belongingness to a family or a common luxury consumption culture;
- Symbols reflecting the world and the value of customers;
- A pleasurable and enchanting social interaction;
- Feelings of well-being.

Thus, the shift from traditional luxury marketing to experiential luxury marketing is based on the implementation and the mastery of two key fundamentals:

- The capacity of a luxury brand to understand the different luxury cultures, meanings, and the experiential needs of its customers.
- Challenging luxury marketing tools, such as marketing mix (4Ps), and the segmentation techniques based on sociodemographic criteria (e.g., age, CSP, income, etc.). These tools must be reevaluated to give luxury brands the ability to offer the ultimate luxury experience, which is adapted to each luxury consumption culture.

Therefore, experiential luxury marketing marks the transition from a logic centered on the luxury goods (product, service) and luxury brands to an era where the meaning, the emotion, the human element, the relationship, and the experience lived by consumers are at the heart of the decision-making process of the individual. The introduction of experiential luxury marketing can be explained by rethinking the following logics at the heart of the traditional approach to luxury marketing:

- The 4Ps (product, price, place, and promotion) – often used by luxury brands to adapt the offer to different consumer segments.
- The functional need, the quality, and the image of the luxury brand are not the only factors that create consumer value and satisfaction. Luxury brands should focus more on the human aspect by placing customers and their emotional needs at the heart of their marketing and communication strategies.
- The loyalty and satisfaction of customers primarily depend upon the quality of the relationships and the experiences they have had with the employees in the luxury sector.

Although a luxury brand is attractive because of its know-how, its history, and its image, consumers who are not satisfied by their experiences can suddenly quit it. They can then switch to another luxury brand that they feel it is closer to them in terms of human and social values. In order to provide quality luxury experiences to their clients and create a strong connection and a durable relationship, intangible aspects such as subjectivity, irrationality, and emotions should be taken into account in the creation process. Indeed, emotion-driven experiences enable luxury brands to improve business performance and thus create growth opportunities by growing sales, building customer loyalty, and opening up to other markets and segments.

Experiential luxury marketing, therefore, invites luxury brands and marketers to understand the expectations and needs of consumers from a perspective that is

Table 2.1 Luxury marketing vs. experiential luxury marketing

	Luxury marketing	Experiential luxury marketing
Focus	Focused on functional benefits	Focused on emotional and social benefits, experiences, and feelings
Product	Defining the artisanal attributes and focusing on ancestral know-how	Consumption is a holistic experience in which the meaning of the product is shaped
Consumer	Consumer is a rational market actor	Consumer is emotional and irrational
Approach	Quantitative and systematic	Eclectic and hybrid
Tool	Marketing mix (4Ps or 7Ps)	Experiential marketing mix (7Es)

consumer-centered since the attractiveness of the luxury brand is not limited to its features or its history and know-how. Indeed, consumers buy luxury brands for the meanings they carry and which speak to them. These meanings add a very strong dimension to the luxury brand while positioning it as a strong symbolic landmark in the spirit of different consumer cultures.

The difference between luxury marketing and experiential luxury marketing (Table 2.1) is that, in the traditional logic, we do not sufficiently integrate the emotional and subjective dimensions of the consumer's decision-making process or the norms and codes of their consumer cultures in which luxury can have several definitions.

As Table 2.1 shows, the transition from luxury marketing to experiential luxury marketing can be enhanced by shifting the focus from the use of the traditional marketing mix logic (7Ps) to a new experiential marketing mix approach (Batat 2019), which provides a set of manageable components that the company can use to design and offer the ultimate customer experience – one that is suitable, enjoyable, and profitable. In the book *Experiential Marketing: Consumer Behavior, Customer Experience, and the 7Es*, I offer a new framework "experiential marketing mix" to help businesses with the design of customer experience. This framework highlights controllable components of the mix that companies can use to implement effective experiential marketing and communication in order to create and share value with their customers. The controllable components of the experiential marketing mix refer to the 7Es (experience, exchange, extension, emphasis, empathy capital, emotional touchpoints, and emic/etic process).

Within this framework, luxury brands should concentrate on seven key decision domains related to the 7Es that constitute the experiential marketing mix while designing the luxury experience offerings and planning their marketing plans. The 7Es, altogether, are interconnected and related to decision-making, which means that a decision in one domain can affect strategic or marketing decisions in others. Each luxury brand should build up such a composition of 7Es, which can help it meet its organizational and strategic objectives and guarantee a strong and sustainable competitive advantage generated by value creation and sharing, ultimate customer satisfaction and loyalty, and positive image offline and online.

2.2.1   The Ten Rules of the Experiential Luxury Marketing Logic

The ten rules of experiential luxury marketing identified in this section can help brand managers and marketers to not only facilitate greater customer satisfaction by meeting rational needs, but they will also enable them to enhance brand identity and maximize the positive outcomes of lived experiences, thereby strengthening customer loyalty through building a strong emotional connection with their customers. For ensuring the growth of luxury brands and offering ultimate and unique luxury experiences, experiential luxury marketing is a real competitive advantage and its implementation should follow ten major rules (Fig. 2.3).

1. **Emotion**. The positive emotion promotes action and consumer loyalty.
2. **Enchantment**. The client should leave the store or the restaurant with a positive and unforgettable souvenir.
3. **Commitment**. It is important for luxury brands to establish their values, so consumers can identify with and remain loyal to the company.
4. **Empathy**. Clients seek to live an empathic experience stimulated by emotional, human, and relational capital.
5. **E-experience**. The Internet shopping experience should be consistent with the actual store experience lived in a physical context.
6. **Embellishment**. It refers to a presentation of the offers focusing on themes, decor, sensory, and aesthetics.
7. **Bewitching**. Surprise the consumer, and generate the WOW effect by designing a sensory offer and storytelling.
8. **Expression of customer values**. Brand managers should integrate consumers' values into their products, services, and concept stores.
9. **Exclusivity**. Each client should be considered as unique and exceptional.
10. **Embracement**. Value sharing and long-term connections allow customers to embrace the company's culture and image.

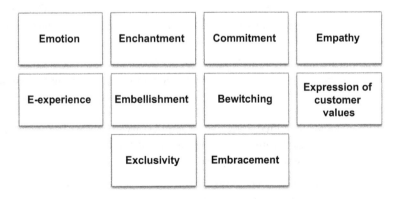

Fig. 2.3 The ten rules of the luxury experience strategy

Table 2.2 The implementation of the experiential luxury marketing

Strategy	Objective
Theming	The theming helps luxury brand marketers order customer impressions when they meet a luxury offer. The objective is to unify the different tangible and intangible elements provided by the product or the luxury brand around a common and coherent history and culture
Producing positive unified impression	This element helps to harmonize customer impressions with positive indicators. It is important for the luxury brand to produce unalterable impressions that customers can keep or carry with them
Eliminating negative elements	It is about eliminating negative clues that affect the quality of the luxury experience lived by customers at all levels (anticipated, before, during, and after)
Producing souvenirs	This strategy leads luxury brands to produce a mix of souvenirs by offering products and services that customers use as a reminder of their luxury experience

By applying the ten rules of the experiential luxury marketing, brand managers and marketers would be able to implement an effective strategy by incorporating, in addition to the translation of the ten rules, the five operational elements of the customer experience: theming, creating positive and unified meaning, eliminating negative elements, producing memories, and committing the five senses (hearing, sight, smell, taste, and touch). These experiential elements are explained in Table 2.2.

Furthermore, experiential luxury marketing can be focused on one or more levels of the customer experience: desired, proposed, lived, and expected.

- **Desired experience**. It is defined by the luxury company and corresponds to the culture and brand identity that marketers and brand managers would like to communicate with their customers.
- **Proposed experience**. It refers to the implementation of the desired experience.
- **Lived experience**. It is the result of all the perceptions and emotions felt as well as the knowledge generated by the consumers in a given situation.
- **Expected experience**. It refers to the anticipation of the experience. Consumers can also live the vicarious experience through stories of others who have already lived the experience.

Experiential luxury marketing is based on the integration of four essential elements of the experiential model: individual characteristics, social and economic interactions, factors related to lived experiences, and the physical environment, as shown in Fig. 2.4.

The four elements identified in the experiential luxury marketing framework can have a positive or negative impact on the quality of the luxury experience. The explanation of these four elements is presented hereafter:

- **Objective and subjective elements of the consumer's personality**. Personal factors, such as personality, previous experience, lifestyle, life cycle, and motivations, have an impact on the luxury experience. Marketing studies have already

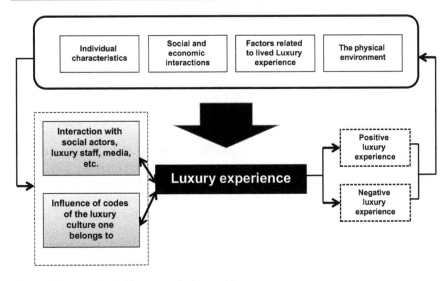

Fig. 2.4 The experiential luxury marketing model

shown that personal characteristics, whether objective or subjective, influence people's reactions to the physical environment around them. In this case, the customer's luxury experience can be modified according to the different intrinsic and extrinsic characteristics of the individuals. Two important factors contributing to the personality of the individual can explain this impact, demographic and psychographic:

- Demographic factors include individual characteristics, such as age, gender, or educational level, that influence consumers' perception of the physical environment and, therefore, its experience.
- Psychographic factors, such as lifestyles, beliefs, values, personalities, etc., can lead to significant differences between consumer groups and market segments, thereby changing desired behaviors and experiences.

- **Social and economic exchanges**. The luxury experience is also influenced by human relations and the social and economic interactions that consumers have with other social agents.
- **Experiential elements**. They refer to factors such as the presence at the point of sale, feeling advised or supported during a buying situation, and feeling valued by sellers and other actors at the point of sale (e.g., other customers).
- **Physical and digital settings**. Two elements that are necessary to take into account when attempting to create a satisfying luxury experience by focusing on the functionality of the product as well as the emotional, virtual, sensory, and relational elements associated with it.

2.2.2 Types of the Experiential Luxury Marketing

Beyond sensory marketing used by luxury brand managers and marketers to create and improve the quality of the customer luxury experience, experiential luxury marketing is also implemented through the use of three other forms of marketing to enhance emotional, altruistic, and empathic dimensions of the luxury experience (Fig. 2.5). These three forms are more than necessary for the success of the luxury experience, customer enchantment, immersion, and satisfaction.

These forms underline the importance of human aspects and social interactions, which are an integral part of the consumer's luxury experience in physical places (stores) as well as in digital spaces (social media, website). Thus, experiential luxury marketing implemented through these three forms demonstrates the importance of the human element, relationships, and social dimensions related to the experiences that luxury brands have to integrate into the design of the offer as well as into their marketing and communication strategies. Indeed, the lack of empathy, emotions, and altruism is one of the main sources of consumer frustration that generates negative experiences when the consumer is in contact with the luxury brand, its staff, products, and services.

2.2.2.1 Emotional Luxury Marketing

Creating emotional connections during a purchasing experience has a very strong impact on the decision-making process. In fact, emotional commitment helps personal selling and brand managers to both increase sales and create lasting customer loyalty to the luxury brand. Given that emotion is often at the heart of any

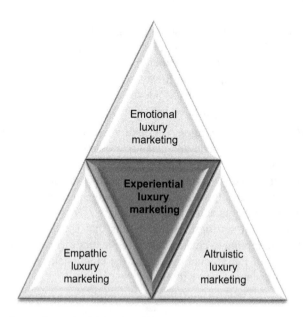

Fig. 2.5 Three forms of experiential luxury marketing

experience, emotional luxury marketing is needed to capture and create the positive emotions that make the in-store customer experience more enjoyable. Prior to defining what we mean by emotional luxury marketing and how emotions may play a role in customer satisfaction, the following questions should be asked: What is emotion? What is the benefit to luxury brands? How does emotional luxury marketing help brands in creating a satisfying customer experience?

While some authors in marketing admit some personal and individual effects on decision-makers, the conventional framework of consumer behavior is mainly cerebral in nature. Others, such as Kotler et al. (2010), state that marketing has moved beyond the age of "messaging" to an age of affecting customers' emotions. Kotler and colleagues emphasized the key role of emotion in studying consumer decision-making: "the essential difference between emotion and reason is that emotion leads to actions while reason leads to conclusions" (2010:170).

As society has evolved into digital and experiential consumption, marketing scholars started to examine the impact of emotions on consumer decision-making. The reason is that the "decision to buy and be loyal to a brand is greatly influenced by emotions" (Kotler et al. 2010:170). Furthermore, emotions are a powerful resource for capturing experience-driven consumer affection for brands and consequently incorporating brands into their everyday habits and their identity projects. Thus, creating emotional connections during the shopping process or the brand consumption experience has a strong impact on the decision-making process and consumer satisfaction. Indeed, consumer emotional involvement increases brand loyalty and sales by improving brand image and positioning. While emotion is often at the heart of the consumer brand experience and behavior, emotional marketing and branding are, therefore, necessary to capture and create positive emotions that make the off- and online luxury experience more enjoyable.

- **Defining the notion of "consumer emotion" and its typologies**. There are several definitions of the notion of "emotion." In 1981, Paul and Anne Kleinginna identified more than 90 definitions of "emotion" that can be found in different disciplines. Following this multidisciplinary and chronological analysis, the two authors proposed a new definition that is more universal and concrete enough to be translated into managerial, marketing, and operational actions: "emotions are the result of the interaction between subjective factors and objective ones attained by neural systems … this induces experiences, such as feelings of awakening, pleasure, or displeasure … that can lead to the creation of adaptive behaviors…." This definition highlights the three main characteristics of the notion of "consumer emotion": physiological, behavioral, and dyad emotion/rationality. The interactions between these three dimensions have a direct impact on the decision-making process in the luxury buying experience.

Whether positive or negative, consumer emotion is composed of a mixture of feelings that emerge within luxury experiences and can be primary or secondary. Furthermore, consumer emotion is not static but evolving through experiences and includes both positive and negative peaks that occur when a consumer is in contact with social actors and other components of his/her immediate environment (e.g., salespeople, brands, services, institutions, other consumers, etc.).

In cognitive psychology, emotions are split into two groups: elementary (primary) and elaborated (secondary) emotions. Elementary emotions are universal and express visible emotions through facial expressions that each individual is capable of recognizing and decoding in different cultures. There are six elementary emotions essential to individual and collective survival: joy, sadness, disgust, anger, fear, and surprise, as shown in Fig. 2.6.

The elaborated or secondary emotions are derived from elementary emotions (joy, sadness, disgust, anger, fear, and surprise) and are influenced by the consumer's personal background, his/her childhood, consumption experiences, and his/her external environment. They often encompass two or a mixture of primary emotions (e.g., contempt is a mixture of two emotions: fear and anger) or from an emotion, such as fear, that creates anxiety.

These emotions, whether primary or secondary, are constructed during childhood and culminate in adulthood. Throughout the brand experience, consumers express both positive and negative emotions, which differ and fluctuate over time,

Joy is produced by the desire for discovery and triggers consumer willing for closeness. It also occurs when the expectations and needs of consumers are met	**Sadness** is often associated with loss or lack. It causes isolation, self-enclosure, and the acceptance of loss
Disgust is induced by harmful attitudes and leads to rejection. It is also important in protecting individuals from unsafe behaviors and risky situations	**Anger** is a defensive reaction that a person prepares for attack when the individual faces a danger or an obstacle in the pursuit of his/her goals
Fear is triggered through a state of alert when there is a threat	**Surprise** can take two aspects: positive or negative. It creates either a reflex of withdrawal or closeness that is driven by curiosity

Fig. 2.6 The six elementary emotions

and sociocultural interactions with the environment. Figure 2.7 shows the different emotions expressed by the customer during his/her purchase experience.

Figure 2.7 shows that luxury experience is an evolving and ongoing process that creates a multitude of negative and positive emotions due to customer's interactions with employees, the welcoming protocol, other customers, decoration, service, etc. In this case, the customer will go through several stages expressing positive and negative emotions throughout his/her experience.

Consumer emotion is therefore a key component that has a strong impact on consumer decision-making and his/her satisfaction. Thus, the most attractive and competitive luxury brands are those that succeed in touching their clients before making them think. Luxury brands can use emotional marketing strategies (e.g., customer-oriented service) as well as communication tools (e.g., storytelling) to target consumers on the basis of their emotions, whether they are positive or negative or primary (fear, joy, anger, etc.) or secondary (guilt, admiration, pride, exclusivity, etc.). For example, among the most used emotions in luxury where sentiment is at the heart of the consumer purchase decision-making, we can cite the following: love, happiness, and admiration.

- **How does emotional luxury marketing contribute to creating a pleasant customer experience?** Emotional luxury marketing is grounded in the idea that the individual behaves in both rational and emotional ways. For example, a young woman wishing to buy her first luxury bag can be divided by opposing rational arguments (I cannot afford it, I do not need this bag, I already have one, it is too expensive, I can wait for sales, etc.) and emotional arguments (it is the same bag as my idol, I feel confident and beautiful with this bag, I like the brand, etc.). Emotional luxury marketing is therefore used to respond to changing

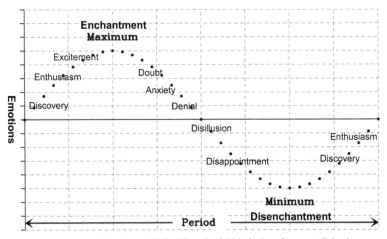

Adapted from Wided Batat (2019), "Experiential Marketing: Consumer Behavior, Customer Experience, and The 7Es," Routledge: London

Fig. 2.7   The evolution of emotions during the customer experience

consumption patterns as well as paradoxical aspirations of consumers. Its objective is to privilege pleasure and establish an affective and reassuring relationship while communicating and sharing the values of the luxury brand.

By using emotional luxury marketing, the luxury brand can then reinforce consumer emotions (positive), which accordingly promote action (purchase) and offer a pleasant dimension to the experience in the store (enchantment). Indeed, when customers experience a strong emotion, they tend to act impulsively and spontaneously, without utilizing their cognitive abilities. Based on emotions, marketers and luxury brand managers seek, above all, to reach the heart of consumers, for example, through advertising messages focused on pleasure. Emotional luxury marketing is also a very effective tool for creating a strong link between a luxury brand and its customers. This relationship can be created and strengthened through:

– The creation of strong emotions, which allows the brand to be memorized or recalled by the consumer. A luxury brand that generates a strong emotion in store or through an advertisement will remain fixed in the mind of the consumer forever.
– The association of the same emotion with each communication or consumer experience that is lived in contact with the luxury brand. This association goes beyond memorization; it will anchor the event and the emotion experienced in the mind of the consumer. Though this technique is not often used by luxury brands, it is more relevant for mass consumer brands (e.g., Nutella displays in its advertisements warm and pleasant family environments that are appealing to our childhood memories).

Emotional luxury marketing is not limited to the creation of emotions; it is also about other important dimensions during the purchase or consumption experience such as:

– Perception of the offer and the brand;
– Time spent in the store;
– Renewal of the experience;
– Loyalty to the brand or the label, etc.

However, implementing emotional luxury marketing to provide customers with pleasant and satisfying luxury experiences is not easy to achieve. It is not enough to smile at customers or offer a coffee to generate emotions; luxury brands should rethink their whole marketing and communication strategies by putting the customer back at the heart of the relationship through the development of social skills, such as altruism and empathy. Indeed, effective emotional luxury marketing goes beyond the idea of smiling to please the customers. Personal selling should make customers leave with a smile by thinking "customer" and then "product." This task can be accomplished if the luxury brand's staff are able to develop a strong potential for empathy that helps them use their social and interpersonal intelligence to identify the personality, aspirations, and mood of the client. In addition, there are several tools such as video, photography, storytelling, sponsorship, mascots, influencers, bloggers, etc. that marketing managers can use with other tools to fulfill this objective and succeed in implementing emotional luxury marketing.

2.2.2.2 Altruistic Luxury Marketing

Altruistic luxury marketing refers to a company's willingness to take an interest in others. An altruistic luxury brand is characterized by behaviors oriented toward others who benefit from it and from which no advantage is hoped for by the company. In his definition of altruism, Claude Raymond Haas (1988) identifies three types of motivations that can encourage brands to develop an altruistic attitude:

- Charitable and commitment motivations that positively contribute to society;
- Motivations related to the brand's image or ego-altruism;
- An idealistic vision of the world that can take two forms: personal pleasure and solidarity.

Although altruism is seen as the future of new customer-centric marketing, its presence is still scarce in the luxury realm, unlike mass consumer brands, many of which have already made attempts to be altruistic. Yet, luxury brands have everything to gain by developing the humility and altruism that facilitate relationships and engage customers in strong and meaningful harmony with the luxury brand. Indeed, when customers find that a luxury brand behaves altruistically and disinterestedly, they tend to feel closer to it. An altruistic luxury brand should develop the following features:

- A modest attitude in accepting criticism and recognizing mistakes;
- Offering customers the opportunity to learn and grow humanly, intellectually, and socially;
- Luxury brands should be courageous and take risks, break taboos, and fight against injustices and inequalities;
- Luxury brands should be responsible and ethically committed to the well-being of their employees and consumers.

Altruistic luxury marketing is almost impossible to ignore, especially in the luxury sector where retailers who are looking for altruistic values are the most innovative brands and are the best prepared for the future and social changes in postmodern, capitalistic societies that demonstrate ethics and altruism. For example, Blake Mycoskie, the founder of the brand TOMS, launched his company by giving a pair of shoes, for each pair of shoes sold, to a child in a poor country – or consider the French designer Philippe Starck who in a conference evoked the future of companies by stating that in the future, "there will be two kinds of companies. On one hand, the cynics who talk about consumers as a 'target' to try to sell them things at any price, and on the other, those who are in business to help their friends and help build a better world." Luxury brands should therefore look to the future and work to improve the world while making a profit (this is not contradictory) and offering unforgettable and enjoyable experiences to their customers who will see their own values and altruistic commitment reflected in the brand.

2.2.2.3 Empathic Luxury Marketing

Empathy is the ability of the individual to put him/herself in the other person's place, to understand his/her reasoning and his/her emotional state. Empathy is a multidimensional concept that involves both emotion and cognition. For a luxury brand, it is the brand's ability to take the customer's perspective and his/her point of view and put itself in his/her shoes.

Empathy is not easy to cultivate when trying to create a satisfied luxury experience. It requires taking into account several human, social, environmental, and other factors. For example, a salesperson who speaks the same language is always naturally suited to create empathy and thus facilitate sales (Fig. 2.8). Or, a client who has just had a bad day and who is, perhaps, in a negative emotional state will appreciate being looked after with more attention, understanding, and additional services.

The lack of empathy in the luxury experience is one of the main sources of consumer frustration. Marketing scholars have highlighted the fact that empathy and responsiveness are necessary conditions for successful interactions between brands and consumers. Indeed, empathy at all levels can transform the customer's luxury experience and generate positive emotions.

For example, the interaction with a passionate seller who values the customer, who is an expert, has proactive listening, and good understanding, will make customers happy and make them want to spend more time in store and also come back, as they appreciated the human exchange and the discussions about the brand and life

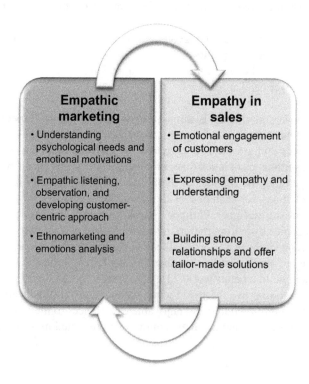

Fig. 2.8   From empathy in marketing to empathy in sales

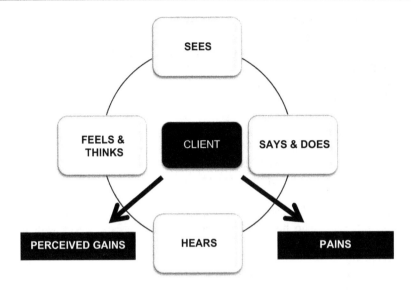

Fig. 2.9 The six components of the empathy card

in general. In a highly competitive luxury marketplace, empathy allows marketing and brand managers to meet two needs: functional and emotional.

Empathy luxury marketing is about satisfying customers and building a lasting relationship between the luxury brand and its customers. Among the tools managers can use to promote and generate empathy in the consumer experiences they offer is the "Empathy Card," an effective and easy-to-use tool (Fig. 2.9).

The empathy card was first introduced in 2011 by Osterwalder and Pigneur who explained how to build empathy, why, and how to use it. The implementation of the empathy card, as part of empathic luxury marketing, enables managers to better understand their customers and help them understand how to create and manage empathy in their luxury experiences. The empathy card is a tool composed of six main categories: seeing, saying and doing, hearing, thinking and feeling, suffering, and gain. These six dimensions give a complete view of the customer and his/her perceptions anchored in his/her experiential setting, specially analyzed according to his/her own standpoint.

The empathy card is a visual tool based on the observations of the client, the description of his/her expectations, and his/her tacit (emotional) and explicit (behavior) attitudes toward the brand. The six categories allow brand managers and salespeople to analyze customers' profiles by asking themselves the following questions:

- What the customer **sees** with his/her own eyes:
  - What are the elements that make up his/her environment – what does he/she see?
  - What is his/her luxury universe?
  - Who are the actors who belong to his/her social setting?

- – Who are his/her friends and colleagues?
- – What is his/her job?
- – What type of offer is he/she exposed to in his/her daily life?
- What the customer **says** and what he/she does:
  - – What are his/her motivations?
  - – How does he/she behave in public?
  - – What is he/she talking about?
  - – What are the topics addressed by the client?
  - – What is his/her behavior with others?
- What the customer **hears** lets us understand:
  - – Who the client is influenced by and how?
  - – Is there a prescriber?
  - – Where does he/she search for information on the brand's products?
  - – Does he/she share his/her buying and consuming experiences with his/her friends?
  - – What are his/her friends saying?
  - – What media does the customer trust?
- What the customer **thinks** and **feels**:
  - – What is really important to him/her that he/she will not dare to confess in public?
  - – What are his/her principles?
  - – What are his/her aspirations and dreams?
  - – How can he/she be moved or upset?
  - – How can he/she be satisfied?
- What might be the **suffering** of the client? This is for understanding the fears that can constitute an obstacle preventing the customer from fully living his/her experience:
  - – What are his/her great fears?
  - – What are the major obstacles facing him/her?
  - – What risks does he/she refuse to take?
  - – What does he/she apprehend?
- What might the customer's perceived **gain** be? Focusing on what the customer expects from his/her buying or consuming experience:
  - – What are his/her wishes and expectations?
  - – What does he/she want to accomplish when buying the product?
  - – What are the criteria for success?
  - – What are the strategies he/she is able to put in place to succeed?

Thus, the use of the empathy card in the empathic luxury marketing logic offers managers the opportunity to establish a profile of their very heterogeneous clienteles. The empathy card therefore allows the brands to adapt the luxury experiences to better satisfy customers by matching their emotional, social, and functional needs. Improving the quality of the empathic luxury experience is also related to other aspects of the offer, such as:

- Improving the perceived value of existing products;

- Designing products that really fit what customers want;
- Providing an adapted answer to dissatisfied customers to win them back;
- Setting up communication strategies and campaigns based on empathic values in line with different profiles.

To use the empathy card, it is essential to call on the collaboration of consumers, who, according to their own subjective perspectives, will help the managers to understand the emotional and functional dimensions related to their luxury experiences.

2.3   Summary

The concept of luxury experience addresses the relationship with the customer in terms of his/her own experience that evolves and changes according to the stages of his/her luxury consumption process (before, during, and after). The luxury experience is closely linked to the quality of service, social interactions, consumer well-being, learning, training, and the experiential marketing mix tools (7Es) that accompany the client in his/her experience. The idea is that the customer evolves throughout his/her "experiential journey" beyond the "shopping journey" usually at the center of luxury marketing strategies. In the experiential approach, the starting point for reflection is the customer through a customer-centric logic, which surpasses the good-centric logic. Instead of focusing on the functionalities of the luxury product, the experiential approach places at the center of its strategic thinking the consumers as well as their buying behavior; functional, emotional, relational, and symbolic needs; customer experience-related standards of quality; service quality; and qualitative staff training.

Therefore, customer experience has become a subject of interest in the field of luxury because the excellence and quality of luxury goods are no longer sufficient in the current context. Customer experience and experiential marketing provide answers to new challenges and emerging consumer trends in the luxury sector. Thus, experiential luxury marketing capitalizes on the idea of building a competitive advantage for luxury brands and houses by moving beyond the idea of the 4Ps in traditional luxury marketing, based on meeting customers' tangible and functional needs, to an experiential marketing mix in luxury that takes the foundations of the traditional marketing model and integrates the irrational, emotional, experiential, and subjective aspects of the behavior of the consumer. Therefore, beyond the sensory marketing often used by luxury houses to create and improve the quality of the luxury experience, experiential luxury marketing allows brand managers to focus on three major forms of the luxury experience: emotional, empathic, and altruistic luxury experiences.

Customer Experience to Keep Up with Changing Consumer and New Luxury Consumption Trends

3

Today's luxury consumers are becoming familiar with instant accessibility and will expect their luxury experiences to be personalized and emotional. Thus, luxury houses need to better understand their customers and the emerging social trends to offer the luxury experiences consumers really want through meaningful messages. Understanding the changing consumer and the emergence of new luxury consumption trends is an essential mission for luxury houses and marketing managers and cannot be examined without considering the key changes in consumer behavior within the actual era that will impact marketing most in the future, such as the transition from a modern to a postmodern consumer society or the common use of technology and digital devices. This chapter seeks to explore key changes in consumer behavior and the new luxury trends that can affect customer experience and help luxury houses design suitable experiences by taking into account functional, digital, paradoxical, and emotional needs of their customers.

3.1 Who Is the New Luxury Consumer?

By analyzing emerging trends in luxury consumption practices, I have identified two main profiles of the new consumer of luxury that should be taken into account by companies when designing luxury experiences: postmodern and transmodern luxury consumer. The next section will present these two profiles and their characteristics illustrated by examples from the luxury sector.

3.1.1 Postmodern Luxury Consumption: Paradoxical and Multidimensional Luxury

In the past two decades, there has been a major shift in consumer values and experiences in terms of drivers for consumers to purchase and recommend products and services. Firat et al. (1995), who imported elements of postmodernism ranging from

© Springer Nature Switzerland AG 2019
W. Batat, *The New Luxury Experience*, Management for Professionals,
https://doi.org/10.1007/978-3-030-01671-5_3

the humanities to marketing and consumer behavior studies, suggest a change of societal paradigm by shifting the focus from a modern to a postmodern consumer society.

As a consequence of globalization, technology, and sociocultural mutations, change in the twenty-first century is discontinuous and occurs faster than ever and in a disrupted manner. Therefore, new schemes of production and consumption (e.g., collaborative consumption, sharing, low cost, just-in-time, DIY, online shopping, and so forth) have progressively emerged over the past decade and are replacing the modern approach to the mass production of standardized goods (products and services).

This new context is also transforming luxury consumption activities and the forms of workforce and marketing strategies required to respond to the postmodern consumer trends in the digital era. These transformations are evidence of the inherent and ultimate change the consumer society faces as it enters a new era of "postmodernism." In order to benefit from these changes, luxury brands should conduct fundamental transformations in their thinking process as well as their consumer approaches, off- and online marketing and communication strategies, loyalty programs, customer services, and so forth to offer the ultimate customer experience.

The shift from modernism to postmodernism can be explained by two key factors: economic context and cultural norms. While the economic aspect of modernity refers to massive production, standardization, and industrialization, the cultural dimension in the modern era highlights the influence of traditions and customs embedded within a particular cultural context in terms of consumer values, beliefs, behaviors, and attitudes toward brands. Frochot and Batat (2013) state that the modern consumer society is uniform, hierarchical, and based on the idea of an objective universal reality. Thus, there are several characteristics of the modern consumer society:

- Product first, consumer second;
- Distinction of production from consumption;
- Industrial progress, capitalism, and productivity improvement;
- Consumer rationality and cognitive process;
- Develop objective science by testing reality through experiments;
- Science, institutions, and politics are the truth;
- Universal morality and law;
- Life is organized according to dichotomies: consumer/producer, rational/irrational, cognitive/emotional, etc.

Postmodernism is characterized by suspicion toward modern totalitarian thoughts, established rules, standardized knowledge, and the absence of diversity resulting in social chaos and the loss of reference points. Individuals should then redefine their identities and values to achieve their own emancipation, affirm their differences, and thus liberate themselves from modern dominant representations. Thus, postmodernism rejects the idea of a universal reality by emphasizing its fragmentation, plurality, and diversity, even beyond human understanding. Furthermore, postmodernism offers marketing scholars and luxury brand managers a thought-provoking framework for examining or reexamining consumption practices and experiences by shifting the focus from product to consumer.

Mini-case 3.1

The perfume "Ma Dame" by Jean Paul Gaultier: A fragmentation of female identity

In September 2008, Jean Paul Gaultier launched his feminine perfume called "Ma Dame." In his communication, he displayed a fragmented feminine model juxtaposing two opposite dimensions: masculine and feminine. This fragmentation is not only reflected by the fashion model who appears in advertising; it is also reproduced through the perfume bottle and other aspects such as a rigid glass bottle with sharp angles (masculine) and a gradient of pink pop color with a vaporizer encircled by a black collar (female).

It was the English top model Agyness Deyn, with her boyish side, that was chosen for the advertising campaign of "Ma Dame" or "My Lady." She is chic and rebellious and has style and spirit to present several feminisms: free, bold, strong, sensual, etc. The model appears in a 40-second clip with a remixed song *Troisième sexe* or "third gender" of the French pop group Indochine.

See the ad on: Madame, Jean Paul Gautier, https://www.youtube.com/ watch?v=DPhNmDCsyS0, accessed September 1, 2017

With the rise of the postmodern consumer society (e.g., Venkatesh et al. 1993), luxury consumption was obviously transformed by a transition from a modern to a postmodern society. Throughout the former, consumption was influenced by the utility value of products and/or services. Consumption was comprehensible and part of a relatively unchanging context in which consumers were capable to choosing conventional commodities. Further, individualism was insignificant in a modernist consumption culture, and thus diversification of commodities beyond their functional properties was limited.

Furthermore, while modern consumer society places the consumer at the end of the process and views him/her as rational, postmodern consumption goes beyond a purely economic vision of the marketplace by focusing on both the emotional and cognitive dimensions of consumer experiences and the meanings the latter gives to his/her consumption practices involving brands, products, services, environment, and social interactions with salespeople, multiple stakeholders, and other consumers. Firat et al. (1995) bring clarity by explaining the rise of the postmodern consumer society through the identification of five main transformations:

- The separation of the private and the public spheres;
- The building of the consumer society through diverse public discourses, practices, and media initiatives;

- The implementation of men in the field of production and of women in the private sphere;
- The conversion of women into consumers;
- The conversion of consumers into shoppers by the use of marketing techniques.

The paradigm of a postmodern consumer society is not new. In former studies, marketing and consumer scholars introduced the idea of the culture of consumption as a framework in which consumer behaviors and purchase habits can be examined. Based on the works of postmodernist scholars who enormously contributed to marketing and consumer behavior fields, I have identified seven key characteristics of today's postmodern luxury consumer: fragmentation, juxtaposition, media culture, tolerance, hyperreality, anachronism, and pastiche. Table 3.1 continues the development of these seven postmodern dimensions.

Table 3.1 Postmodern luxury consumer characteristics

Characteristic	Definition	Example
Fragmentation	The fragmentation of the individuals due to the weakening of their identity leads them to no longer project themselves into traditional models and aspire to a greater flexibility of identity	Jean Paul Gaultier perfumes: the fragmentation of feminine and masculine identities
Juxtaposition	It emphasizes the erasing of hierarchies established (elitist culture/popular culture, masculine values/feminine values, etc.). It also reflects the coexistence of opposing elements	Stella McCartney's vegan products Mix of materialistic values (luxury) and altruistic values (eco-responsibility)
Media culture	It is the consequence of the intensive exposure to media content resulting in the creation of strong media knowledge and shared media cultures	Dior and Sincerely Jules: fashion bloggers who become muses for luxury brands
Tolerance	It stems from fragmentation and juxtaposition and refers to the multiplication of consumer values	Saint Laurent The first fashion shows where model tops belong to ethnic groups or minorities
Hyperreality	It is the representation of the image in communication. The image stands out from its referents and becomes a strategic component in marketing discourses	The LV logo of Louis Vuitton or the horse of the Ferrari brand
Anachronism	It refers to the explosion of temporal references through the mixture of styles where old representations and icons are updated and mixed with new references	Fashion designers: Dior, Chanel, etc. who revisit the trends of the 1920s
Pastiche	It refers to the era of recycling media references and content. Creation is none other than the copying and pasting of what already exists. We do not invent anything; we do recycle	Copy and paste luxury hit bags: Hermes, Dior, etc.

According to Thomas (1997), the postmodern consumer lives in a society filled with "doubt, ambiguity, and uncertainty." It is this situation that brands and marketing professionals should attempt to understand by identifying the macro sociocultural forces influencing consumer behaviors, attitudes, and motivations in order to satisfy the needs and expectations of the consumer in terms of brand experiences if they wish to subsist in the postmodern marketplace. The postmodern luxury consumer displays two key features: multidimensionality and paradoxical behaviors.

- **Multidimensionality**. It refers to the fragmentation of society, behaviors, individuals, and their identities that results from the proliferation and diversification of offers, brands, images, products, discourses, and so forth. Consumption experiences become fragmented by replacing single attitude/behavior with multiple realities that make sense to consumers according to their own perceptions. Multidimensional behaviors and the fragmentation of consumer experiences contribute to the rise of emerging representations and behaviors that are more or less accepted, depending on the cultural context. Multidimensionality allows the postmodern consumer to choose different roles, behaviors, and identities at the same time (e.g., being a wife-consumer and mother-consumer or student-consumer and worker-consumer). The multidimensional aspect of consumer experiences often requires a fragmentation of the self in order to deeply experience each consumption setting in which consumers may express multiple behaviors and attitudes toward the same brand, product, and service. Firat, Sherry, and Vankatesh (1994) refer to this situation as "multiphrenic selves," which means that the postmodern consumer changes his/her image frequently by including all consumption practices and can embrace his/her multiple consumer identities rather than conforming to a single one (e.g., purchasing a luxury watch, renting it, buying a secondhand one, and getting a countrified luxury watch).
- **Paradoxical behavior**. Almost all postmodernist authors agree with the idea that consumers' paradoxical behaviors are a key characteristic of the postmodern consumer society. The paradoxical juxtaposition and combination of opposites lead to contradictions and confusions in consumer attitudes toward brands. The postmodern consumer expresses his/her paradoxical behavior by mixing and matching opposites or by combining contradictory consumption styles. The postmodern consumer can juxtapose opposed emotions (loving and hating the same brand), opposed behaviors (buying authentic luxury and counterfeit luxury), opposed thoughts (beliefs and doubts), and opposed feelings (great and bad hotel/service experience) in order to cumulate different cognitive, pleasurable, and meaningful experiences.

3.1.2   Transmodern Luxury Consumption: Green Luxury

Transmodernity reflects the evolution of a culture of economic and individual performance, competition, opposition, and exclusion toward a culture of cooperation, respect for the environment, social justice, union, and integration. Transmodernity is a cultural movement that goes beyond modernity (nineteenth century) and postmodernity (twentieth century and twenty-first century) in terms of consumer practices and values. Luxury consumption practices are recreational and central to rethinking the relationship between the consumer and his/her engaged consumption practices (luxury and the environment) or between affluent and underprivileged individuals in an eco-collaborative perspective. This responsible consumption of luxury gives an ethical sense and a social utility to the act of purchasing and allows the consumer to develop a thoughtful approach to his/her consumption practices. Today, companies and luxury brands should incorporate the idea of a consumer who can no longer be passive because he/she has a value system that controls and influences his/her consumption of luxury.

Mini-case 3.2

Louis Vuitton green luxury policies

Louis Vuitton emphasizes respecting nature, a heritage that belongs to humanity and is the origin of their products' excellence. LV has made designs that have passed from generation to generation since 1854. The luxury group is constantly renovating to eliminate negative impacts on the environment by applying more accountable practices respecting ISO certification. Louis Vuitton has successfully managed energy consumption and minimized carbon footprint by reducing greenhouse gas emissions and wastes. In addition, the luxury brand thrives to make eco-friendly designs with its leather goods and accessories.

The transmodern luxury consumer is aware of the impact of his/her consumption on the environment and adopts consumption practices that generate values such as social justice, sustainability, and well-being. The transmodern consumer represents a responsible and engaged dimension of its luxury consumption practices. He/she follows a "green luxury" ideology, and his/her criticisms are directed to the process of manufacturing luxury goods. There are several representations related to transmodern luxury consumption (see example in Mini-case 3.3).

Mini-case 3.3

Porsche sustainable development policies

Porsche is meeting a challenging goal in response to the new transmodern consumer trends by implementing different programs, actions, and policies to play a social role within the transmodern society. Among these policies, we can cite the following:

- **Porsche reducing carbon dioxide emissions**. The sports car manufacturer is transforming its rail logistics transport into a completely carbon-neutral

---

(continued)

Mini-case 3.3 (continued)

process, and thus in 2018, the transportation of finished Porsche vehicles was done by rail, which is powered by renewable green energy.

- **Home for bees**. Porsche is getting involved in nature and species conservation work, and, therefore, a total of 1.5 million honey bees will be given a new home on the 40 hectares of untouched natural land. The honey will then be processed and used in employee catering at the Porsche plant in Leipzig. There are also plans to sell the honey at the Porsche Leipzig customer center.
- **Porsche planting campaign**. Thanks to the support of Porsche, the drinking water forest, which is composed of coniferous trees, will produce 1.2 million liters of clean drinking water each year. Considering that one person consumes 1000 liters of drinking water per year, the planting of these young trees will ensure a lifetime supply of drinking water for up to 1200 people. According to Michael Steiner: "By having the drinking water forest in the immediate vicinity of our Development Center, we are able to emphasize the commitment we have made to take responsibility for people, the environment, and society."
- **New training centers and projects**. Porsche has opened new training and recruitment centers. A total of 75 men and women from socially disadvantaged backgrounds will be trained as service mechatronics. Hence, with the opening of the new training centers, Porsche is investing in the future of its trainees. It is worth to mention that Porsche will qualify more than 120 trainees as industrial mechanics, tool mechanics, mechatronics engineers, and automotive mechatronics engineers at its site while preparing them for working life.
- **Combined annual and sustainability report**. The new unified report format of Porsche highlights the significance of the relations between economic, ecological, and social factors for a sustainable and profitable growth. The format is designed to be simultaneously informative and inspirational. The first part of the report is about the performance of financial figures as well as environmental and energy data. It also features a review of the year's important events. On the other hand, the second part, which is called Perspective, provides entertaining but also reflective insights into the company. Porsche has supported more than 100 projects as part of its charitable donations and CSR sponsorship activities during the reporting year. The firm funds such projects as part of its corporate responsibility in keeping with its commitment to local and social causes. Its support is focused on five key areas: education and science, culture, social affairs, sports, and the environment.
- **Porsche's focus on female workforce**. Porsche is increasing its focus on women. The proportion of women in leadership roles directly below executive board level has increased. To meet Germany's Law on Equal Participation by Women and Men in Leadership Positions in the Private Sector and Public Services, standards were set for the percentage of women who should be on the supervisory board, on the executive board, and on the first-tier management at Porsche AG.

Transmodern luxury consumption is the expression of a consumer who acknowledges the economic weight of his/her consumption and who decides to consume in accordance with his/her values. His/her fundamental ideology is to consume only if it is really necessary. The responsibility of the transmodern luxury consumer leads him/her to take responsibility for his/her act and makes his/her consumption "fair." Therefore, the transmodern consumer displays his/her citizenship and his/her ideology. Luxury companies should then adapt their products as well as their communication and marketing strategies by rethinking manufacturing processes that use animals and by developing eco-friendly practices while guaranteeing the exceptional quality of the luxury goods manufactured.

Mini-case 3.4

Gucci, a transmodern brand that renews with eco-responsible practices
Gucci announced in a statement that the company was setting up a more sustainable model for deliveries of its shops in major European cities by using electric vehicles as well as designing products from eco-friendly and biodegradable plastic materials. This approach highlights the new eco-responsible strategy of the luxury brand to appeal to its transmodern customers who are concerned about the impact of their consumption acts on the environment and the society in general.

3.2   New Luxury Consumption Trends

By analyzing studies and reports focusing on the changes within society in terms of luxury consumption, four major luxury trends have been identified and are important to consider by luxury houses when designing their experiential offers, their communications, and their services. Figure 3.1 introduces these four luxury trends which are detailed and illustrated by examples from the luxury sector in the following section.

3.2.1 "LuxDisneyfication" or the Art of Destocking Luxury Without Damaging the Brand Image

In order to destock luxury products while preserving brand values, new retail spaces should be created to provide pleasant and memorable customer experiences. Indeed, to sell their stock of unsold products without damaging their image, luxury brands are now present in destocking shops and outlets called "Villages." All the big cities have their own Village: "La Vallée Village" in Paris, "Bicester Village" in London, "Shanghai Village" in Shanghai, "Las Rozas Village" in Madrid, etc. These Villages have become tourist sites that compete with great monuments and tourist attractions.

Fig. 3.1 Four new luxury consumption trends

In the Village, the consumer is immersed in a universe of entertaining luxury, combining both the codes of luxury (through the presence of a large variety of luxury houses) and entertainment (the codes of the Disneyland universe). This is what I call "LuxDisneyfication."

LuxDisneyfication refers to a phenomenon of globalization in a world of fantasy and feeling linked to luxury, its products, values, and practices. It is all about applying the idea of a Disneyland theme park to discount or outlet luxury practices. Disneyland values are global and popular among a large number of consumers. They are also known to everyone and their service to discount luxury offers enjoyable, entertaining, and memorable experiences in different villages across the world.

The concept of "Village" emerged in the early 1990s. It was initiated by Scott Malkin, an American Harvard graduate from a family of real estate investors. He created the company "Value Retail" in London to launch destocking centers and outlets dedicated exclusively to luxury goods. There are now nine in Europe, attracting more than 32 million visitors. Each Village includes a set of luxury outlets: Gucci, Celine, Cerruti, Burberry, Dolce & Gabbana, Givenchy, Kenzo, and Valentino. In these Villages, there are no "discount" banners displayed in the windows, even if a 30% or sometimes 70% discount is offered on the products of major luxury brands. In practice, the process of LuxDisneyfication can be translated strategically and operationally using five essential components (Fig. 3.2).

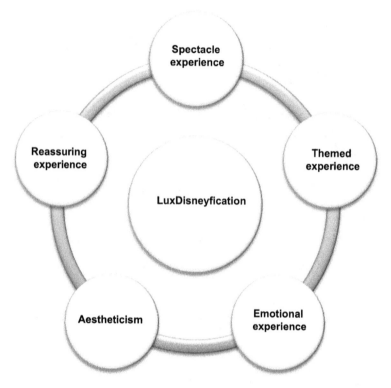

Fig. 3.2 Five components of LuxDisneyfication strategy

- **Offering a spectacle experience**. The experience should be designed as a big show. The expanse of its immense landscape combining luxury and enchantment aims to control and direct the emotions and desires of the visitors as in an amusement park. Thus, the LuxDisneyfication meets the needs of a society regarding the element of spectacle. It implements the globalization of the show through entertainment in the service of the destocking of luxury goods. Therefore, Villages are attractive to the average consumer because of the prices. Villages also help eliminate the real characteristics of luxury boutiques that can be intimidating, inaccessible, arrogant, and so forth. The goal is to make the luxury experience more enjoyable, re-appropriable, and easy to understand.
- **Themed experiences**. The theming of luxury Villages can be achieved by using narratives and telling a story in a universe of refined luxury that combines fairytales, globalization, and accessibility (a sort of Disneyland for adults). The Disneyland theme adds entertainment to the world of luxury. Although all luxury Villages have the same theme, grouping the Disney Parks codes, the thematic bases, may vary depending on the country and the Villages. For example, Disneyland's original theme was a combination of US history and a celebration of American popular culture. But other themes can be chosen as part of a LuxDisneyfication process, such as sports, cinema, fashion, literature, etc.

- **Enhancing the emotional experience**. The emotional experience includes both consumers and employees in the luxury sector. The emotional dimension of employees working in Villages should be consistent with the values of luxury brands, as they are embodied in the stores of major avenues. Village employees should then respect and defend the values of the luxury brand. However, the emotions generated in a LuxDisneyfied experience are globalized and can be perceived as too artificial. These emotions also vary between the Villages and the real world of luxury, where the consumer may be disenchanted because of the gap between his/her LuxDisneyfied experience in the Village and the real experience in the real boutique.
- **Focusing on aestheticism**. The aestheticism of the Villages and the discounted sale of luxury brands allows the consumer to immerse him/herself in a luxurious world with its codes: a VIP lounge, an art gallery, a valet, grooms carrying bags, and personal stylists. The playful dimension is guaranteed by the codes of the Disneyland universe with the same small and cute houses, walk-in shops, big clocks, etc. These elements provide, beyond the impression of getting a good deal by buying luxury goods at low prices, pleasure, aesthetic interest, and emotion that make the experience unforgettable.
- **Offering reassuring experience**. The LuxDisneyfication allows the middle classes to access luxury brands in a universe that speaks to them, namely, the

Mini-case 3.5

Bicester Village: An ultimate experience of LuxDisneyfication

The luxury outlet destination located near London is a home to more than 160 boutiques of world famous brands, each offering exceptional luxury experience and value with savings of up to 60% on the recommended retail price all year round. Most of its stores are in the luxury goods and designer clothing sector. It is among the most popular tourist destinations in England for foreigners attracting over six million visitors every year. The center is the second most visited location in the United Kingdom by Chinese tourists after Buckingham Palace. Besides tourists, fashion editors and journalists are regular visitors as well as the Duchess of Cambridge Kate Middleton who was once spotted buying goods for Prince George. After all, from time to time even royal family members like bargain and discounts.

Nowadays, travel trends around shopping are changing as more of the shoppers are going abroad. In order for the Village to continue attracting the wealthiest tourists, the outlet must keep offering exceptional experience for guests, so that they have stories to tell to their friends about the experience lived and the savings they did on high-end brands such as Burberry, Gucci, and Armani. To ensure visitors enjoy an effortless shopping experience, together with a selection of restaurants and cafés with unique and tasty foods

(continued)

Mini-case 3.5 (continued)

on menu, the Village offers a team of bellboys and doormen, hands-free shopping, personal shopping, valet parking, and luggage drop, in addition to staff throughout the Village and tax refunds for visitors from outside the EU. Also, to make the visit more rewarding, guests can earn miles from different airways as they shop in the Village. Although in the United States people can find fashion outlets as "Jeremys" in California and department stores with 80% discounted luxurious designer merchandise, however, these outlets don't offer the amazing experience that Bicester Village offers to its visitors.

In terms of digital usages, the Bicester Village app allows users to navigate through the Village, enjoy fashionable question and answers, style tips, videos, and much more. One can also find an interactive map of the Village where you can search by name or category of the brand. Also it includes all the information you need about the resident restaurants, live music events, exclusive offers and treats, luxury services, and opening hours of the boutiques.

---

popular culture conveyed by Disneyland codes. It reduces the social anxiety of consumers who are not really the target of luxury brands and makes them want to live new luxury consumption experiences and strengthen their self-esteem.

Therefore, LuxDisneyfication offers opportunities for both luxury brands and middle-class consumers. For luxury brands, it is all about attracting a customer out of their target or who has low purchasing power. Without this initiative, the consumer would never have dared to go to a luxury boutique on a high street. The LuxDisneyfied experience, typified in concepts, such as Villages, would, therefore, encourage consumers to invest in luxury items and visit the real boutique to live a full luxury experience. The challenge for luxury brands, therefore, is to offer a continuum of the LuxDisneyfied experience in their stores by ensuring that the real world of luxury does not represent too many challenges in terms of psychological accessibility or relational, social, and emotional obstacles.

3.2.2   Masstige: A Cheap and Chic Luxury

The phenomenon "masstige" has existed for about 10 years and explains why luxury brands should focus more on creating luxury experiences rather than only luxury goods. Masstige is the grouping of two words "mass" and "prestige" and refers to the marketing of luxury goods at very low prices, making them accessible to a large mass of consumers. The masstige can be set up through an association between luxury brands and other popular consumer brands. For example, the Karl Lagerfeld collection for Macy's or Stella McCartney for H&M and Adidas.

Mini-case 3.6

Stella McCartney masstige through collaboration with Adidas

In 2004, Stella McCartney and Adidas proclaimed their long-term collaboration in New York. It was the first time a luxury brand creates sports clothing selection for women. The collection included attire for running, workout, swimming, and other exercises. By taking this initiative, Bill Sweeney, the head of apparel at Adidas Sport Performance, claims that this specific range enabled to offer women what they want: clothes that allow them to work out and at the same time look good.

McCartney claims that women give major importance to both their style and sports life, and given that fact, she believes these two elements must coexist without compromising one for the other. Stella's collaboration with Adidas achieved success simply because of the vision that arose from an existing reality, triggered by Stella to come up with this effective partnership. Stella states that men were always well dressed, even in the sports domain, while women lacked that and seemed like they didn't have anything good to wear like men did. This issue insulted Stella and prompted her to put her passion into work through the collaboration. Moreover, McCartney's designs represented the Olympic Games, and she is the only designer that took such a step and achieved a breakthrough.

Stella's action of uniting with Adidas to launch a brand new sportswear line aimed at a younger, fresher, and a more vibrant target audience. Her goal was to join style and sport with daring branding and vibrant colors and prints, giving the active wear line a new attitude and style, ensuring to reach out to the targeted age group. Designed for what is known as "Action Girl," this collection can be worn at the gym or even on the streets.

The brand has been inspired by and working with a very well-known model Cara Delevingne, who has a significant influence on her fans worldwide. In addition, an important matter that people/clients today give a great deal of importance is sustaining the environment. McCartney with Adidas together ensure to keep their products environmentally friendly and safe by eliminating the use of leather and fur, by using PVC-free garments (polymerizing vinyl chloride, a synthetic thermoplastic material used in shoes and clothes), and by including materials that are woven to have less waste. Her purpose to keep the environment safe and healthy by using eco-friendly materials influenced her collaborators (Adidas and H&M) to also adopt eco-conscious business strategies.

Masstige can also be perceived as cheap commercial opportunism. Taking advantage of its public and mass consumption, the masstige is increasingly practiced by big names in fashion and luxury. Indeed, designers can participate in unusual associations with large retailers or other popular mass brands (e.g., Coca Cola). For Karl Lagerfeld, it is not only a desire to democratize luxury and make it affordable, as he

Table 3.2 Examples of luxury masstige

Sector	Exclusivity	Accessibility
Automotive luxury	BMW Sedans, price from $55,000	BMW 1 Series, price from $23,000
Luxury clothing	Armani Haute Couture, price from $1,500	Armani Jeans, price from $130
Luxury watchmaking	TAG Heuer Link, price from $5,500	TAG Heuer Formula 1, price from $650

stated: "I've always wanted, since I have a mainstream [...], to do things affordable." For him, it is also a question of modernizing the luxury "mass elitism, it is the way of the modernity... To be present at the two ends of the market, here is the peak of the luxury..." Table 3.2 presents some examples of major luxury brands that apply the masstige strategy.

Masstige offers mutual opportunities to luxury brands and retail chains. For luxury brands, it is about seducing a clientele who is out of reach by giving consumers with low purchasing power access to the symbol of the brand that, in turn, becomes accessible in the mind of the consumer. Without this initiative, the consumer would never have dared to go to a luxury boutique. Luxury brands are hoping the masstige will encourage consumers to invest in the luxury goods offered by the brand in its stores.

On the side of retail and consumer brands, the most immediate goal is to enhance their image through an association with luxury brands with very strong brand equity. It is also a communication campaign to attract media and thus generate significant profits by focusing on the temporary and exceptional nature of the collection offered by luxury brands. However, major luxury brands, who are overzealous and want to conquer the market, risk losing their legitimacy and their loyal customers who genuinely belong to the high society and no longer see themselves reflected in these new values. Indeed, masstige is often associated with mass production, which has a negative impact on brand image, customer experience, and quality.

Therefore, the masstige signals, most of the time, the entry of a luxury brand into a phase of illegitimacy, which can entail the loss of its luxury dimension and its exclusive character. Hence, the interest for luxury brands that practice masstige is to democratize luxury and convert potential customers into brand customers, to build on the experience that will help maintain the unique luxury brand, which is lacking in its luxury masstige offer. The masstige is therefore an attractive strategy, but it is also a perilous one if the brand does not integrate the customer experience in parallel in its shops or in continuity consistent with the masstige offer.

3.2.3 Commoditization of Luxury

The commoditization of luxury can be explained by two main emerging consumption trends: secondhand luxury and luxury rental.

- **Secondhand luxury**. Unlike other sectors that are experiencing a difficult economic context, the secondhand market continues to grow thanks to new consumption patterns. The luxury secondhand market can involve exchange among private individuals or between individuals and secondhand businesses. The discount of certain luxury goods and brands can range from 30% to 70% of the price of brand new luxury items. This shows the importance for luxury brands to focus more on the customer experience to distinguish themselves from these offers considered by consumers as attractive but which may lead to the commoditization of luxury. Luxury brands also need to work closely with key offline and online market players to protect the exceptional and exclusive values of luxury.

Mini-case 3.7

Vestiaire Collective, the luxury secondhand market in the digital era: When secondhand luxury becomes trendy

Vestiaire Collective was launched in October 2009 with the aim of offering a community platform on which members could buy and sell, under the best conditions, high-end fashion and luxury fashion clothes and accessories. The launch of the website benefited from the explosion of the secondhand luxury market and new consumer behaviors and attitudes toward luxury. Vestiaire Collective is considered a new competitor and a must-have pure player, who has paved the way for the uberization of luxury.

The website offers a catalog of luxury items from the personal wardrobes of hundreds of thousands of users around the world. Additionally, to ensure user confidence, something that is a major hindrance when purchasing secondhand luxury goods on the Internet, the website offers a unique quality control process. Absolutely 100% of items sold are physically controlled by experts. Nearly 100,000 new users sign up each month, joining an international community of four million members.

Destocking luxury goods is, in fact, more reserved than luxury brands that impose the place, price, date, destocked products, big brands, etc. on the website where users can find all luxury brands, even those that do not adhere to destocking, for a question of image and prestige. Users make the law; they choose which product to sell with prices that range from 100 dollars to 30,000 dollars or more. The Vestiaire Collective website responds to new emerging behaviors and the advent of the new hybrid and paradoxical consumer who can buy in stores and on the website in search of the best quality/price ratio.

- **Luxury rental**. The rental of luxury goods, such as clothing, watches, etc. is one of the new consumer trends that is attracting more and more consumers. Initially, rental is reserved for cars or wedding dresses, but in the luxury sector, rental practices are booming today for two main reasons: the response to the economic crisis and the responsible sense of the consumer. The responsible consumer prefers to preserve the environment by rejecting the purchase of cheap products, a purchase that must be renewed due to wear and repetitive washing or use. Instead, this consumer will move toward luxury to ensure exceptional and sustainable quality – and the act of renting facilitates access to it. Luxury brands should, therefore, follow these new trends and offer an alternative through an experiential offer that promotes craftsmanship and the economic sustainability of artisans. The combination of this alternative with the purchase of luxury goods allows luxury brands to differentiate themselves from the luxury rental market, and, therefore, to revive the desire to buy the luxury product.

Mini-case 3.8

Mabonneamie.com, a French website to rent haute couture evening dresses

Mabonneamie (my good friend) is a rental service for haute couture evening dresses and accessories of major luxury brands. Mabonneamie offers a Parisian showroom in a Parisian apartment for customers wishing to rent a dress for one evening or more. The idea is not only to rent haute couture dresses by great designers for parties and special occasions but also to rent dresses designed by young designers.

Mabonneamie also offers a makeover and an image coaching service to help women get to know each other better and to feel comfortable, especially in the chosen dress. For founder and fashion enthusiast Axelle Bonamy, the idea of this service is to recreate the role of the girlfriend who comes to pick a new holding of luxury brands. The rental price for dresses that are worth up to $5,000 ranges from $40 to $150 for 4 days rental plus $15 for cleaning and a deposit check (not cashed) of $550. This luxury rental practice is becoming more popular and is paving the way for other products and brands such as luxury watches, art pieces, etc.

In addition to these three factors (LuxDisneyfication, commoditization, and luxury rental), which explain why luxury brands need to focus more on the customer experience and integrate it into their offerings, another important factor has changed the way consumers approach the luxury market. Here, we are talking about the uberization and the digitalization of the luxury market.

3.2.4 The Digitalization of Luxury

Digital tools give a practical convenience to luxury, which should not be in contradiction with its exceptional dimension. The challenges for luxury brands are multiple; that's why the quality of customer service that is reflected in the welcome and other considerations is principal in the world of luxury but almost inapplicable to the digital world, which has rather pragmatic, efficient, and fast aspects of the luxury experience. Most of the digital strategies of luxury brands rely on "brand content," which is not enough today to emphasize the specificity and exception of luxury. For this reason, luxury brands should offer digital experiences rather than digital content.

Mini-case 3.9

Burberry and its digital revolution

Burberry is, today, the leader of the digital market and was among the first luxury brands to open up to digital in the early 2000s. In the 2000s, the marketing strategy of the luxury house was marked by a digital shift toward becoming the first luxury brand to be fully digital. The brand posts regularly on its website and interacts with consumers via social media and other community platforms by adding innovative, exclusive, and interactive content to differentiate its offers from its competitors.

Burberry applies offline and online marketing strategies through a 360° approach to reach a wide audience. The Facebook account of the brand has more than 17 million likes, making it the luxury brand with the greatest number of fans. Burberry was also one of the first luxury brands to enable its followers to follow and comment on live shows of its collection on Twitter and Facebook. It has also offered its followers a service that allows them to order what they see live on the show so that consumers can enjoy items well before they are available in stores.

The luxury digital element should then allow customers to circulate between different physical (offline) and digital (online) channels so that they can pass from one to the other without any difficulties. This should guarantee consistency in the experiential journey from the physical to the digital context and vice versa. For luxury businesses, it is essential to create effective, high-performance digital customer experiences that are firmly rooted in consumers' daily habits both offline and online. Yet, designing thematic points of sale equipped with touchpads or other screens giving access to the brand's website, as is available to any other consumer at home, is only a minimalist solution that will only provide a small, in-store phygital purchase experience.

The transformation of physical stores involves the use of digital tools to support the customer throughout his/her experiential journey – and it starts well before the customer opens the door of the store. Luxury houses should then combine different tools and strategies to offer the ultimate customer experience and enhance the continuum between the real place and the virtual space and vice versa. Among the tools and strategies that can help luxury brands create a phygital experience, the following can be considered:

- Mobile and mobile payment. The mobile phone has become an essential object in commercial relationships. Firstly, the connection that technologies now offer allows companies to establish a close contact with the customer, to identify and log his/her data, and to personalize the messages that are addressed to him/her. But also, in terms of payment technologies, the phygital concept will revolutionize the act of purchasing goods and services, allowing, for example, customers to pay for their purchases at any time or as soon as they enter the store.

- Click and collect and e-booking. With click and collection, customers can buy online at home or on the go and retrieve their item in-store without paying shipping costs. With e-booking, the customer reserves an article before going into the store without obligation of purchase. In the first case, the customer ensures that the product is available before purchasing and retrieving it. In the second, the customer comes into physical contact with the product he/she intends to buy, something that is not possible in e-commerce until the receipt of the product ordered is in the hand of the consumer.
- Range extension and the break. The customer orders an article from the store that is either not available on site or out of order. This new practice can be either in the form of a catalog extension that enriches the still limited supply of the physical store or in the form of product customization, as is the case in luxury items. But the most important thing about this approach is that it restores the value of the sellers, who take their place in the heart of the relationship with customers to advise and guide them.
- Shopper-centric focus. One of the main differences between traditional marketing, sales, and phygital is that the company has to think not in "consumer-centric" terms but in "shopper-centric" terms – that is, to focus not on the customer but on the buyer. The idea here is that digital must put itself in the customer's shoes and offer him/her digital solutions that are useful and enriching while streamlining his/her experience.

Luxury brands can also use numerous technologies such as iBeacons, quantified self apps, connected objects, and augmented reality, among others to connect real places with virtual spaces, thus, designing suitable phygital customer experiences.

Mini-case 3.10

Gucci's offensive digital strategy to keep up with a digitized consumer society

Gucci creates and enhances the customer experience by implementing a robust and offensive digital strategy to fit with the expectations of digital consumers. First, Gucci started with a new design of its website. The site offers free returns, find-in-store options, product information, and gift-wrapping. Gucci also places customer service options on each product page so that customers can easily get in touch with salespersons. Gucci also differentiates itself by using specific language. For instance, "complimentary delivery" instead of "free shipping" and "place in cart" as opposed to "add to cart."

(continued)

Mini-case 3.10 (continued)

These small differences in language can sometimes help deliver the high-end nature of the brand.

Furthermore, Gucci developed a new tech image through its strategy. The company has launched an immersive retail experience for its customers. Thanks to the latest technological innovations, Gucci's customers can experience an interactive type of engagement where fast-forward, rewind, freeze, and full 360-degree views allow customers to examine a product from every angle and in great detail. Additionally, Gucci focuses on creating a 3D e-commerce experience and online awareness. The product pages are filled with high-quality images. Additionally, these images can be viewed from multiple angles and consumers can zoom in on the photos.

Another aspect of the digital strategy integrates the in-store Gucci experience. Shopping in Gucci's majestic stores is a unique experience due to the astonishingly high-tech experience available for in-store shoppers. Gucci's displays are highly interactive and put the customer in control and transport them to a different world. It also uses creative methods of storytelling about the heritage and history of the brand. It's worth mentioning that Gucci pays a lot of attention to details that are relevant in translating the brand's personality to the digital space. Gucci's mobile application was a great innovation that allowed consumers to connect with digital clients due to the fact that customers spend a lot of their time on smartphones; mobile has become a crucial aspect of engaging with them. Gucci uses its application with a focus on brand awareness and keeping in touch with their customers. It features new collections, videos, or photos from fashion shows, and fashion trends that are attractive and delightful.

- The use of iBeacons is a good example that illustrates the importance of merging physical and digital spheres. iBeacons enable the digitalization of the physical customer experience at various points of sale. It is a small box with Bluetooth technology that allows the company to interact with customers in the store or provide them with contextual information through their smartphones. Introduced by Apple in 2013, iBeacon technology works on the principle of micro-location. It estimates the proximity of a smartphone to a given point represented by a tag. Two conditions are necessary before the reception of the signals: (1) the possession of the dedicated application and (2) the activation of Bluetooth by the holder of the device. iBeacons and other indoor location services have become commonplace. In 2016 and 2017, brands mainly used iBeacon systems to send coupons or geolocalized messages. In the oncoming years, brands will use this technology beyond simply pushing brands to the customers.

Mini-case 3.11

Fragrance Outlet uses iBeacons to advance customer loyalty

Fragrance Outlet, a chain of perfumes and cosmetics, launched a campaign of iBeacons that aimed to build on the current loyalty program and attract new buyers. As part of the campaign, the cosmetics chain worked in partnership with a Beacon Award platform to pilot its reward programs by adding fragrance samples to the rewards. To start, tags have been deployed in approximately 100 Fragrance Outlet stores.

When customers enter the store, the application activated by the beacons welcome them through the door. They are then rewarded with a "kick" (rewards on app-activated beacons) for the visit. These "kicks" can then be exchanged for discounts. For Fragrance Outlet, the "kick" can lead right to samples of products for brands such as Calvin Klein, Lacoste, Escada, Hugo Boss, etc.

Fragrance Outlet has also adopted Shopkick's associated credit card program. This program offers cash rewards to customers paying with a Visa or MasterCard. Pedestrian traffic has been driven to stores by attracting new customers and offering rewards. By coming to the stores, customers have generally had a great experience.

3.3   Summary

This chapter has examined the key changes in luxury consumer behavior and the new emerging trends that affect customer experience in the luxury sector: those related to the LuxDisneyfication, luxury masstige, luxury commoditization, and luxury digitalization. These trends all together emphasize the shift from a modern to a postmodern luxury consumer society. In this chapter, I have explained how luxury brands can rethink their customer experiences by focusing more on the changes emerging and how they can benefit from them by designing unique luxury experiences that match customer expectations, thereby potentially increasing customer satisfaction, loyalty, and advocacy.

Part II

The Big Five Strategies to Designing the Ultimate Luxury Experience

Capturing Luxury Customer Values

4

The perception of luxury value is essential to the enjoyment and the satisfaction of consumers and is consequently of huge significance to luxury brands. The concept of value has always attracted significant interest in customer experience and experiential marketing fields. Most studies have attempted to define value according to consumer perception by identifying several categories of value, ranging from economic utility to emotional value. Customer experience studies have highlighted the importance of the perceived value sought by customers in their shopping and consumption experiences. This chapter aims to examine consumer value as a relevant component that luxury houses should integrate into their strategies and communication campaigns. In fact, one of the big five strategies for attracting consumers and connecting with them is based on capturing luxury consumer values. Given that luxury goods (products and services) are also bought for what they symbolize, it is critical for luxury brand managers to know what kind of outcomes their brands and offerings (products and services) endorse in the eyes of actual and potential customers.

4.1 What Exactly Is Consumer Value?

The key values luxury businesses should capture and address are reliant on the consumers' personal perceptions: economic, functional, individual, and social outcomes of their customer experiences that are strongly interconnected but not indistinguishable from each other. Although the four dimensions cited above are commonly used in marketing and consumer studies, the definition of customer value is still a topic of discussion. Several authors have different categorizations of customer value. An analysis of the literature in marketing has led us to consider the following classification of consumer values:

- **Value-in-exchange**. It includes four main forms of values: (1) low cost, (2) what the consumer needs in a product or a service, (3) the quality a consumer gets for the price he/she pays, and (4) what the consumer gets for what he/she gives.

© Springer Nature Switzerland AG 2019
W. Batat, *The New Luxury Experience*, Management for Professionals,
https://doi.org/10.1007/978-3-030-01671-5_4

Value-in-exchange refers to the economic aspect of consumer value and is the most widespread in the marketing field. Value-in-exchange is also used by Kotler and Keller (2006) and continues to dominate research today; customers perceive value in the exchange of product for the price they pay.

- **Value-in-marketplace**. This is based on Woodall's (2003) comprehensive description of value, which describes five forms of consumer values: net value, marketing value, sale value, rational value, and derived value.
- **Value-in-time**. Woodall's longitudinal perspective on value provided four temporal and staged forms. Value-in-time covers concepts that correspond with four stages of experience: (1) ex ante (anticipated) value, (2) transaction (purchase) value, (3) ex post (consumption) value, and (4) disposition (remembered) value.
- **Value-in-use**. It is related to service-dominant logic and the findings of Vargo and Lusch (2006) who emphasize the idea that supports the value-in-use logic – the service. In other words, the service is what is usually traded, and goods become a unique way of service delivery. This perspective emphasizes customer-orientation and the relationships with the service provider, showing profound and more composite relations between sellers and buyers. The service attitude generating qualitative and positive connections allows suppliers to develop a full understanding of co-creating and sharing value with their customers.
- **Value-in-possession**. Another category, which defines material values as the propensity to position possessions and their purchase as fundamental in a consumer's life. Possessions are then seen as a means to happiness and as an indicator of one's success. Furthermore, possessions involve an extension of the self (Belk 1988) and demonstrate a meaning receptacle and produce an affiliation.
- **Value-in-experience**. Holbrook (1994) proposed a typology of consumer value-in-experience with three dimensions:

  - Extrinsic/intrinsic: the consumer perceives value in using or owning a product or service as a means to an end versus an end in itself.
  - Self-/other-oriented: the consumer perceives value for the consumer's own benefit versus for the benefit of others.
  - Active/reactive: the consumer perceives value through the direct use of an object versus apprehending, appreciating, or otherwise responding to an object.

4.2   Consumer Value in the Luxury Experience

The aim of building a customer experience is to understand the value of a luxury experience and its multiple dimensions (functional, relational, emotional, etc.). Due to the specificities of the consumption and purchase of luxury goods (symbolism, aesthetics, hedonism, snobbery, emotion, functionality, etc.) and the characteristics of the customer experience that is related to other external factors and can be influenced by direct and/or indirect social actors, the disenchantment of the customer in the luxury sector is often unavoidable because of the incoherence and the discontinuity between the five big strategies cited in this book that luxury brands should follow to design the ultimate customer experience. This break is an indicator of the quality of the luxury experience and the consumer's perceived value sought. Therefore, a consumer's perceived value is a key element in helping retailers and luxury brands improve the quality of the overall lived experience from a consumer's perspective. In other words, it is important to give the customer the "perceived value," he/she wants and not what the luxury brand wants to offer as "desired value."

In the luxury experience, the perceived value is a result of the customer's interaction with luxury goods and services as well as other components of the experience. Value is, therefore, a bonus that the consumer derives from his/her luxury experience. This gratification can take many forms and can have a positive or negative impact on an individual's consumption experience. Furthermore, luxury businesses should better understand the values that consumers associate with their luxury brand experience as well as how these values can be used to offer customers satisfying, enjoyable, and memorable luxury experiences. The value expected from luxury experiences can include several factors that are related to the following aspects:

- Utility of luxury good;
- Cost and economic dimensions;
- Consumer's perception of luxury good quality;
- Usage value and the benefit perceived by the consumer;
- Emotional dimension at the heart of the brand/customer relationship;
- Time-saving and convenience;
- Hedonic aspect of luxury experience.

Luxury brand managers and marketers can then use all or some of these values to deliver satisfying and memorable luxury experiences to their customers.

Testimonial 4.1

Edouard Meylan, CEO. H. Moser & Cie: A hedonic and disruptive approach to traditional watchmaking

1. **Who is H. Moser & Cie. and what makes it different from other watchmakers?**
   H. Moser & Cie. is an independent Swiss high-end watchmaking brand based in Schaffhausen. It was founded in 1828 by Heinrich Moser, descendent of a family of watchmakers in Schaffhausen. Today, H. Moser & Cie. is one of the few family-owned and family-run watch brands. It employs 60 people and produces less than 1800 watches per year. It develops, constructs, produces, and assembles all of its movements in-house. In terms of positioning and image, H. Moser & Cie. differs from other brands as it subtly combines tradition and modernism. H. Moser & Cie. features some the most innovative mechanisms with highest level of finishing and manages to

(continued)

Testimonial 4.1 (continued)

sublime it by reducing it to the essence by removing everything that is not necessary (incl. logo and indexes) to focus on the essential.

H. Moser & Cie. is also known as the Swiss watch brand with a rebel touch. H. Moser & Cie. has built a transparent communication based on its values and willingness to protect traditional watchmaking. H. Moser & Cie. got into the spotlight, thanks to polarizing campaigns combining humor and provocation on important topics such as Smart Watches, "upgrade to a mechanical Watch," or Swiss Made – "Make Swiss Made Great Again."

2. **How do you define the disruptive approach of H. Moser & Cie.? And why is it relevant to apply it in the sector of watchmaking?**

Our disruptive approach is unique in our industry for two reasons: (1) it is linked to important topics related to traditional Swiss watchmaking, and (2) it uses unconventional tools (social media) and communication languages (humor and provocation).

(continued)

Testimonial 4.1 (continued)

It is relevant because traditional watchmaking is not famous for its sense of humor and because there is some kind of lack of transparency in this industry. As the Swiss watch industry grew very successful in the last years, it became in many cases pure marketing machines which started to forget its origins and what made the traditional Swiss watchmaking so successful.

There is a big gap between the watchmakers working on the movements and the communication, all glitter and sparkle. H. Moser & Cie. took the responsibility to initiate a debate and to come back to the roots of watchmaking. In addition, the Swiss watch industry is very old fashioned and conservative. Very often, communication is too slow and loses its attractiveness toward younger generations. H. Moser & Cie.'s approach has therefore contributed to making the Swiss watch industry reconsider its approach.

3. **What are the values of your company and how do you share them with your customers?**

Our values are:

We are entrepreneurial. We are an independent, Swiss, family-run business. We believe in challenging the norm. H. Moser has a history of entrepreneurialism. This is very rare.

We manufacture in-house. All our movements are manufactured entirely in-house. Every watch is built and finished by hand. Hence we make very few watches. This is very rare.

We make ingenious products. Our watches house unique features. Our complications are simple and functional. We do everything in our power to make better watches. This is very rare.

Our strategy is to build a community of fans. We try to engage them as much as possible through different activities from dinners/events/presentation around the world where key people from the Moser family are present or through our digital initiatives which are gathered under the platform www. pioneerchronicles.com.

4. **How should watchmakers evolve and innovate in order to offer new experiences and share values with their customers?**

The most important is to keep the connection with the end customers while remaining authentic. Mechanical watches used to be important tools used to guide ships and planes. Today we don't even need them anymore to read time so their function is different. Mechanical watches bring emotions and build a connection to a traditional world we can comprehend in opposition to a digital world which is very abstract for most people.

(continued)

Testimonial 4.1 (continued)

5. **How can digital help you to create the ultimate luxury experience?**

H. Moser & Cie. has a beautiful museum in Schaffhausen hosted in the castle built by Heinrich Moser for his wife Charlotte 150 years ago. It is located next to the largest waterfalls in Europe and very close to our manufacture where 60 amazing craftsmen and watchmakers create the beautiful H. Moser & Cie. watches. These are the most important elements of what we do, but unfortunately it is impossible for me to transport our museum and manufacture around the world or to bring all my customers to Schaffhausen.

Digital is a tool that helps us bring all those elements as close as possible to our clients. If done well, it can be very real, emotional, and engaging. It also allows us to better target our audience which is a key element for brands with limited budgets. I don't want to reach everyone, only the right people. Today, thanks to the digital tools, I can personally answer in a few minutes or hours any request or question from end customers around the world. This is the solution to get connected to them in order to build a human relationship with them. Beyond the product, this is the most important element.

Therefore, luxury value results directly from the consumer experience. Following the logic based on a consumer standpoint as well as on Holbrook's values, we identified four main typologies of values related to customer experience in luxury: utility/functional, social, experiential, and ideological. Table 4.1 introduces these four values, which are also illustrated by luxury brand examples.

Value is also a result of personal experiences in the field of luxury. Personal experience can therefore have a positive or negative impact on the perception of luxury and, in turn, on the customer's satisfaction and loyalty to the brand.

4.3   Consumer Value and Personal Luxury Experience

Personal experience in luxury is associated with hedonic, emotional, cognitive, and social stimulation leading to enchantment, which is the ultimate degree of satisfaction. The dream is an essential dimension in luxury. It is very important for the brands to provide a "break" of reality by offering unique and symbolic moments. Through experience, luxury brands nourish the imagination and offer a promise of self-expansion, that is to say, an opportunity to extend one's field of knowledge, sensations, and emotions. By providing discoveries and providing access to new capabilities, luxury brands contribute to enhancing consumer's self-esteem.

Table 4.1 Four types of luxury value

Type of value	Dimension	Definition	Example
Utility/ functional	*Efficiency*	It refers to a functional value based on the attributes of the luxury good	Hi-fi high-end experience
	Excellence	It reflects the quality and unique know-how of the luxury brand	The unique know-how of Swiss *haute horlogerie* houses
Ideological	*Ethics*	The purchase of a luxury good appeals to consumer consciousness and his/her system of value	Luxury leather brands committed to the animal cause
	Spirituality	Refers to religious, ideological beliefs, etc. related to the consumption of luxury	Fashion and haute couture designers who adapt to the local culture, values, beliefs
Experiential	*Hedonism*	Looking for fun, escaping daily life by searching for surprises in the lived experience	Hyper-luxury experiences that thrill by plunging the consumer into a magical world far from his/her everyday life
	Affection	An emotional value which is characterized by the feeling that emerges within luxury consumption	The emotion generated by the experience of gastronomic restaurants
	Aestheticism	A value relating to the beauty of the artistic manifestation "pleasure for the eyes, for the ears"	Luxury brands that organize private events and parties in which VIP customers are immersed in a universe with images, sounds, colors, etc.
Social	*Status*	It refers to the social bond sought by the consumer and which brings together three other dimensions: interaction, practice, and social communion	Brands and private clubs that offer social activities and personalized services to their customers in a spirit of "getting together"
	Esteem	It reflects the consumption of some luxury products to enhance self-esteem and self-confidence	Luxury brands that manufacture in limited series or engage in a hyper-personalization of their products

Mini-case 4.1

How does Porsche attract the youth segment through youth cultural values?

Porsche confronts the challenge of retaining its heritage and attracting a younger and more female audience by using segmentation based on the idea of sharing youth values. Using segmentation based on youth luxury values, Porsche can reach this target audience and create messages and products for

(continued)

each segment. Porsche's targeted marketing efforts focus on reducing the high average age of the Porsche owner and increasing the number of female owners.

The car brand achieves the ultimate goal of positioning the brand in the consumers' mind and differentiates it in terms of attributes or benefits, quality, price, and use or user in order to position itself as a high-priced, high-quality, and exclusive sports car. Porsche uses psychology to understand young consumers' wants and needs. To attract the young who love speed, power, and the roar of the engine, Porsche took part in the famous movie Top Gun where the person driving the car cares about the power and control expecting to be noticed. On the other hand, other young targets see Porsche as a reward for their hard work, similar to the case in the movie Proud Patrons. So, the young believes that driving a Porsche equates with excitement, performance, achievement, success, status, and high income.

Furthermore, Porsche's legendary association with racing and numerous appearances in television, movies, and books gives it a unique position in automotive industry history and the power to attract the attention of young generations. Famous movies like Top Gun and Risky Business by Tom Cruise as well as new generation movies such as "Cellular," "Twilight," and "Cars" contain many scenes where the luxurious brand becomes the center of attention. In addition, almost all the sport, music, and movie celebrities own the luxurious brand and post fascinating images of their cars on social media where young generations are the most active.

In a context where the distinction between luxury and non-luxury sometimes is blurred, a result of the temptation of luxury brands to widen their target market and attempts by premium brands to copy the codes of luxury brands, the experiential dimension becomes an essential means of identifying true luxury. The decision to buy luxury brands is essentially dictated by psychological motivations rather than by the functional qualities of the product. The creation of the experience allows luxury brands to go beyond utilitarian expectations to fulfill symbolic and hedonic needs. Luxury is then drawing new frontiers, getting closer to more intimate motivations, such as well-being, living strong experiences, or personal fulfillment through the consumption of luxury brands.

The types of personal experiences we can find in luxury are multiple and can be grouped into four main categories that include senses, emotions, interactions, and knowledge.

- **Sensory luxury value**. In this experience, the pleasure provided comes from the stimulation of the senses (smell, taste, sound, visual, and touch). The luxury experience generates physical sensations. Whether by the extreme quality of the products or services or by the beauty of the environment in which luxury items are presented, it is a matter of awakening the senses. For example, the Ladurée brand of macaroons invites customers to a very rich, sensory experience in its stores, thanks to a magnificent storefront with bright colors, the delicious smell of macaroons, packaging that compels consumers to touch products, and the promise of an incomparable pleasure of taste. Another example in the automotive sector shows that a premium car brand, such as Infiniti, emphasizes the physical pleasure of driving in comfortable cars with materials that are pleasant to touch, beautiful lines to look at – all with the ability to listen to music on wireless Bluetooth devices.

- **Emotional luxury value**. In this personal experience, a consumer's feeling is more psychological. Positive emotions are generated by the feeling of living an exceptional moment and being recognized symbolically as a unique person. For example, the experience that Singapore Airlines offers in business class gives the lucky beneficiaries the pride of feeling privileged and treated as an important person, to feel surprised by unexpected attention (like receiving a small gift for their children or chocolates with coffee), to have positive emotions like joy at the prospect of immersing one's self fully in a comfortable and entertaining journey without any stress. Furthermore, the Krug Champagne brand invites its best customers to exceptional "Krug In Capital" dinners in Parisian restaurants where chefs create menus combining fine food and champagnes of the brand. Guests live a unique experience with a certain excitement of being a special guest who will live a special evening.

- **Relational luxury value**. In this experience, engagement is produced by active participation in a brand-related activity. The co-creation experience offered by luxury brands illustrates this notion of the interactive experience that allows consumers to come into contact with the brand and to feel part of its community. The clothing brand Miu Miu invites its customers to a real relational experience by allowing them to create a personalized video in which they mix music and visuals from the shows of the brand. Through this creation, customers live a new experience in connection with the brand. Another example is the fashion brand Burberry, which allows the consumer to create a sealed letter with a kiss in the colors of the consumer's favorite lipstick (of the brand) and send it by email to a person of his/her choice. This brand interaction experience brings the customer into the world of the Burberry brand.

Mini-case 4.2

Burberry creates relational value by interacting and co-creating with its customers

Burberry is one of the most important fashion brands in the world. Founded in 1856, the brand has always been forward-thinking and implementing strategies that go beyond just designing and selling clothes. Burberry's first store

(continued)

was opened in London, in 1891, and ever since the company has developed a network including more than 200 stores worldwide. Its online business is growing within a web in more than 40 countries globally. The brand partnered with tech companies, published ads on Snapchat, and expanded on social media. These steps resulted in business growth marking 86% in 1 year and a brand value of $3.38 billion. The marketing strategies Burberry adopted to achieve success and create relational value with its customers include the following actions

1. **Burberry Bespoke**. This approach allows clients to customize their own trench coat. The brand helped customers to pick their own color, style, choice of fabric, and materials to design their own trench coat. Customers can first choose their gender on the brand's website and then proceed to design their own coat on a model that appears on the screen. The customization process is easy, and the users can pick from ten different styles that have many choices and looks.

2. **Burberry Kisses**. Its concept is to send simulated kisses to anybody in the world.

    Burberry Kisses is a lipstick line. The brand's aim was to deliver the notion of love through a kiss, the universal sign of human affection, while promoting its beauty product.

    Burberry took into consideration that the millennials are technology driven and admire the online world, so it collaborated with Google to invent a very unique tech experience.

    The procedure included Google's face recognition technology, where users could send private messages sealed with their own kiss. The web camera later captures the kiss and the computer makes a replica of the user's lips. The message then was sent as soon as it was written and sealed by the kiss. This experience makes customers witness their messages spread in a 3D manner. As a result, Burberry Kisses achieved remarkable results. It had 253,000 search results and users from 13,000 countries sending kisses in the first 10 days.

3. **Snapchat to convey exclusive content**. Burberry knows what millennials want and love, and this is one of the reasons why it started promoting its collections from clothing to fragrances on Snapchat. The brand gave the users a "snapcode" that can be used to explore and see exclusive content. The snap gave all the details from the events happening in the campaign. It even exhibited the brand's spring/summer 2016 collection on Snapchat just a day before its publication.

4. **Burberry Regent Street-linked in-store and online shopping**. In 2012, Burberry opened its Burberry Regent Street in London to help customers have a standalone and a significant e-commerce encounter. The goal of the

(continued)

Mini-case 4.2 (continued)

Burberry Regent Street is to bring the e-commerce and the digital world to life by allowing customers to experience and perform whatever they were doing online practically. The CEO of Burberry Angela Ahrendts states that when someone walks through the store doors, it's like going to the website. Moreover, the store interiors have large screens that display catwalks and can be watched live. The store is also equipped with many mirrors that show the product's images just like it is shown during the catwalk. Finally, Burberry's huge success is achieved by:
- Allowing product customization;
- Partnering with tech companies;
- Using Snapchat to showcase content;
- Marketing by using word-of-mouth strategy;
- Combining in-store shopping and online experience.

- **Cognitive luxury value**. In this personal experience, the intellectual stimulation provided by the knowledge of the brand bears a sensation of one becoming a brand aficionado. The experience of an initiatory journey leading to the discovery of the history, the know-how, and the heritage of the brand makes a strong impression in the mind of the consumer. That is why Hermes (a French high fashion luxury goods manufacturer specialized in leather, lifestyle accessories, home furnishings, perfumery, jewelry, etc.) organizes the "festival of trades" during which the craftsmen of the house share their specific know-how and disclose their clothing techniques. Similarly, Louis Vuitton offers "special days" to discover behind the scenes of the brand. These cultural experiences provide an intellectual pleasure and a divinely rewarding feeling of being part of the true "connoisseurs" of an elitist brand and an expert in its field. Cognitive luxury value is then about sensing a past, registering as a link in a chain, being part of a story, and integrating a community of passions.

  Therefore, through the use of personal experiences and the values they provide, luxury brands can initiate the demonstration of their excellence, differentiate themselves from non-luxury brands, and maintain a strong attractiveness. Indeed, in a materialistic world, it is the experience that make the difference.

- To create memorable and unique experiences, luxury brands can take advantage of the following: their brand heritage, which must be an inspiration to create stories that bring the consumer into the world of the brand. It is about understanding the roots and preserving a certain coherence in the transmitted values.
- Through the story, the brand will be able to create an immersive experience, where the customer feels transported and forgets his/her daily life.

The four types of luxury values described above use the sensory dimensions (through the excellence of the quality of products/services), emotional dimensions (by the elitist character of its accessibility), relational dimensions (by the integration of its customers in the co-creation process), and, finally, cultural dimensions (by the initiation of the know-how of its customers). The personalization of each luxury experience, made possible by knowing its customers, will help luxury brands create ever more bridges between brand-related associations and the personal memories of each encounter with the brand. Luxury brands should then imagine stories that are appealing and consistent with their identities that highlight the links between the brand and the personal experiences of customers and their own values.

Mini-case 4.3

Centurion card from American Express: A unique value for ultrahigh elite consumers

The American Express Centurion Card, also known as the Amex Black Card, is an elite card used most often by the very wealthy and rich celebrities noting that anything could be purchased with it. There are three different challenges of the Centurion Card: personal, business, and corporate. However, the luxury card has been used to proclaim status, both in spending and in creditworthiness. In order to have the luxury card, there are some requirements:

The card is available by invitation only. Like most elite experiences, the card is invite-only. The cardholders are most likely the target market for those on the VIP list, including both long-time business and personal charge card customers.

Be a multimillionaire. The card is available to 0.1 percent of the population according to The Motley Fool, and it's only offered to those who can handle its high limits and spending power.

Cost to join. To get the card, one must pay an initiation fee of $5,000 to $7,000 in addition to annual fee of $2,500 for the privilege of using the card.

Benefits of the card. The card provides travel benefits by giving $200 annual air travel that can be used for baggage fees and in-flight purchases. In addition to airport lounge access, it offers elevated hotel membership and Platinum Medallion status that allows holders unlimited first-class upgrades 5 days before their fly with Delta. Also benefits include VIP treatments at spas and hotels as well as priority seating at restaurants and get first dibs to ticket sales, meet-and-greets, and other opportunities offered by the card. Not to forget that the card itself is made of anodized titanium with the information and numbers laser etched into the metal.

Since the centurion cardholders are among the wealthiest individuals in the world, there have been stories and accounts of excessive purchases all done by the card. For instance, Victor Shvetsky purchased a private jet by its centurion card. This is known to be the largest centurion purchase on record. Also Centurion cardholders purchase Bentley, Ferrari, Gucci, LV, and many other luxurious products. It's worth to mention that most of the items purchased by the card cost more than most Americans earn in a year.

4.4 Summary

This chapter has examined one of the big strategies that focus on how luxury houses can capture luxury consumer values. Luxury houses can implement this strategy to design and offer the ultimate luxury experience to their customers. Consumers' perception of values is the only strategy that can connect the luxury brand with its customers and create a long-term commitment by transforming the major consumer values, utility/functional, social, experiential, and ideological, into strategies, offers, services, and communication opportunities thanks to the understanding what consumers value in terms of luxury experiences.

Experiential Branding of Luxury

5

Another essential component of the luxury experience strategy is the experiential branding of luxury products and services that are carriers of content, values, emotions, and experiences. Luxury houses can use this strategy to create an emotional luxury experience with a strong link connecting the customer to the luxury brand. The experiential branding of luxury refers to the way luxury companies should use consumption culture elements to connect with their customers. Instead of using brand promotion, as in the Ps of the traditional marketing mix, the emphasis on brand cultural meaning provides a necessary complement to promotional strategies by including a focus on the meanings that are embedded and shaped by particular cultural settings that the brand shares with its customers. This chapter will expose the shift from brand content to brand culture and the tools for experiential branding which are important components of the luxury experience design.

5.1 The Rise of Experiential Branding

The rise of experiential branding refers to the shift from the logic of content branding of luxury (implemented through editorial content created by a luxury brand that aligns itself with symbolic, cultural, historical, and artistic elements, which is the basis for creating original content in the form of short films, documentaries, books, and various visual and textual elements) to a logic based on branding luxury goods (products and services) through creating, telling, and sharing experiences with customers. The next section presents the transition from branded content logic to the experiential branding of luxury.

© Springer Nature Switzerland AG 2019
W. Batat, *The New Luxury Experience*, Management for Professionals,
https://doi.org/10.1007/978-3-030-01671-5_5

5.1.1   From Branded Content to Experiential Branding

Branded content has several functions according to the objectives given to them by the marketing managers and which can be grouped as follows:

- **Identification**. Branded content focusing on the function of identification guides customers in their choice of the luxury brand to meet their needs for quality, usage, price, etc. In its identification function, branded content also plays the role of memory marker to recall the previous experience related to the luxury brand.
- **Credibility**. Branded content provides customers with credibility and trust-based information that informs choice and decision-making.
- **Values**. Branded content is directly linked to the values of the luxury brand. These values can be divided into three main categories: use, exchange, and symbolism.
- **Justification**. Branded content is also used to justify the price of luxury goods (products and services).
- **Positioning**. Branded content helps to position the luxury brand and differentiate it from its competitors by highlighting its unique know-how, services, and its symbolic distinction that marks the minds of customers.

For luxury brands, there are several strategies that brand managers and marketers can use to create branded content to reach the abovementioned goals. Four main strategies can then be implemented to create branded content (Fig. 5.1).

- **Informational luxury content**. These strategies focus on the product as well as its functional and cognitive aspects. For example, a gourmet Michelin-starred restaurant can highlight on its website practical and functional information content, such as information on menus, accommodation, teams, reservation, and other available services (e.g., valet).

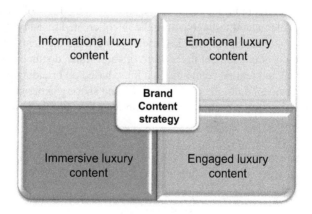

Fig. 5.1 Four luxury brand content strategies

Mini-case 5.1

The creative and informational website of the champagne house Ruinart

Ruinart, the first champagne house, founded in 1729 by Nicolas Ruinart offers a creative website that is divided into six segments, each part having its influence on visitors. The first and second parts, known as the "Maison" and "Know-how," explore how the journey of Ruinart started and inspired others in addition to the steps undergone including the harvest of the grapes to the creation of the wine. The fourth part highlights the different kinds of wine Ruinart has and how each has its own blend and extraordinary taste. The fifth part discusses the art and its collaboration with Ruinart which maintains close links with contemporary art giving carte blanche to well-known artists and providing support for major art fairs throughout the world. The last two parts are the "Rendez-vous" and the "Experience." The former helps visitors to take quick appointments, and the latter welcomes them to the center of Maison Ruinart where they can take a journey through reality and imagination during a virtual visit to REBOND, the fresco by Ugo Gattoni, and find out more about Ruinart's know-how from the artist's perspective. It describes steps and the expertise needed for the transformation from grape through to shipment of the bottle, an expertise which has been transferred across almost three centuries, the unique taste of Maison Ruinart cuvées.

Furthermore, Ruinart takes dining to a new level using 3D technology innovation, called "Petit R" that offers visitors a journey through the Maison's rich history, using a process called anamorphosis. The amazing experience is created using an animated film projected on a "screen" on a dinner table, set with plates, glasses, and tableware. The experience creates a contemporary vision of the Maison and the distinctive French art de vivre. It is now available to the public with dinner reservations in the reception room at Ruinart's historic home.

In terms of hospitality and architecture and as a family business, the champagne house Ruinart ensures a warm and friendly service whether one shops in store or online. The brand strives to create an environment of trust, an experience to enjoy, and a product to recommend. Receptions, which may revolve around either dinner, cocktail, or seminar, are held at the Domaine Les Crayeres in a historic building renovated by celebrated contemporary architect Elliot Barnes. The house of Ruinart's chalk mines are like underground cathedrals of chalk that were first exploited during the Gallo-Roman period. These magnificent cellars were classified as a historical monument in 1931. They were dug by hand – the deepest measuring 38 meters in height beneath the vault. Luminous white, these chalk mines that are spread over three levels offer a total absence of vibrations and a constant temperature that are ideal conditions for the fermentation and maturation of Ruinart cuvées.

- **Emotional luxury content**. Luxury is a highly experiential field that generates a variety of emotions. Luxury brands use the emotional dimension in their communication to meet different objectives, such as creating strong connections with their customers, involving and engaging them within sensory and immersive luxury experiences, sharing values with them, etc.

Mini-case 5.2

Hermesistible: When Hermes reinvents emotions

Hermes has launched a communication campaign using videos in which it offers a new reading repertoire of emotions, as well as a new vocabulary, understood through the prism of the brand and its symbols. It is an innovative, fun, and refreshing approach to creating emotional content that drives the universe and the values of the brand.

Hermes proposes new words that do not exist in dictionaries, but rather in the one invented by Hermes. Each word accompanies a product of the brand: bag, scarf, or bracelet.

Consequently, one can connect several emotions to the names imagined to introduce the brand's products, such as accessories. This innovative approach can make consumers want to visit the store or the website of the brand. Among the French words invented by Hermes and which consumers can find in the dictionaries of emotions created by the luxury brand, we can find the following:

- Retournelle n.f. (Re-turn-nel). Irrepressible need to repeat the same things.
- De-retox n.f. (De-re-toks). Ability to defeat any good resolution.
- Wifidèle n.f. (Oui-fi-Del). Obsessive search for the permanent connection.

- **Immersive luxury content**. These strategies aim to involve the consumer through content that requires real or virtual interactions. In order to interact with consumers, the luxury brand can use several strategies. For example, Barneys New York "On the Window" brings the consumer backstage of luxury by creating immersive content that allows consumers to get behind the scenes of their favorite designers or even the artists who worked on decorating the windows of the luxury store. Consumers find themselves immersed in the universe of fashion designers and can learn more about the inspiration behind the clothes and jewelry they wear and they enjoy. Furthermore, to enhance the immersion off- and online, the website of Barneys New York includes videos, photos, and articles about designers and creators. One can see how luxury designers imagine and create the windows and identify the symbols associated with the theme. Consumers feel, therefore, that they are privileged to participate in discovering what is behind the scenes.

Mini-case 5.3

Burberry "The Art of the Trench": Involving customers in daily experiences

Burberry launched "The Art of the Trench," a campaign that brings together photos of professionals and consumers wearing the "Burberry Trench." This campaign that shows people around the world wearing the famous trench on a daily basis has helped to popularize this product and the brand by linking it more to the daily lives of people who use the trench in their own way. This campaign has contributed to inventing trends in style – "the way to wear a trench" – that are valued by the brand through posts.

The trench is a symbolic product of Burberry which, with its "The Art of the Trench" campaign, highlighted the importance of its famous trench in the lives of people from different countries and cultures around the world by offering a unifying immersive and close experience that remains unique for each individual.

Therefore, Burberry allowed its customers to exhibit the brand's important products among its outstanding trench coat line instead of letting celebrities or models to do so. Burberry developed a unique social media strategy where customers can upload pictures of themselves in their trench coats. These same users appeared on the website home page for 15 whole minutes. Customers then could like these pictures and even share them on Twitter, Facebook, etc. The users could categorize their pictures by the color of the trench, the type, their gender, and the weather, and then they could end up buying the product when visiting the main Burberry site. This exceptional marketing method made the campaign have a natural and a personal feel while promoting the products.

- **Engaged luxury content**. It refers to the brand's commitment to a certain social cause or ideology. For example, luxury brands can be involved in the fight against discrimination, racism, violence against women, and homophobia, or they can also support and encourage positive values such as promoting eco-friendly behaviors and attitudes. Luxury brands can express their moral values and their ideologies through the use of communication mix tools, such as public relations, sponsorship, etc.

Mini-case 5.4

OMEGA and its commitment to women with "Her Time"

On its website, OMEGA's content strategy highlights the history of the house's know-how and watch sales to women. The brand has a strong link with women who wear its watches. The watch brand does not only seek to position itself as a seller of women's watches, but also hopes to reconnect with its feminine roots and enhance its commitment to this cause in every communication campaign or press release issued.

Although content branding allows luxury brands to connect and share values with their customers, there is a need to shift the focus from branded content to creating experiential content. The new consumption trends (see Chap. 3) and the rise of luxury and premium brands (some with meaning and clear content and others create more confusion on positioning) should encourage luxury brands to favor experiential branding strategies instead of content branding. Indeed, experiential branding is needed to create a luxury brand with a strong content that targets all its segments by creating a set of meanings through the construction of particular stories, which Holt (2004) calls "identity myths." Customers will then use a luxury brand's myths of identity to meet their emotional and identity expectations.

According to Holt, brand's identity myths can be created by using several techniques, e.g., marketing, which is an important and effective tool for creating myths by anchoring them in the cultural context of the brand. Identity myths will then be conveyed through communication, advertising, and other media and social media. Luxury brand myths appeal to imaginary worlds far from the reality in which people live their daily lives and can act as a mirror for a new identity that aspires and inspires consumers in a positive way. The myths created are very important because they enable individuals to overcome the tensions of a difficult economic environment, a lack of security, a rise in racism, international terrorism, and so on. Therefore, by creating an identity myth, the luxury brand rises to the status of icon in the minds of its customers and its myth is anchored in its cultural context and in the experience lived, thus, avoiding any disconnections and endowing itself with a sustainable credibility built by the clients of the luxury brand.

Mini-case 5.5

The Hermes Kelly bag: The story of a myth

Originally, Hermes' first Kelly bag was much larger than the current shape and was meant to carry saddle and rider boots. In 1930, the brand Hermes decided to create a smaller version of the bag adapted to a more feminine target by proposing elegant shapes with a clasp equipped with a padlock. But it was not until 1954 that the Kelly bag was popularized, thanks to the actress Grace Kelly, who became a princess and discovered the Hermes bag during a film shoot. Alfred Hitchcock even proposed to his costume designer to choose the accessories for the film from a Hermes boutique in Paris.

Grace Kelly immediately adopted the brand, and it was then that the bag of Hermes was renamed "the Kelly bag," and since then, it has risen to the rank of one of the most mythical bags of the Hermes house. In addition to its mythical and symbolic dimension, the Kelly bag is manufactured with the most luxurious materials and benefits from a unique know-how. It takes 3 to 4 years of waiting to get a new Kelly for an average price of 7,000–20,000 USD.

5.1.2   Why Do Luxury Brands Need Experiential Branding?

Experiential branding is the future of the luxury branding strategies, as it allows the content, experience, and culture of the luxury brand to adapt to its environment by integrating all the values of its targets. Luxury experiential branding, therefore, brings more substance, density, and meaning that help brand managers capture and create suitable shared values as well as customer satisfaction and loyalty. Experiential branding has several advantages, which should encourage luxury brands to rethink their branding strategies. Some of the advantages for luxury brand managers when applying experiential branding are summarized as follows:

- A reputational advantage: the luxury brand is perceived as a reliable and high-potential partner that aspires to trust. Experiential branding is then vital to enhance the attractiveness of the luxury brand and attract customers with high purchasing power.

Mini-case 5.6

Church's and its ancestral know-how: A historic reputation with royal recognition

The history of Church's house is a significant portrait of a brand that values traditions, the legacy it conveys to future generations, and the quality of its unique shoe-making expertise. The origins of the Church family date back to 1675, when the great-grandfather Stone Church founded the company in a city renowned for its flourishing leather and footwear industry since the days of Cromwell. This ancestral know-how is transmitted from generation to generation.

At the brand's second royal meeting, Her Majesty Queen Elizabeth II visited Church and awarded the company with the prestigious Queen's Award to Industry for its outstanding export performance. This accomplishment is proof of Church's growing recognition as a leading brand in the international footwear industry. In 1999, Church's was acquired by the Prada Group, an ideal ally (Prada products have an international reputation) to help the shoe manufacturer move up a gear.

Source: Church's website http://www.church-footwear.com/en/heritage, accessed June 3, 2017.

- A proximity advantage: it is about developing a strong relationship with customers who identify with the luxury brand and its values.

Mini-case 5.7

Luxury hijabs: Dolce & Gabbana cultivates its relationship with the Middle East market

In 2016, the Italian fashion brand Dolce & Gabbana announced the launch of a line of hijabs (veil concealing the hair) and abayas (long dress covering the whole body with the exception of the face, hands, and feet) in chic shades of beige and black, with luxurious materials, lace, embroidery, and prints. This line is aimed at wealthy women in the Middle East and responds to the religious beliefs and traditions of Middle Eastern customers. The brand has created a robust proximity by incorporating the values and beliefs of this clientele into its proposed collection.

According to the 2013 Thomson Reuters study, Arab countries are a thriving market, and creators are looking for new customers to cope with the declining purchasing power of Western customers. The Italian brand Dolce & Gabbana has fused fashion and the Muslim religion by offering a line that respects the codes and obligations of clothing while being in tune with the trends of the moment rather than those of the West.

- A symbolic capital advantage: the luxury brand becomes an identity builder for its customers who buy certain brands because they convey a state of mind they claim to have (e.g., a dynamic and young luxury brand, innovative, elitist, committed, refined, etc.).

Mini-case 5.8

The Orient Express: A timeless luxury symbol of the art of travel

The Orient Express has marked the history of which the myth begins in Paris at the train station Gare de l'Est, in 1883. A symbol of refinement, bourgeois, love, and detective literature, it is one of the jewels of the railway heritage of the SNCF French railways. It is also a luxurious train that crosses Europe from North to South and from East to West.

From its launch, the Orient Express has combined innovation and sophistication by offering modern, luxurious, and over-equipped cabins with upholstered interiors and spotless beds and bathrobes marked with the seal of the company for travelers.

In the Orient Express, the best materials are used, such as silk sheets, marble sanitary ware, cristal cups, and silver cutlery. The myth of the Orient Express was built later through literature and cinema. Many writers, such as Ernest Hemingway and Agatha Christie, have found inspiration on the Orient Express.

Therefore, experiential branding forms a durable competitive advantage for luxury brands and allows them to be positioned very strongly in the minds of their actual and potential customers. The image created through experiential branding will always be anchored in the culture of the brand and in line with the expectations of the targets that will adopt it because it symbolizes something very meaningful and strong for them. Customers will therefore remain loyal to the luxury brand, which is considered an "icon" or "identity myth." Thus, customers recognize themselves in the values of the luxury brand, its unique know-how, its history and culture, and its universe. They will always communicate positively with other targets, and thus generate a positive word-of-mouth effect.

Moreover, the transition from branded content to the experiential branding of luxury is a result of three main changes that have affected communication strategies and the content of messages to fit with the emerging consumption trends within a digital and experiential era:

- **The media context**. With the rise of the Internet and the digitalization of societies, access to advertising is becoming easier and consumers are more and more involved. Thus, it becomes difficult to reach a large number of consumers with a multiplicity of media that results in the fragmentation and the dispersion of audiences. Previously, there were only few media sources (e.g., television, radio, cinema) that exposed a large number of people to the content of advertisers. Today, the viewer has changed and developed new, powerful attitudes that can be summarized in four points:

  - Consumers decide about the selection of the type of medium (e.g., TV, web, etc.);
  - They select the place, time, and content, which can also lead to advertising avoidance;
  - They decide if they want to react (e.g., comments, criticism);
  - They can produce, publish, and share content since the essential technical and financial means are less important than in the past.

Therefore, the democratization of technologies gives ideas to marketing and communication professionals, who occasionally ask their consumers to create their advertising.

- **The socioeconomic context**. In recent years, society, more specifically Western society, has begun to develop certain feelings that communication cannot ignore. The movement for ecology enhanced by the disbelief of capitalism and the global economic crisis of 2008 led to the rise of new behaviors. Consumers today are expecting a more "responsible" communication content. The social and environmental responsibility of the companies is a crucial element that should not be neglected as today's consumers are very sensitive to social and ecological issues.
- **Historical context**. The evolution of communication can be divided into three stages: modernity, postmodernity, and alter-modernity. Modernity is a way of communicating that aims to value the brand as an agent of humanity's progress toward the satisfaction of its desires. In the postmodern era, communication and

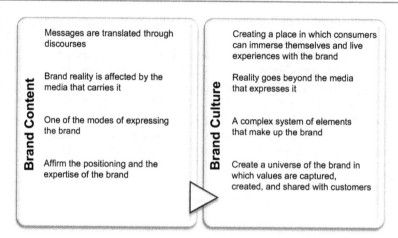

Fig. 5.2 From brand content to brand culture

advertising were marked by self-deprecation, derision, and mockery; the brand made fun of itself. The current era refers to alter-modernity that shows that communication is no longer conceived as a message centered on the brand, but as a service, a content for the benefit of the consumer.

The shift from brand content to the experiential branding of luxury can be explained by the motivation of consumers to live experiences with luxury brands that are charged with meanings. The main differences between brand content and brand culture are summarized in Fig. 5.2.

Furthermore, in order to connect and share values with their customers, luxury brands should set up an experiential branding strategy that incorporates consumer's consumption cultures. To become iconic, luxury brands should anticipate avant-garde consumption and social trends. In order to do so, Holt recommends a methodology following six steps to develop an effective experiential branding strategy:

- **Step 1: the analysis of the cultural orthodoxy of the context and the competitors**. Brand managers should first examine the cultural context that an innovation should circumvent, what we call cultural orthodoxy that refers to the conventional cultural expression (ideology, myths, and cultural codes) used by the competition.
- **Step 2: identification of social disruptions that will replace orthodoxy**. At every instant, societal changes take place, and they end up disrupting consumer identification within conventional expression categories. Whether driven by technology, the economy, the media, or even something else, these changes will drive consumers to desire a new ideology.
- **Step 3: uncovering the ideological opportunity**. It is necessary to evaluate how the disruption will act on the consumers. What are the new cultural expressions? How do they evolve? To which emerging ideology do consumers' values gravitate?

- **Step 4: collecting the appropriate source of materials**. A cultural innovation is usually about cultural expressions coming from subcultures, social movements, or even the content of the brand. This is the source of material that will be used by brand managers to respond to the ideological opportunity.
- **Step 5: applying cultural tactics**. Many techniques can serve as tactical improvements to a cultural strategy. For example, it may be to provoke ideological fighting, to mythologize the brand, or to revive a dormant ideology.
- **Step 6: shaping a cultural strategy**. A cultural strategy needs to detect a precise occasion that is practical at a specific instant, in a certain social setting, and replies to that occasion with a specific cultural manifestation. In fact, for a brand, to take benefit of a cultural precursor is certainly a paying strategy of innovation and development.

Therefore, within the experiential branding framework, luxury brands are not seen as mere intermediaries of their cultural significance or their DNA, they become moral standards that form cultural practices, commercial activities, and public rules regarding the individuals who belong to a particular consumption culture. For example, strong and competitive luxury brands continually advance referent models to define consumers' goals, desires, and thoughts as well as the way they behave and the way they might feel. Furthermore, luxury brands may anticipate cultural aspects of faith, ideology, politics, and legend, as they normally endorse a philosophy and thought process related to religious and political systems that associate luxury consumption with happiness and consumer well-being.

5.2 Tools to Create Luxury Experiential Branding

There are two main tools luxury companies can use in their strategies to create luxury experiential branding and thus strongly connect with their customers: (1) storytelling through two major lenses, which consist of the hero's journey and the implementation of the brand's positioning, and (2) the storydoing. These two techniques are detailed and illustrated through luxury brand examples in the next section.

5.2.1 Storytelling

Already ancient Greek philosophers, such as Plato and Aristotle, have proposed different literary genres, but it was especially Russian Vladimir Propp who initiated a structuralist approach to storytelling. In a marketing context, we can offer different criteria to evaluate the approach to storytelling, which has been the subject of a lot of attention in recent years; it is an approach that has been used for many centuries and was developed heavily by politicians and marketers alike. The idea behind storytelling is to influence the consumer through his/her feelings by using the solid expressive associations that stories deliver. The purpose is, by telling stories, to provoke feelings (rationality will only come in later to motivate the purchase) that should lead customers to be more open to the brand's communications. The stories are created to capture the consideration of consumers, and the tale will help consumers be more profoundly immersed than by using conventional communication modes.

- Emotions are seen as the key element, as it engages consumers and creates involvement with the place/product.
- Narratives will use anecdotes, entertaining stories and details about a brand/destination, and portray authentic pieces of information (even if legends are often brought in).
- The message has to convey sincerity. It needs to be seen not as a commercial message, but as a communication in which a consumer/local or inhabitant/destination shares a story with other like-minded customers.
- Memories are triggered when context and relevance are created through the story wherein the emotions elicited will also feed into long-term and meaningful souvenirs.

For example, a hotel room could be described using a traditional communication mode: description of the location, standards of service, and amenities. A storytelling approach will aim to describe the place by explaining, for instance, what the visitor will see from the hotel room (describing the landscape and nearby sights) and what can be undertaken close by, for example, a visit to a local farm that produces a memorable food products (it is even better if the owner is named personally, as a friend). The narrative may also have suggestions for types of activities that can be undertaken nearby (for instance, if it is cycling, brief explanations of the type of roads available, degree of difficulty, etc.). The description does not need to be too long, but if it involves references to various senses, it will necessarily elicit emotions from the reader. The idea is to give the basis from which the reader can project him/herself into the experience. It is not so much a promise (as a traditional advertisement would be) but rather a sincere description of a rare and emotional moment.

Mini-case 5.9

The Shangri-La applies the art of a moving storytelling

The Shangri-La luxury hotel wanted to expand its reputation globally, and for this purpose, the hotel produced a 3-minute promotional film titled "It's Our Nature," a moving storytelling that ends up with, "To embrace a stranger as one's own. It's our nature." The spot was broadcast on television and on the Internet, in airplanes, and in cinemas. During the first 3 months of the campaign, the film was seen more than one million times online. The brand's website has recorded additional visits and also an increase in bookings.

Storytelling is a strategic tool for narrative communication. Its approach is characterized by an emphasis on cultural, experiential, and emotional aspects that are very important for allowing luxury brands to communicate in order to immerse their customers in meaningful experiences and share common values with them. Instead of promoting brands, products, and services by using traditional communication tools (e.g., advertising, sales promotion, direct marketing, etc.), customer experience should incorporate storytelling, which consists of telling a story to consumers to promote brand awareness and values by creating an emotionally charged universe, identity, and story. In fact, stories are made and told by companies to reach their customers and create a strong relationship with them. Storytelling is an integral part of the building process of customer experience since it allows companies to:

- Differentiate themselves from the competition by making customers aware of the brand's history, allowing them to share common values, and build loyalty.
- Place the customer and his/her lived experience at the center of the brand's history to create closeness.
- Highlight authenticity and values as well as ideological, symbolic, experiential, and emotional dimensions of the company's brand, products, and services.

Furthermore, in some cases, in order to create a strong and emotionally charged storytelling, companies do not hesitate to call on artists and filmmakers to give the brand more human, emotional, and historical significance that consumers can capture and share. Additionally, the making of a story varies depending on the vision and the objectives of the company. Storytelling can be developed from the point of view of business, communication, media, and artists (novelists, writers, etc.) as well as from the perspective of social sciences, especially in the mythology field.

Mini-case 5.10

Storytelling in luxury experiential branding: Inside Chanel

For many communication agencies, Chanel represents the perfect illustration of the way storytelling can emphasize the brand identity and share cultural meaning with its customers. The brand, created more than a century ago by Gabrielle Chanel (aka Coco Chanel) and regarded as a symbol of French luxury, is indeed a master in the art of telling its story. Through videos, short films, or photos, the products, values, and know-how of the house are scripted, allowing the universe of the brand to be consistently more accessible.

Chanel's storytelling strategy is reflected, for example, in the web series that the brand has created to trace the story of its creator: *Inside Chanel*. We note, in particular, in Chap. 16 of the we series, which focuses on the passion of Coco Chanel for the camellia, a flower that became the symbol of the luxury brand. The voice-over is a feminine voice embodying the personification of the camellia, which narrates throughout the video, the place of the

(continued)

Mini-case 5.10 (continued)

camellia in the life of the creator, how she used it, how she was inspired by it, and how it is found in her creations (in jewelry or later with the wedding dress imagined by Chanel's famous designer Karl Lagerfeld – entirely covered with embroidered camellias). The anaphora "I remember" allows the luxury brand to establish a relationship of intimacy, a dialogue with the viewer (customer) – as if Gabrielle Chanel came back to life and was able to converse with customers.

Therefore, the question that comes to mind is: what types of storytelling can we find in luxury? Most luxury brands, in fact, offer stories around the product and/or the brand. For example, in recent decades, Hermes has developed a storytelling around the "hands of Hermes," that proposed a metaphor (e.g., tradition, quality, etc.) and a synecdoche (e.g., craftsmen holding the know-how of the box). On the other hand, a brand like Chanel could be designed as a narrative storyteller, that is, as a brand whose role is not only to manufacture products but also to create stories for its customers. Chanel is a true storyteller, as demonstrated by its advertising campaigns and the website series Inside Chanel. Therefore, we can say that there are luxury brands that use storytelling to tell stories about their products and others, a strict minority, in fact, that place storytelling at the center of their activity and talk to their customers.

A second factor to take into account to distinguish storytelling as a tool of luxury experiential branding is to separate the brands of luxury that build stories about the brand, or even the product, from brands that create stories marginally or not at all related to the product. Guerlain Shalimar is a story about perfume itself, which is presented as the first fragrance with an oriental bouquet, hence, the link to the myth of the Taj Mahal. On the other hand, Prada has often engaged renowned filmmakers, such as Ridley Scott ("Thunder Perfect Mind"), Roman Polanski ("A Therapy"), or Wes Anderson ("Castello Cavalcanti"), to shoot short films in which the brand aims to tell another story.

Luxury brands differ according to the level of control over the construction of narrative content. So far, luxury brands remain largely reluctant to open the story-telling of their own brands to consumers. Beyond the risks associated with the loss of control, there is a need in luxury (or an impression of need) to maintain a hierar-chical relationship within the market, a relationship that would boost the sanctity of luxury brands. In rare cases, luxury brands allow, and even favor, circulation of stories fueled by their customers and, more generally, by their audience. Apple has exploited this participation to turn passionate consumers into evangelizers. American Girl, an American brand of high-end dolls, actively involves its customers in creat-ing stories around the experience of being a woman in the United States. Therefore, to create an immersive and emotionally charged luxury experience, marketers can use storytelling tools to respond to specific strategic objectives that integrate one or more elements of experiential branding. These elements are presented as follows:

- **The myth of the founder.** The history of the brand is often linked to its founder, who by his/her character, his/her personal story, his/her career, and his/her genius contributes to forging the myth of the luxury brand and its uniqueness. Telling the story of the luxury brand is, therefore, linked to the narration of the story of its creator, often elevated to the rank of icon or myth (e.g., Yves Saint Laurent, Coco Chanel, etc.). The luxury brand benefits from the mythical status of its creator by integrating his/her values, identity, and philosophy of life. Telling the story of these creators in an experiential branding has several objectives:
  - Promote the unique know-how of the brand and its related craft and creative trades;
  - Humanize the brand through the life course of its creator;
  - Communicate on the values of the brand;
  - Promote causes supported by the brand;
  - Disseminate the ideology of the brand;
  - Highlight the authenticity and historical anchoring of the brand;
  - Reinforce the legitimacy of the luxury brand, and create a distance with mass market, fast fashion, and retailers who often have boutiques located in the main avenues usually occupied by major luxury brands;
  - Capitalize on its past and use the brand's history of antiquity to introduce luxury;
  - Educate a new audience on the history of brands, the milestones they have gone through, such as the Rolex brand, which highlights its unique know-how and the elements used in the manufacture of watches.

- **Know-how.** Luxury goods differ from other product categories because of the unique know-how that explains their price. Generational and ancestral know-how combining specific manufacturing techniques is often highlighted in narrative communications to value luxury products and especially justify their high prices. In addition, the know-how can be linked to a cultural tradition, such as French gastronomy, products made in France, Bordeaux wines, Suisse Made, Italian leather, etc.

Mini-case 5.11

Cristal Room Baccarat: The way the French cristal house is extending its offer from know-how to luxury experience

Cristal Room restaurant is nested among the several first-floor lounges of the beautifully decorated and extravagant Baccarat Museum. Originally, French designer Philippe Starck transformed the former dining room of Marie-Laure de Noailles into one of the most breathtaking restaurants in Paris

(continued)

and later in 2018; this place was reborn to create an exclusive moment. The building itself is gorgeous and with no doubt this restaurant turned to be the one of the most satisfying and atmospheric restaurants in the city. It is a different story inside, an outstanding place in terms of setup, where as much attention is paid to the taste as to the presentation.

Right from the entrance hallway, the pleasure is born, and it goes up with the customer as he/she climbs the grand staircase. The magnificent Baccarat chandelier and the imposing marble fireplaces will elevate customer's Parisian experience and excite him/her for the upcoming scenes. Customers can experience a room with glittering cristal chandeliers, white table covers, high ceilings, large mirrors, exposed brick walls, and intimate lighting.

As this luxurious restaurant unveils its new setting by the famous designer Jacques Grange, one will come to live the upscale experience of this breathtakingly spectacular looking place, including the innovative new bar that offers a collection of Baccarat glasses in which the guest can enjoy his/her drink of the day. On the first floor, we can find more colorful and modern displays with exquisite dining experience, where the serving ware is all impressive Baccarat branded and wine is served in exquisite cristal glasses. The restaurant lately left multi-starred chef's, Guy Martin, dishes behind to promote chef Mathieu Mécheri's subtle cuisine, who as well promotes a kind welcome and a variety of elegant refined dishes with a setting as sparkling as the cristal decorations itself.

Beyond all these extraordinary experiences, before the client leaves the cristal Room, the restaurant will invite him/her to visit the Baccarat Museum, to discover Marie-Laure de Noailles' great smoking room and some historical pieces of the Lorraine cristal, dishes, glasses, and carafes.

- **Creativity to guarantee the WOW effect**. Brand managers should highlight the creativity of the brand to retain current customers and attract new ones. The creativity of the brand communicated through the storytelling emphasizes the brand's potential and capacity for renewal, which would be more likely to surprise its customers by offering them new and unique experiences at each store visit or restaurant and hotel outing.

Mini-case 5.12

Anne-Sophie Pic: A gourmet three Michelin-starred restaurant that focuses on the Wow effect via a concept of disruptive cuisine

Chef Anne-Sophie Pic combines emotion, know-how, and innovation to imagine each recipe, which is based on associations of flavors that are dear to her. She selects each ingredient individually and works with fresh and seasonal produce. Beyond taste, she also seeks textures, temperatures, and colors that participate in the pleasure of the table.

With its territory of assertive expression, Anne-Sophie Pic creates associations of new flavors, highlighting the power of taste and the delicacy of expression, which summarize the culinary experience in the Pic universe. For the chef, the dish is a living organism just as tasting is not a linear exercise. Each bite must provide a disruptive taste that leads to an intense emotion.

- **The power of visual**. The use of visuals and images allows luxury brand managers to express the values and the discourse that the brand wishes to communicate to its target. Luxury businesses need to focus more on the use of visual storytelling in setting up an immersive and authentic customer experience. The visual comes in addition to a simple and concise textual discourse to avoid flooding the consumer with functional information about the product. For visual storytelling, in order to seduce consumers, it should include three main components: aesthetics, refinement, and originality. For example, Rolex relies on the visual scripting of its watches on its website. Thus, the visual allows the visitor to start to project with the product and integrate it into his/her own history and identity.
- **Sound to create and amplify emotions**. Music in storytelling allows the luxury brand to create its own musical identity. The sound elements also influence the emotions of the audience and allow them to share a similar sensation. The music chosen and the context of diffusion are more important than the choice of style made for expressing the luxurious aspect. Luxury brands should not be locked in a given "musical style," such as classical music or jazz, but they should innovate and affirm their identity through their own sound signatures that, if successful, can be elsewhere, thus contributing to the development of a sound line linked to the original signature (e.g., sound signatures on the Hermes and Cartier websites).

By analyzing the literature in both marketing and narratology (narrative studies), I identified two main pathways that marketers can follow to construct the story of their company or brand: (1) the transformation of brand positioning into a history and (2) building a storyline that retraces the "hero's journey," a framework developed by Joseph Campbell in his book *The Hero with a Thousand Faces*, first published in 1949 and reissued in 2008.

- **Transforming a brand's positioning into storytelling**. To transform a brand's positioning into an emotional story, the brand manager should start from the DNA and the essence of the brand and then build around the narrative elements that highlight the values and positioning of the brand. In order to achieve a successful transformation process, several elements should be taken into consideration:
  - The values and DNA of the brand as well as the history of the company;
  - A narrative that can include the history of the founder and the brand, customer experiences, anecdotes, tales, etc.
  - The temporal and spatial dimensions of the narration process;
  - The roles assigned to each character in the story;
  - The articulation of episodes with a common thread – several related stories that constitute the final story, stories interrupted by negative or positive events, etc.

  The transformation of the brand DNA and its positioning into a strong storytelling requires four main steps: identity, relation, story, and incarnation. These steps are presented in Fig. 5.3 following a methodological logic highlighting the main objectives related to each step.

- **The hero's journey**. The hero's journey is a concept and a tool established by Joseph Campbell in 1949. It is a classic of narratology extensively used even today in narrative communication to build stories with myths. The hero's journey is about building a story by describing the initiatory journey of a hero who goes through several phases during which he/she is likely to meet moments of happiness as well as difficulties that he/she will have to overcome during his/her initiatory journey. By passing from a known world to an unknown universe, the hero is realized and creates a myth that fascinates, inspires, and touches the audience. The hero's travel method is often used by novelists and filmmakers and recently in video games (e.g., Tale of Dragon Age: Origins).

  This model is particularly relevant in the development of narrative communication as it is based on the study of the main myths in different cultures that have survived through time and have retained their status of myth in our contemporary societies (e.g., the myth of Beauty and the Beast). Table 5.1 summarizes the principal characteristics related to each phase of the hero's journey model that brand managers can take into account in their communications for telling a story and creating a strong myth around the founder of the brand, its history, etc.

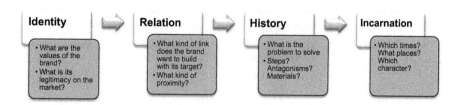

Fig. 5.3 Steps in storytelling construction

Table 5.1 The stages of the hero's journey

Stages	Characteristics
The hero in his/her ordinary world	This is an introduction that will bring out the extraordinary nature of the adventures that will follow
The call for adventure	It presents itself as a problem or a challenge. The hero is initially reluctant, and he/she is afraid of the unknown
The hero is encouraged by a mentor	The mentor will give his/her advice, but he/she will not accompany the hero who must face the tests alone
The hero passes the "threshold" of the adventure	The hero enters an extraordinary world, and he/she cannot turn back
The hero undergoes trials	Hero meets allies and enemies
The hero reaches the most dangerous place	Often in depth where the object of his/her quest is hidden
The hero undergoes the supreme test	More serious, the hero faces death
The elixir	The hero seizes the object of his/her quest
The way back	It is still about escaping the revenge of those from whom the object was stolen
The hero is transformed by his/her experience	The hero comes back from the extraordinary world where he/she had ventured, transformed by experience
The triumphant return	The return to the ordinary world and the use of the object of the quest to improve the world (thus giving meaning to the adventure)

Hence, what will be the future of storytelling in luxury? The advent of the digital realm is obviously a major change in storytelling, with multiple challenges for luxury brands. Commercial communication is not dying, but it is changing. Consumers are increasingly connected and able to filter advertising content if they do not engage the interest of the audience. Therefore, the time when we could hope to force communication upon the audience declines, making way for a time when the communication of the brand itself should become content that is exciting enough to attract the audience and facilitate sharing (like, share, retweet, etc.). This is where storytelling comes in to transform traditional factual communication into narrative content.

In addition, storytelling can also go beyond traditional means of commercial communication to express its potential in the fields of packaging, point of sale (take the example of Eataly in the context of luxury Italian food), and even staff training. If it is true that customers transported by a story are more convinced and responsive to the brand that transported them, the same thing would happen to employees. Managers transported by the brand they work for would be more motivated and more attached to their company. In luxury, where know-how is essential for maintaining its competitive edge, being able to retain key employees is not insignificant. Furthermore, it is also important for luxury brands to make a transition from experiential storytelling to experiential storydoing and sharing with the customers as well as employees by transforming their stories into actions.

5.2.2   Storydoing

History has meaning and value only if it is lived first, if it reflects an emotion, or if it creates an exchange between the brand and its customers. Without this unique breath, the story, beautiful as it is, remains an empty shell. And that is the difference between companies that "tell" stories (without real foundation) and those that "make live" their story, those that create shared experiences so rich that the customer wants to live and to extend the experience. Indeed, luxury businesses should allow their customers to live their stories because it creates for them emotions and the desire to belong and share. Each company has its own story and should make it livable and sharable with its customers.

Unlike "storytelling," which consists of imagining stories to appeal to consumers, storyliving or storydoing combines story and action through lived experiences in order to put customers at the heart of the story. In fact, while engaging customers is an effective strategy, telling a story is not enough to build loyalty. Brands should also engage in "storydoing" projects where they engage customers by turning the brand's storytelling into concrete actions. The term storyliving is derived from anthropology (e.g., Emigh 1996), which uses the term "lived story" to define social practices of people. Table 5.2 summarizes the main differences between storytelling and storydoing.

Storydoing (lived story) or an experience of living is an ongoing experience narrated in real time. It could, in any case, be closer to "storybuilding" or even "storyliving" since there is something that is occurring in the present. Storytelling and storydoing do not have to be opposed since storyliving is a form of lived storytelling. It is in the field of virtual reality (VR) that storyliving has flourished. Storydoing gets rid of any element of contextualization or past in relation to the brand and inscribes its target in the present time. Behind slightly vague terms, the idea is to involve customers in relation to the brand.

Far from being a new whim created by decision-makers and advertisers, storydoing logically follows the growth of new methods of communication and content

Table 5.2 Storytelling vs. storydoing

Storytelling	Storydoing
Based primarily on a story told and conveyed through the media	Builds on the company's ability to turn a story into a customer-centric strategy
The company owns the history of the brand	Consumers co-construct history and participate in actions related to it
Fiction is part of the symbolic universe	Fiction takes place in reality
Telling emotionally charged stories	Bet on the action
The goal is to build brand awareness	The goal is to consolidate the utility of the brand
The brand defines the customer experience	It is the customer experience that defines the brand
Communicate about the brand and its products	Create products as an extension of the story told
Create the desire to buy products	Create products that consumers want

creation on the Internet. Social networks play a major role in the expansion and success of storyliving. The heart of the transformation lies in living experiences with brands. With Snapchat, Instagram, Facebook, Periscope, or even YouTube and other video platforms, more and more creators and influencers are turning to live video to reach their subscribers. It is here that the complete deconstruction of storytelling is based on a short or even medium-term reflection toward an ideal of spontaneity that seduces a rather young target heart. The storydoing takes place more in a sort of permanent duration considered as a present (at least that of an event), such as the Periscope function that broadcasts live the lived moment allowing people to interact and add comments.

The primary goal of storydoing is to share the experience with users rather than just let them read and comment on the messages they view. The first luxury brands to have started the storyliving trend immediately adopted virtual reality, augmented reality, videos where the user/customer is the hero, and, of course, a host of live tools, participative debates, tutorials, challenges, etc., with content that is likely to attract the user, to involve him/her, to make the buzz, and, in return, to attract the curiosity of the whole world. By consolidating its affective community base, storyliving is undoubtedly a major challenge for marketers in designing the ultimate customer experience.

The storydoing refers to the luxury brand's ability to bring its values and history to life by offering customers immersive and interactive experiences. These experiences can be shared in the real space (e.g., shops, events, etc.) and in the digital world (e.g., e-commerce site and social media). This guarantees a continuum between the "offline" and "online" customer experiences. Storytelling is then the starting point of any successful storydoing and has to include the following elements:

- Covering all the actions of the company and engaging its various functions (e.g., marketing, communication, HR, R&D, etc.);
- Putting the customer and his/her expectations at the center of the brand's history.

It is obvious that brands that have storyliving approaches to communicating with consumers will perform better than those that limit their actions to storytelling.

Mini-case 5.13

The Montblanc brand writes and makes history: From storytelling to storydoing

Montblanc with its "power pen," as nominated by Wall Street bankers, associates its name with the culture of writing since its birth 109 years ago. It was in 1906 that the company's story began. Two German contractors, August Eberstein, an engineer, and Alfred Nehemias, a banker, returned to Hamburg from a trip to the United States, where they discovered the first fountain pen

(continued)

Mini-case 5.13 (continued)

with its own tank. They decided to partner with Claus-Johannes Voss, a stationery trader, to design an easy-to-use fountain pen that did not stain.

In 1910, a new pen with a white Montblanc star on the hood came on the market. The design of the iconic pen was modified in 1934 and would remain almost unchanged even to this day; only the channel that allows the ink to feed into the tip has been improved. Another feature of this hand-made pen is the number 4810 engraved since 1929 on each of the gold feathers. It is the estimated height, at the beginning of the last century, of the mountain of Europe. Since its origins, Montblanc has been linked to the culture of writing. With Montblanc's commitment to UNICEF since 2004, the brand writes and makes history to put an end to illiteracy and promote writing by making it accessible to as many people as possible.

5.3 Summary

In this chapter, I have examined one of the big five strategies that luxury brands can implement to design unique luxury experiences through the experiential branding of their products and services. Experiential branding is then a central strategy in building a strong luxury brand since it is co-constructed by incorporating cultural and experiential dimensions embedded within different luxury experiences. Even if the luxury house is strongly related to its brand, it cannot alone generate values, attitudes, and shared behaviors among consumers in their experiences with the brand. In this chapter, I explained how luxury brand managers and marketers can implement and emphasize two strategic communication approaches: an experiential branding based on storytelling through two main techniques – that of the hero's journey and brand positioning – as well as the technique of storydoing, which will transform story to action and thus to experience. These communication strategies are very critical for luxury houses that are willing to design a valuable luxury experience in which the brand shares the same values with its customers who, in turn, view the luxury house' offerings as meaningful and close to them.

Experiential Setting Design

6

Nowadays, consumers can move through a variety of spaces each day, including both digital (e.g., website experience) and physical ones (e.g., in-store experience). These experiential settings have been designed over time, adjusting to the functional needs of individuals to optimize their navigation and usages without even focusing on how new ways of designing both digital and physical spaces can help companies, especially luxury houses, design experiential settings which are phygital and that can help consumers be fully immersed in their consumption and shopping experiences. This chapter will explore one of the big five strategies that luxury houses can implement to design their experiential settings by conceding the continuum between digital space and physical place. By designing experiential settings, luxury houses will be able to create a memorable and rewarding luxury experience through considering not only the physical but also the digital environment in which the experience with the luxury brand is lived in a virtual or connected universe.

6.1 Components of the Experiential Environment

The experiential environment of luxury encompasses three key components: immersion and multisensory, theming, and hyperreality. These components (Fig. 6.1) are necessary for luxury houses in order to offer a rewarding and pleasant luxury experience and enhance a customer's positive feeling within a highly experiential setting in-store (during the purchase) and out-of-store (pre- or post-purchase).

6.1.1 Immersion and Multisensory

To offer immersive and multisensory luxury experiential settings in luxury boutiques, as well as in luxury hotels and restaurants, brand managers and marketers can use sensory marketing tools that include the five senses (sight, sound, smell,

© Springer Nature Switzerland AG 2019
W. Batat, *The New Luxury Experience*, Management for Professionals,
https://doi.org/10.1007/978-3-030-01671-5_6

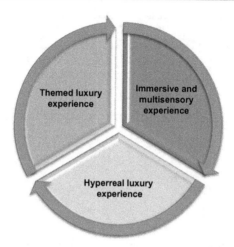

Fig. 6.1 Factors of luxury experiential setting

taste, and touch), which can induce emotions, sensations, and enhance the immersion of consumers in enchanting luxury experiences. Most studies in the marketing field highlight the idea that a consumer who feels good in a luxury store or restaurant tends to spend more time, consume more, and speak positively about the brand. An immersive and multisensory luxury experience brings together different types of marketing that target the five senses and enhance luxury brand signature and identity: olfactory marketing (smell), auditory marketing (sound), tactile marketing (touch), visual marketing (sight), and gustatory marketing (taste).

Testimonial 6.1

Simon Sproule, Chief Marketing Officer and Vice President at Aston Martin: An immersive multisensory driving experience

1. How does Aston Martin reinvent the luxury driving experience?
   Owning a luxury car like an Aston Martin should be more than just providing mobility. Our owners are buying a car but also joining a family, and as such, we need to ensure the experience lives up to the promise of the brand. We don't, for example, see much value to our customers in providing a concierge service as they typically have this already in their lives. However, our customers do want to have interesting and engaging experiences with us that

(continued)

Testimonial 6.1 (continued)

are unique to ownership of an Aston Martin. That could be a private visit to our factory or access behind the scenes at an F1 race. If there is a reinvention of the customer experience in general, I would submit this would be around personal contact between a company and its customers beyond just a digital relationship.

2. **What is the DNA of Aston Martin multisensory driving experience?**
   Our driving experience DNA is rooted in high-performance grand touring. This is the ability to have a car that is dynamically gifted on a track but provides the ability to drive large distances effortlessly and in comfort. Our brand promise is "for the love of beautiful," and we aspire to make our cars every bit as beautiful to drive, as they are to look at. Going forward, we will enter new segments for Aston Martin such as SUVs and mid-engined supercars. Although we will need to dial in different driving characteristics to suit customer expectations in these segments, we will ensure that every Aston Martin has a consistent dynamic feel.

(continued)

Testimonial 6.1 (continued)

3. **Why does Aston Martin use experiences to help reach luxury shoppers?**

As a percentage of our marketing and communications investments, traditional advertising is relatively small compared to other luxury brands. We are a brand that is naturally oriented toward experiences. Seeing, touching, and driving an Aston Martin is the most compelling way to bring new customers to our brand, and so we orientate our marketing toward that objective. Our experiences can range from a visit to our factory to a hot lap of an F1 circuit during a race weekend. We also work very closely with our retail partners to create launch events, test drives, and unique experiences that allow customers to not only experience driving an Aston Martin but to also gain a deeper insight into the brand.

4. **What is the digital strategy and UX of Aston Martin on mobile phone? Do you use digital devices in store to create immersive and multisensory driving experience? How?**

In 2016 we undertook a total overhaul of our website and configurator technology. Today we have a site that has richer content, a more sophisticated and luxurious UI, and is enabled for viewing on multiple devices. The parallel investments in configurator technology were equally important as this is where our customers will come and start to create their personal Aston Martin. We have extended this technology into our retail network and are now working on next-generation technologies incorporating virtual reality.

5. **How can digital help you to create the true luxury experience targeting millennials?**

I don't think millennials are the only demographic that seeks engagement through digital channels. Before we select a communications platform, we start with our story – the narrative of the brand – and then look at the desired outcomes for a given product or experience. Although different customer segments might have a preference for communications via one channel vs. another, we find more common ground in the content of the experience.

- **Olfactory signature**. It allows the company to reinforce its identity and values. The olfactory signature is spread regularly and can also be integrated into products and other types of media, such as magazines and brochures, which continuously reinforce the olfactory atmosphere of the luxury brand. The interest of luxury businesses in using the consumer's sense of smell is to appeal to memories that can generate emotions, well-being, and nostalgia, thus encouraging a purchase or making the luxury experience enjoyable and memorable. The sensations and feelings generated by spread perfumes lead the consumer to develop a strong connection with the luxury brand and identify it among others.

- **Auditory signature**. Sound/auditory marketing is intended to broadcast sounds and music in order to influence the purchase decision-making of customers. Several marketing studies have shown that the type of music and the rhythm of the melody chosen have an influence on the time spent in stores and, ultimately, on consumer spending. Also, studies show that consumers will move toward aisles or choose products that are closest to the sound signal. Additionally, the rate of diffusion and the quality of the sound have an impact on the behavior of the buyers. In luxury, the auditory signature is a key element in creating an immersive and memorable luxury experience. An auditory experience helps luxury brands influence behaviors at the point of sale or at an experiential setting by acting on three main dimensions: emotional, cognitive, and conative/behavioral.

  The sound identity of a luxury house or brand can include a collection of sounds, voices, melodies, or musical compositions. Therefore, auditory marketing can be used by luxury businesses to convey the universe and the identity of their brands in order to strongly position themselves in the mind of their customers. The dissemination of the auditory identity of luxury brands can be achieved through different channels:

  - Social media and Internet websites;
  - Point of sale (e.g., popup store, boutiques, corners, etc.);
  - Switchboard;
  - Headquarter (e.g., reception, elevator, etc.);
  - Advertising and institutional films;
  - Events, conferences, conventions, etc.

  The dissemination on the various channels reinforces the coherent positioning of the luxury house allowing the consumer to distinguish it from its competitors by identifying its unique experiential signature conveyed through sound. Although audible marketing has an impact on consumer purchasing decisions and is essential in creating and improving customer experiences and identifying the brand's DNA (brand colors, logo, typo, forms, etc.), luxury businesses never use them and limit the use of sound to the broadcast of impersonal playlists and pieces of music in hotels, restaurants, and shops; sometimes the same playlists are used by both luxury fashion brands and by fast fashion brand stores, such as Zara and H&M.

  Nowadays, luxury houses, hotels, and restaurants should take into consideration auditory marketing when developing their own sound identity and their auditory signature, which is an integral part of a successful luxury experience. Although auditory marketing is not the priority of luxury brands, which prefer visual marketing (logo, graphic charter, etc.), it is nevertheless essential for the following reasons:

  - Audible signature guarantees a 360° global coherence on all broadcast media (Internet, telephone, institutional film, advertising, etc.) between visual elements and luxury brand identity;
  - Audible signature has a very high power of persuasion related to the emotions generated by the music;

- Audible signature helps to establish a strong relationship between the luxury house and the client;
- Audible signature and music facilitate consumer immersion in the luxury brand universe as well as contact with products and staff;
- A stimulating audible signature that is in line with the image of the luxury house can increase turnover by 28% (World Luxury Tracking,[1] 2016);
- Audible signatures significantly influence the time spent in the store.

The sound dimension is, therefore, an essential element of living a pleasant and enjoyable luxury experience in an immersive and emotionally charged experiential setting. The audible signature allows the optimization of the quality of service and that of the customer experience by making it more comfortable, pleasant, and memorable.

Mini-case 6.1

Sonos: A luxury sound experience

Anyone who's into sound has undoubtedly heard of Sonos, a modern wireless home audio company that offers high-fidelity speakers to be connected, to create an immersive listening experience. Sonos' vision is to fill every home and every room with music, helping people to listen to incredible sounds and make listening a valued practice. Basically, Sonos speakers make one's home sound like he/she is at the stadium. The best way to discover about it is to experience in action the flow of the sound as it comes through these speakers naturally, clearly, and crisply disappearing into the background.

In terms of retail experience, Sonos which is one of the prime brand names in the industry aims to do its activities differently when it comes to marketing. The company's first goal is to replicate the home listening environment at retail and deliver a real, personalized Sonos sound experience to its visitors, convincing them that purchasing its smart sound system is worth it. That's why the company has designed its own branded stores, places that are made to feel and sound more like home than a store, ensuring the customers listen to their preferred music as it should sound, suitable to their home needs. Sonos' 7 acoustically perfect listening rooms resemble tiny houses each with a custom interior design to characterize different styled homes. There, clients do not find boxes on top of the shelves; Sonos does not even have ten different products to sell, but it has voice platforms and music services for the clients to play and queue in an immersive way, discovering different combinations of Sonos speakers and how each would work in their own home.

(continued)

---

[1] Source: website https://www.ipsos.com/en-hk/world-luxury-tracking-2016, consulted on February 13, 2018.

Mini-case 6.1 (continued)

Furthermore, Sonos speakers are designed to sit underneath the TV or be mounted to the wall of homes or offices while using Wi-Fi to pump the music to the preferred surrounding. Sonos embraces excellent and budget-friendly speakers from Play:1 to the higher-end Play:3 or Play:5.

The design of Sonos products is clean and modern; but after all, they all look like what they are: a piece of electronic. Their color options are two: black or white with a metallic-gray grill. Sonos lately changed the look of its products for marketing initiatives, turning its electronic devices into more sculptural objects that can fit anywhere and into any interior space.

- **The tactile signature**. Tactile marketing uses touch and contact with materials to create a pleasant luxury experience. Touch gives an impression of quality, softness, and comfort and can influence purchasing decisions or the time spent in the store. Customers need to touch the product to get an idea of its quality, shape, texture, and materials used. Luxury brands should, therefore, develop a tactile signature that makes customers want to take products into their hands, explore them tactually, and buy them. The signature should also differentiate a brand's products from those of competitors. Many luxury brands have employed tactile marketing strategies that allow customers to become acquainted with the spirit and DNA of the luxury house (e.g., the thickness of cristal Baccarat glasses, the soft pillows in hotels luxury, etc.).
- **The visual signature**. The visual aspect distinguishes the identity of the luxury brand. Visuals are important, especially regarding the packaging of products, decoration, choice of colors, layout of stores, shelf products, etc. Colors are also important and can have a positive or negative influence on the customer experience. To develop a visual signature, luxury brands should create a visual identity in tune with their universe and their DNA. Managers can use visual marketing for the power it has to act unconsciously on customers and influence their perception and reactions at a product or point of sale.
- **The gustatory signature**. It is an essential sensory element of the luxury experience that can be associated with other sensory elements, such as sight or touch. Taste is not only for food products; it can also be used by luxury brands to create taste experiences by associating a specific taste with a luxury universe. The aim of the gustatory signature is to seduce consumers by stimulating their taste and associating it with the subtle and refined universe of the luxury brand (e.g., the cristal brand Baccarat created a gustatory signature through the launch of its Baccarat chocolates).

6.1.2 Hyperreal Experiential Setting

Hyperreality is one of the key characteristics of today's postmodern consumer societies, which merges two realities: real and virtual, both of which are constructed and shared by members of the same consumption culture. Hyperreality originated in the art movement born in the United States at the end of the 1960s called hyperrealism, which refers to the reconstruction of reality by proposing themed universes in which the recreated reality (hyperreality) brings together universes that may be more suited to consumers' expectations than the "real reality." The reconstructed reality has the advantage of offering reality with its advantages and without its constraints. Thus, in hyperreal settings risks are almost inexistent. In order to offer hyperreal experiential settings, luxury brands should follow two main steps of the hyperreal process:

- Step 1: a simplification of the direct natural customer experience, replaced by a recreated and simulated luxury experience whose meaning is reconstructed through the simulated situations.
- Step 2: a metaphorization through the use of media representations that speak to all customers.

To build hyperreal luxury settings, six main characteristics inspired by Rodaway's work on hyperrealism (1994) and hyperreal spaces can be considered by luxury brands: sensuality, hegemony, consumerism, security, transparency, and automation.

Mini-case 6.2

The World and Palm Jumeirah in Dubai, the hyperreal luxury world

Completed in 2006, the Palm Jumeirah hyperreal space is an artificial palm-shaped archipelago that offers houses nearly 500 apartments, 2000 villas, 25 hotels, 200 luxury shops, and tourist leisure attractions. Since 2005, it has featured a shopping center with an indoor ski slope in one of the hottest cities on the planet.

Another example of hyperreal luxury tourism, The World, is a construction project of 250–300 islands whose layout will mimic a world map. The idea is to remind consumers and travelers that Dubai also pretends to simulate the whole world in its commercial malls.

6.1.3 Theming the Experiential Setting

Theming refers to the process of creating a specific theme that allows the customer to dive into a deep thematic experience as defined by the luxury brand. Theming is a good illustration of today's contemporary societies in which the enjoyment of consumption settings can be enhanced through decors and creative themings. Baudrillard (1983) states that our societies are characterized by simulation and simulacra. Simulation involves a service provision where the whole core product can be entirely created for the pleasure of the consumers.

Although the objective of the theming process is to create an atmosphere, above all its purpose is to unify the decor of the customer experience. This can be achieved by ensuring the consistency of the theme through diverse elements of the servicescape and the physical environment that give compliance throughout the experience journey. Compliance is an essential element for successful customer experiences. It allows customers to gradually immerse themselves in the consumption and purchase experience and remain immersed throughout the duration of the experiential process. Luxury companies should consider theming for the following principal reasons:

- Theming allows for better immersion of the consumer and can be used in many consumption areas, such as retail, services, leisure, and so forth.
- Theming also generates a magical dimension that allows to transpose the consumer into another consumption universe. The customer will, therefore, disconnect from his/her daily world characterized by external pressures related to environmental and social relations.
- Themes selected by luxury brands will be used as a mental reference by consumers and will facilitate pleasurable memories (e.g., Schmitt 1999).
- A theme will help consumers unify the provider and organize their impressions about lived experience (e.g., Pine and Gilmore 1999).

An uninterrupted themed consumption experience is regarded as a new way to re-enchant the consumer during his/her purchase and consumption experiences. Marketing professionals and brand managers can apply several forms of theming that can be designed to meet marketing objectives, ranging from increasing sales volumes to creating value and the formation of branded communities. Though, Gilmore and Pine (2002) argue that it is only when a theme is used that an offer (service or product) will become an experience. Furthermore, theming refers to the idea of recreating reality to make it look more real than the real object. Luxury companies can recreate reality through two approaches:

- Offering authentic consumption experiences to satisfy consumers with high expectations in terms of "real authenticity" (e.g., World Heritage Sites).
- Offering reconstructed authenticity through hyperreal theming to meet the expectations of consumers who accept the idea of "fake authenticity" and enjoy the entertainment provided by non-authentic artifacts (e.g., Las Vegas) mixing both real and false elements.

Mossberg (2007) defines three main factors that contribute to successful theming: an arena (experiencescape), characters (personnel and other customers), and structure (construction of the story).

Mini-case 6.3

The Bentley Suite: A themed luxury hotel experience

The five-star St. Regis has partnered with the luxury car brand Bentley to offer a themed hotel experience that plunges hotel guests into the luxury automotive world. The hotel offers luxurious suites decorated with noble materials in a universe developed by the car manufacturer Bentley.

Partnership and openings. St. Regis, which is one of the world's most luxurious hotel brands, collaborated with Bentley in an amazing partnership with a mutual goal of delivering truly astonishing levels of excellence. With this exclusive partnership, St. Regis provides its guests with the opportunity to discover extraordinary destinations in classy settings and gorgeous craftsmanship they have come to expect from these world-class brands. It is worth to mention that their partnership is a true example of both brands' shared vision of design excellence and ideal attention to detail, combined with the desire to balance legacy and heritage with art design.

The Bentley Suite at St. Regis New York was launched in 2012 and was a huge success, winning many luxury design awards. The second suite opened in the vibrant St. Regis Istanbul with designs inspired from the adventurous spirit of Bentley Continental GT. Also in 2016, the third attractive suite opened at St. Regis Dubai in Al Habtoor City. However, this one was styled according to one of the models of Bentley called the Mulsanne being one of the world's finest handmade cars having the combination of both luxury and performance.

Unique design. Everything is inspired by Bentley, from the curves of the room to the furniture that uses the same leather pattern as the auto brand's seats. A light monument hangs above the bed giving the image of both the headlights of the Bentley Continental and the curves of a racetrack. The sofa is modeled after the luxurious cabins inside Bentley's cars. It features Bentley diamond materials and unique illuminated tread plates. Also hidden in the sofa, guests can find a built-in champagne bar, which slides open to reveal.

Amazing experience. Due to the suites distinctive Bentley designs and unique craftsmanship, guests enjoy the incomparable beyond expectation service of St. Regis hotels which also includes personal butlers. The Bentley suites give customers the opportunity to enjoy the Bentley experience in a completely new way, in adventurous and exciting locations. It provides its guests with modern luxury lifestyle that not only can be driven but also lived. To add more St. Regis provides luxury-driving experiences to its guests during their stay. Guests arrive and leave the hotel with beautiful Bentley cars and enjoy tours around town giving them the luxury home from home experience.

6.2   A New Luxury Experiential Setting: Phygital

The digital revolution began with the transformation and transposition of many activities and functions of "real life" into corresponding digital entities. Today, the trend is reversing in a more and more obvious way; the virtual begins to reveal itself in the real. In terms of experience marketing strategy, phygital suggests the multiplication of bridges connecting the two worlds, physical and digital, to give consumers a more fluid and richer luxury experience.

The alliance of the physical and the digital ("phygital") enables customers to live a new luxury experience of purchase in the store and online. This is the reason why luxury brands and luxury retailers have to offer customers the possibilities of optimizing their experiential journey on the shelves according to their running list (indoor location), of reducing their waiting time at checkout (thanks to self-scanning and payment technologies contacts), or using a promotional program or dematerialized loyalty, etc. Designing a phygital luxury experiential setting is, thus, one of the primary challenges that luxury brands will face in the future when creating the ultimate customer experience with a continuum offline and online. Thus, luxury houses have to find a way to adapt dimensions of the physical environment to the digital space. Therefore, sensory, mobile, and interactivity are also very important dimensions to consider in order to ensure the continuum between online digital luxury experiences and in-store ones. Table 6.1 presents the five sensory elements and their operational implementation within a digital experiential environment.

6.2.1   From Digital to Phygital Luxury Experience

Digital luxury marketing is not only about Internet use and marketing techniques applied to a website. It can be associated with several activities, techniques, and tools according to the objectives of the digital strategy defined by brand managers and marketers. The definition of these objectives will influence the type of digital devices, tools, and platforms that luxury brands can use for an effective and optimal implementation of their digital strategy. In order to facilitate the implementation of an effective digital strategy, it is important for luxury brand professionals to understand the specificities of digital marketing and its digital resources so they can choose the right digital channel. Indeed, understanding the specificities of digital marketing and its contribution to creating a new phygital setting with the purpose of guaranteeing the continuum of the experience from a real (physical) place to digital space and vice-versa will enable brand managers to make a more informed decision about which digital tool will be best suited to meet the goals of the luxury brand.

Among the specificities of digital tools for luxury, five properties can be named: vivacity, synchronization, stimulation, interactivity, and transfer mode. These features should be taken into account by luxury professionals prior to setting up the

Table 6.1 Five sensory elements of the experiential website

Sensory elements	Implementation of experiential website
VISUAL	Propose a homepage with strong visuals. It should have a strong impact from the first visit to the site Put forward a concept and a design specific to the brand and its site Propose harmonized colors and HD images with a coherent graphic Work on the style of the text font Integrate interactive avatars
TACTILE	Propose a global view with a selective zoom Integrate quality slideshows and full-screen videos Offer a 3D display of objects, a 360° vision, and augmented reality Integrate interactive and alternative views with demos
GUSTATORY	Propose a detailed description of the product Propose storytelling and strong content Propose tasting events on the site so that the universe of the brand is associated with a taste Develop collaborations with chefs and propose taste references to describe the products Communicate about taste through quality images
AUDITORY	Propose a specific sound signature linked to the identity of the brand Diversify the music on the website and offer several options Propose sound control tools Propose a soothing soundtrack Integrate sound at a click Offer a choice of vocal narration Use a balanced tone Offer a possibility of pulling text or narration in several languages
SCENT	Suggest an olfactory signature Integrate broadcasters into connected objects in stores or on broadcast screens

digital strategy of the luxury brand. The properties of the tools change and evolve during the transition from Web 1.0 to Web 3.0, which is characterized by a strong interactivity through social media platforms (e.g., Facebook and YouTube), a multiplication of technological platforms and devices, and high-speed Wi-Fi. Table 6.2 summarizes the main characteristics of the evolution of the digital from the era of Web 1.0 to Web 3.0 and its impact on consumer expectations, in terms of digital luxury experience.

Nowadays, luxury brands have entered the digital experiential era, marking the transition to Web 3.0, which is increasingly immersive and interactive. This evolution has contributed to the emergence of new approaches in the digital luxury field. The shift from digital to phygital luxury experience reflects three main eras of digital luxury: static digital luxury, social digital luxury, and immersive digital luxury.

- **Static digital luxury (2003–2007).** The first years of the digital era in the field of luxury were marked by the Web 1.0 used as a top-down distribution channel by luxury brands in different sectors. In the era of static digital luxury, the two

Table 6.2 From luxury 1.0 to luxury 3.0

	Web 1.0	Web 2.0	Web 3.0
Type of luxury marketing	Informative and functional marketing	Interactive and social marketing	Sensory and experiential marketing
Luxury marketing approach	A "push" approach	A two-way approach	A collaborative and immersive approach
Role of luxury marketing	Buying	Socialization	Living
User behavior	Passive	Passive and active	Collaborative
Interactivity	Machine interactivity	Machine interactivity and interactivity among users	Overall machine and user interactivity
Luxury product/ service offering	Content production	Co-production of content	Co-production of experiences
Communication model in luxury	One (the brand) to many	One-to-one and many-to-many dialogue	One (the consumer) at the center of many
Priority	Focus on the content or the website of the luxury brand	Place the user at the heart of the relationship	Involve the user in a memorable virtual luxury universe

main elements of the Web were technology and content, which were used to facilitate the dissemination of information enabling offline and online transactions as well as the delivery of content or tangible products. Marketing and branding in the digital static era included various aspects:

– Delivery of goods purchased on the website of the luxury brand;
– The downloading speed of content on the website (e.g., details, etc.) luxury digital tools;
– Online reward offers such as vouchers or points luxury digital tools;
– The location of a luxury brand store by search engines luxury digital tools;
– Visual interface of the contents luxury digital tools;
– Ease of navigation and good ergonomics of the luxury brand's website luxury digital tools;
– Personal offline assistance.

For luxury brands, it was, therefore, essential to remain vigilant about the appearance of a new technology, a new tool, or a new use that could generate new behaviors and usages. Marketing actions related to static digital luxury in the era of Web 1.0 included aspects such as the replication of offline luxury marketing strategies by using websites to disseminate content in the form of static brochures or adding conversational content. Luxury brands had the power to delete, control, or disclose information that they deemed in the best interest of the brand image or the sale.

• **Interactive digital luxury (2007–2012).** This era refers to the social 2.0 Web, which moves away from the top-down model characterized by one-way, hierarchical mass communication. The emergence of interactive digital luxury and the development of social media platforms and forums have facilitated the delivery of content by users as well as co-creation and sharing between users. Unlike static digital luxury, interactive digital luxury integrates the user into the heart of its strategy as an active participant and co-creator of content. Interactive digital luxury includes the following features:

- It is multichannel and based on a multiuser approach in which each user has the power to share information and communicate it in a positive or negative way.
- In interactive digital luxury, the success factors of digital luxury (e.g., speed of download or the appearance of the site) are no longer part of customer satisfaction. In fact, the new elements of user satisfaction are now human factors that luxury brands cannot control.
- Human factors can positively or negatively influence the image of the luxury brand, its marketing strategy, and its communication.

Mini-case 6.4

The luxury Group Richemont and the digital "TimeVallee" experience setting

The Richemont Group has called on Carlipa to digitize its new multi-brand watchmaking concept: TimeVallee. The concept brings together 12 luxury watch companies and has been entirely designed to make digital a central part of the customer experience.

Special features of the concept are management and synchronization of the different digital devices.

Delivery through application development and a platform dedicated to TimeVallee and integrated into Carlipa Online. It allows the automatic upgrade of applications as well as the modification of contents from this platform.

Benefits: these tools allow the brand to interact with the customer and also collect information about him/her at each stage of the experience to better advise and offer him/her fully customized, high-end service.

In order to make the customer experience more exceptional in watchmaking, the digital agency Carlipa has worked on the creation of a new concept of multi-brand haute horlogerie shops where the digital experience serves the customer journey. This is how the TimeVallee concept came up with four main digital experience zones: Watch Bar, Watchslate, Style Book, and Secret Room.

Luxury brands can also use social media to create interactivity with their customers and enhance their online social experiences in which users can exchange information as well as get involved in a co-creation process with the luxury brand.

Mini-case 6.5

Louis Vuitton offers an interaction with customers through an online customization of its bags

To develop a luxury experience in the era of Web 2.0, Louis Vuitton offers to its customers the possibility of personalizing online luggage with a monogram. Of course, this service is not recent because it has always been possible to have initials stamped on one's Vuitton bag, but today, Louis Vuitton goes much further with online customization through the concept of "My Monogram" which allows the consumer to have a unique bag.

How does it work? On an interactive site, the consumer has the choice between three different models (in all sizes): the famous Speedy, the Pegase suitcase, and the Keepal. It is also possible to have one's initials written (3 letters maximum in 8 different sizes) and matched with bicolor bands (17 colors). In total, more than 200 million combinations are possible with these 3 customization options.

To respect the codes of luxury and the authenticity of the brand, the customization of the bag is entirely made by hand, but this service is completely free. Delivery times for a customized bag are a little longer than non-personalized bags: between 6 and 8 weeks. The Louis Vuitton brand also offers its online customers the opportunity to not only buy the product and personalize it online but also to share it with friends through email or Facebook with a simple click on the brand's website. Furthermore, Louis Vuitton designs its experiential setting to create an enjoyable and efficient customer experience by focusing on four main aspects:

1. **In-store experience**: Louis Vuitton's unique characteristic is that it creates an in-store experience for the customers that emphasizes legacy, enables them to customize the products, and provides distinct areas in the boutiques to make it easier for the clients to explore the items. Moreover, even though the French house's social media presence is prevalent, it is still unwilling to completely incorporate digital networks into the customer experience as a means to maintain the customer's trust.
2. **Remove omnichannel conflicts**: for the leather luxury brand, omnichannel marketing has become a vital success since it facilitates interactions between customers and companies by various means, including stores, websites, mobile applications, catalogs, and social media. Luxury boutiques have to be modified to be similar to the online experience.
3. **Place collective emotions at the center of the experiential setting**: the use of digital channels has to be created in a way that is appealing emotionally. Luxury fashion brands should reflect a positive mood that is accepted by customers so that they will all interact through the brand's impression. Louis Vuitton is the most valued luxury brand on social media, and the customers have admitted that their love toward this brand is a result of its

(continued)

Mini-case 6.5 (continued)

genuine customer experience. After all, by applying the omnichannel strategy, the brand can effectively correspond to the customer's personality and preference, ensuring successful marketing.

4. **Friendly customer service**: not only does Louis Vuitton ensure that its staff members greet customers in a friendly manner, but they also offer a drink and a seat to the clients once the clients arrive.

- **Experiential digital luxury (2013–until now).** Experiential digital luxury is very important for luxury brands as it helps to improve the quality of both the offline and the online experience. With the evolution of digital technologies and social media, luxury brands are now facing a major challenge related to the creation of a coherent and effective online luxury experience with the added value of the physical experience lived in-store. In the era of Web 3.0 and 4.0, online social interactions can be facilitated by immersive technologies such as 3D and 4D, avatars, augmented reality, connected objects, 3D printing, etc. However, while the role of immersive technologies as a tool for creating the digital luxury experience on websites is confirmed every day, there are still many questions as to the elements that can bring to life online luxury experiences for individuals. Implementing luxury experience that has been studied in a physical environment and adapting it to a virtual context raise two questions:

  - How can luxury brands integrate the components of the luxury experience into commercial and noncommercial websites in order to create a pleasant and memorable virtual luxury experience?
  - How can luxury companies translate sensory, emotional, cultural dimensions, etc. (characteristics of the luxury experience) in a digital context?

Mini-case 6.6

The "Factory" experience: Jean Paul Gaultier's virtual reality campaign

To promote his two cult fragrances, Classique and Le Mâle, Jean Paul Gaultier presented a new 360° advertising campaign in virtual reality. The 3.0 advertising campaign features a 2-minute spot, designed by the Mazarine agency and produced by OKIO Studio. The advertising campaign allows viewers to immerse themselves into the world of Jean Paul Gaultier. Accessible on a computer, a smartphone, or a virtual reality headset, the individual lives an immersive experience alongside the inevitable sailors and pinups that characterize the perfumes Classique and Le Mâle so well.

The experience of the "Factory" is extended by offering the viewer the opportunity to put him/herself in the bottle's place, in the heart of the action,

(continued)

Mini-case 6.6 (continued)

and interact with the sailors and courtesans of the Factory. The device #BeTheBottle is relayed online on the brand's website (https://www.jeanpaul-gaultier.com/fr//bethebottle/), on Facebook, and on YouTube as well as through a smartphone application.

The experiential digital luxury brings together three main characteristics: immersion, co-creation, and efficiency.

- Immersion in the digital world should be designed to allow users to live virtual experiences by incorporating immersive and interactive technology tools linking the physical environment of the luxury brand and virtual context. These two elements bring a realistic dimension to the online luxury experience. Thus, customers can live virtual experiences similar to experiences in the real context (in-store, hotel, etc.) because they can interact with online brand virtual agents and physical agents (staff, salesman, etc.).
- Users should be involved in the process of co-creating luxury products or services, as well as in the marketing strategy and communication of the luxury brand. They can give their opinions on products and services and customize the products according to their needs.
- The experiential digital luxury should provide a cognitive response (e.g., convenience, time savings, comparison, customization, etc.) and an emotional response (e.g., pleasure, hedonism, online socialization, etc.).

By changing their practices, luxury brands will, therefore, have more opportunities to understand the online needs of users before implementing a digital marketing strategy to ensure the development of the luxury brand.

Mini-case 6.7

Giampiero Bodino, the fine jewelry house launches its experiential website

The fine jewelry house Giampiero Bodino, created by the Richemont Group in 2013, recently presented its new website. To discover the world of this house, the agency Mazarine Digital has imagined an experiential site conceived as a labyrinth of curiosity. The user discovers the website through a navigation within an artistic universe and gradually accesses the secrets of the house in a sort of intimacy and shared secret.

The website is a translation of the DNA of the luxury brand. Each of its creations and unique pieces figures into the great Italian tradition and a passion for antiquity and contemporary design. To express the rarity of the creations of Giampiero Bodino, the brand created a unique website with immersive navigation at the heart of the fairytale story of the brand, which encourages the renewal of the experience.

Consumers increasingly buy experiences rather than products or services (e.g., Pine and Gilmore 1998). As a result, designing valuable consumer experiences has become a top priority for marketers today. In fact, 89 percent of marketers expect to compete primarily on the basis of customer experience (Sorofman 2014). As digital technologies become pervasive, marketers are growing particularly interested in understanding the influence of digital technology on customer experience. Today, a new set of hybrid consumption experiences is flourishing that is neither purely physical nor purely digital experiences, but a convergence of characteristics of both worlds (e.g., Castelli 2016) – e.g., augmented reality, experiences derived from the consumption of 3D printing, digital concierge services, or wearable tech. While some consumers find digital-physical experiences novel, exciting, and useful, others discard them as unnecessary technological gimmicks. This is because, as digital-physical experiences are new, marketers have limited experience in designing them, and very little is known about what makes them valuable for consumers (e.g., Rigby 2014).

Digital contexts build distinct and unique experiences due to their sociomaterial characteristics. These contexts immerse consumers in a world which material functioning is different from physical reality: geographical boundaries are irrelevant, events from the past can be reenacted by accessing archival data (e.g., Kozinets 2010), and impossible dreams can become real by creating virtual objects (e.g., Denegri-Knott and Molesworth 2010). Digital contexts also permit high levels of interactivity so that consumers can play a proactive role in designing valuable experiences (e.g., Hoffman and Novak 2009). As a result, consumer cultures specific to the digital environment have emerged (e.g., Phillips 2015) giving birth to experiences specific to that environment (e.g., Kedzior 2015). As digital technologies become pervasive, marketers are particularly interested in understanding the formation of an experiential value in digitalized contexts (e.g., Drell 2014). Marketing practitioners are encouraged to generate an "online value proposition" to design consumption experiences tailored to the digital context (e.g., Chaffey and Ellis-Chadwick 2012:232).

A large stream of research has investigated digital experiences, looking at the particular gratifications that consumers gain from using digital technologies. Overall, digital consumption has been found to promote positive, utilitarian, relational, entertaining, and aesthetic experiences (e.g., Punj 2012). Yet, it is not clear in that literature how digital experiences differ from their physical counterparts.

With regard to utility, research indicates that consumers search for products and services and buy them online because it is more convenient. Purchasing online is more time effective and cognitively and physically less demanding than. Digital consumption is also perceived as more effective, allowing consumers to make better decisions. Consumers feel that they are able to find the product or service that fits their needs or desires best because they have much more information available and access to a wider range of choices. Consumers also feel that they can obtain the best price for a product, thanks to price-comparison tools. Using Holbrook's terminology, this indicates that digital technologies enhance experiences of efficiency (convenience) and excellence (better decisions).

Digital technologies also promote the emergence of playful and aesthetic consumption experiences. Playful experiences are common because the interactive nature of digital technologies promotes the emergence of flow when searching for information (e.g., web surfing) and using a product (e.g., playing video games). Rich media also allow brands to produce aesthetic experiences by building aesthetically pleasing and attractive images and sounds (e.g., Mathwick et al. 2002) as well as developing elaborate stories for transporting consumers to imaginary worlds where they can escape reality and revel in their dreams.

Finally, social media have been shown to produce feelings of we-ness, that is, feelings of fellowship and togetherness in a group, and to allow the development of strong social relationships, providing consumers with pleasurable experiences of social integration. When consumers become core members of a community, they gain status in the group and receive approval and praise from their peers in the community, generating pleasurable experiences of social enhancement. Because communications on social media are digitally mediated, consumers can bond with like-minded individuals with whom they could not have otherwise connected because of geographical and time constraints. Altogether, digital technologies, therefore, facilitate the emergence of relational value in consumption.

Testimonial 6.2

Antonio Carriero, Chief Digital and Technology Officer at Breitling: The Breitling digital luxury experience

1. **How Breitling is running its digital transformation? How can you define Breitling digital approach?**

   At Breitling we don't speak about digital transformation. Digital and transformation are at the core of our operating model. It is not a specific program or initiative. After 20 years of digital, customer experience has definitely changed, and there is no way back. Digital transformed economies into egonomies, where the customer is at the center. Empowered customers expect a new level of experience, and digital is all about fulfilling customer experience. We operate a clear shift in focus from the product only to the customer and of course still the product. Digital is triggering and allowing this shift: from large campaigns to 1:1 interactions, from controlling the message to collaborative relationships (macro and micro influencers), and from generally accessible to active in the right places and the right time.

2. **How digital devices can improve Breitling customer experience offline and online?**

   Customer digital ecosystem is also our digital ecosystem. We share the same experience; we act in the same ecosystem. Google Apple Facebook Amazon + Baidu Alibaba Tencent: this is the ecosystem and our customers move inside its boundaries. They changed the way brands connect with

(continued)

Testimonial 6.2 (continued)

customer, online of course but also offline. Nothing is more intimate than our relation with our mobile phone.

Customer experience is about services. Online we focus on mobile only, leveraging data and technology to better-fit customer new behavior, personalizing the experience. Offline we empower the sales staff with digital capabilities to better engage with prospect and customer, before and after the visit in a boutique. 1:1 communication and clienteling solution, natively integrated with local social platform (like WeChat in China or Line in Japan), bind customer with the brand. A solid and never-ending link is digitally curated and nurtured by the sales staff but also directly available to the customer.

3. **How artificial intelligence (AI) can be used to create ultimate luxury experiences?**

Consumers crave recognition of their individuality. Technology real power lies in its ability to make it happen and create perfect consumer experience. This is what AI and ML will bring to luxury: anticipation, deep understanding, and the highest instant ultimate personalization of the experience. The vehicle is the digital ecosystem itself; any interaction from search in Google to a specific targeted advertisement in LinkedIn will be AI optimized (I should say decided) to anticipate my expectations. Tools and applications will embark AI capabilities to further help sales staff to better engage with customer.

(continued)

Testimonial 6.2 (continued)

4. **What are the challenges for Breitling in terms of setting up suitable and satisfying digital experiences?**

   Speed, change. Speed of change. Digital ecosystem is rapidly evolving new capabilities, new platforms, global, and locals. It requires flexibility and agility in the organization and the way we work. We have to react fast, build, shape, and reshape to match the continuous changes in the digital ecosystem. Beyond our hyperawareness, we need a network of partners that are capable to scout and anticipate. Working together, we master the technology and the platforms to build unique customer experiences that would influence the customer decision to purchase and repurchase.

Altogether past research indicates that digital technologies produce experiences of enhanced efficiency (convenience) and excellence (best fit) as well as facilitate the emergence of play (flow), aesthetic experiences (narrative transportation), and the development of relationships, which would have been otherwise impossible to build (linking value). Such characterizations of digital consumption experiences are very similar to that of offline physical consumption experiences where these different types of value coexist. It provides a picture of digital experiences as being quantitatively different from their offline physical counterparts (stronger or weaker experiential value, more positive or negative experience) rather than qualitatively different (a different thing).

Sparse research has started to characterize how digital experiences are qualitatively different from their physical counterparts. Digital experiences have been characterized as virtual and imbued with transience, instability (e.g., Watkins 2015), fragmentation, and a sense of augmented reality. Social media experiences have also been characterized as networked and polyvocal (e.g., Kozinets et al. 2010), wavering between private and public conversations. However, these results are preliminary and fragmented calling for further research on the topic to build an integrated framework.

Luxury consumption has attracted a lot of interest in marketing literature in the last 20 years given the reinforcement of luxury as a cultural category in contemporary societies and the consolidation and growth of the economic sector since the 1990s (e.g., Okonkwo 2009, 2010). From investigations of the determinants of legitimate and counterfeit luxury brand purchases to typologies of luxury brands (e.g., Kapferer 2008) and studies on the consequences of luxurious consumption on societal well-being (e.g., Berry 1994), luxury has developed into a marketing research domain.

Luxury is not an essential quality of a product, service, or lifestyle but rather an experience. It is the combination of a symbolic meaning, subconscious processes, and nonverbal cues resulting from consumption and characterized by fantasies, feelings, and fun. Luxury is a specific type of experience lived as desirable and more than necessary and ordinary. Luxury consumption experiences involve living the consumption activity online or offline as the enactment of a lifestyle, recognizing brand elements as holy (brand stories are myths, brand visuals are icons, brand shops are temples, brand followers are believers), and personalizing products through rituals (e.g., Grigorian and Petersen 2014). Various types of luxury brand experiences have been distinguished. For example, Kapferer (2008) distinguished luxury brand experiences as experiences of craftsmanship (e.g., heritage furniture), of modern art (e.g., Yves Saint Laurent clothes), of timeless and internationally recognized quality (e.g., Chanel perfume), and of rarity and exclusiveness (e.g., Ferrari cars).

Yet, the digital context creates a unique set of constraints for the development of luxury experiences. The craftsmanship and the artist's "griffe," normally conveyed through all senses, cannot be experienced given the lack of physical contact with the product or service provider (e.g., Okonkwo 2009). Fast-paced innovation in digital practices contradicts the notions of traditional craftsmanship and timelessness. Further, digital media are democratic, allowing anybody to engage with the brand from anywhere, lessening the sense of exclusiveness associated with luxury. In spite of those constraints, digital luxury consumption experiences exist. Luxury consumers have embraced the digital environment, while many luxury brands have successfully developed social media communication strategies, e-shopping platforms, and digital products in order to be more accessible and create memorable luxury experiences.

The constraints of the digital context raise the question of what digital luxury consumption is. Digital luxury experiences are different from their offline counterparts. In luxury literature, specific phrases like "luxurious webmosphere" or "luxemosphere" were developed, indicating the need to adapt traditional conceptualizations to the digital context (e.g., Okonkwo 2010:308). Descriptive accounts have highlighted that luxury in a digital environment involves different approaches to storytelling (e.g., Kretz and De Valck 2010) and consumer-brand relationships. Anecdotal evidence also suggests that luxury in a digital environment places more emphasis on convenience, innovation, and consumer control (e.g., Tran and Voyer 2013). However, what a digital luxury experience truly is remains unclear. In the digital marketing literature, online consumption experiences have been characterized as "digital virtual," a liminoid experience between the material and the imaginary (e.g., Denegri-Knott and Molesworth 2010), but what this means for luxury has not been addressed.

6.2.2   What Does Phygital Experiential Setting Mean?

The term phygital is the fusion of the terms physical and digital. Phygital explains the unstoppable digitization of society over-all and particularly of business and trading. It is propagated by e-commerce stores that have had to reinvent themselves in order to meet the needs of more and more connected, mobile, and demanding customers.

The phygital concept first appeared in the marketing field in 2013. It was developed by the Australian Marketing Agency Momentum, whose signature is: "An Agency for the Phygital World." This word, which could have been an ephemeral buzzword, however, is being rooted in our vocabulary as it perfectly reflects a reality that no one disputes. Phygital refers to the transformation of physical stores in the digital era: concepts are completely redesigned to offer a new customer experience and use digital tools as sales support.

The phygital logic has given rise to a series of equally evocative terms and marketing jargon, such as connected commerce or responsive retail, an interesting concept, and created by analogy with responsive design, which appeared in 2015. Phygital refers to the idea that today's e-commerce and retail stores should be flexible, attentive, and able to respond to the instantaneous, while simultaneously being able to interpret the paradoxes inherent in luxury consumption experiences. Phygital is then the ultimate solution to adapting to smart purchasing behavior and responding quickly in a multichannel way to the expectations of impatient and zapper consumers. It also helps luxury companies develop successful relationships with their customers by offering better personalization that takes into account the symbolic meanings of consumption that emerge within their experiences.

Phygital leads luxury businesses to rethink the relationship between real and virtual in order to meet the evolving expectations of their customers. Therefore, the phygital experiential setting will be a major challenge for luxury companies in the years to come. In fact, luxury brands need to understand its components and typologies to create phygital luxury experiences that are continuous, coherent, and satisfying at all levels: technical, functional, emotional, and social.

Mini-case 6.8

Sublimotion, Ibiza: The new restaurant that invites customers to a unique phygital and luxurious culinary experience

Paco Roncero (two Michelin stars) is an internationally recognized chef of the Sublimotion restaurant, which opened its doors for the first time in 2014 on the island of Ibiza. After 2 years of intense work and collaboration with professionals from different sectors, such as chefs, designers, engineers, illusionists, decorators, architects, choreographers, and screenwriters, to achieve the experiential fusion of gourmet haute cuisine and the most advanced technology with a unique staging, Sublimotion became the first phygital gastronomic showdown between the real and virtual world. That same year, the restaurant was awarded the title of the best innovation in the world.

The objective of Sublimotion is not only to offer a culinary and gustatory experience, but rather sensations and emotions by integrating the digital dimension in order to offer a unique customer experience. More than 28 waiters were present to serve the 20 dishes on the menu. Unlike all other gourmet restaurants, Sublimotion is a global experience. It allows initiating its customers into the world of refined food through the stimulation of the five senses by combining dishes and external effects. For example, at the same time that images and live sounds are being diffused, the temperature and humidity levels are also modified, all in line with the content of different dishes served. Thus, during a dinner experience at Sublimotion, the client can enjoy a gourmet meal, orchestra, and staged experience, thanks to the effects of sounds, lights, smoke, and projections of images. Each dish is made from a highly sought-after recipe, and tasting combines the creation being served with multiple emotions and sensations.

Table 6.3 Digital tools for designing luxury experiential settings

Sector	Digital tools
Luxury retail	Improve the customer experience by offering click and collect services that offer consumers more flexibility, choice, and convenience
	Use geolocalization and iBeacons for better customization of local offers
	Improve online and offline behavior monitoring, facial recognition, and avatar usage
	Link purchase online and offline and reduce the border between the two worlds
Luxury travel	Social media has a big influence on buying decisions
	Customers will have more and more channels and communities for sharing good and bad experiences
Private banking and luxury financial services	Big data and data analysis are essential to customizing offerings and anticipating future expectations for luxury banking
Luxury health and wellness	A medical self-help in line with the lived experience
	Automatic tracking of the patient's stay in private clinics: booking, alerts, cancellation, and any other changes
	Improve health and well-being through technologies and applications that allow each individual to control his/her health

Additionally, in order to enhance the phygital experiential setting, luxury brands need to integrate five key elements: social media, creative design, virtualization, mobility, and the cloud as a platform for solutions and services. Table 6.3 presents a multitude of technologies that can be used by luxury brands to improve the phygital luxury experience and enhance the immersion and positive feelings of customers.

Delivering a memorable and enjoyable phygital luxury experience requires the integration of digital tools and devices, such as smartphones, tablets, connected objects, etc., that meet three main functions of the customer experience:

- Function 1: create a contextualized, emotional, and sensory phygital luxury experience.
- Function 2: strengthen the link between the virtual and real experience on several devices and platforms – laptops, tablets, apps, websites, etc.
- Function 3: offer engaging experiential content using storytelling techniques. The video can be used to tell stories. This technique is very effective, requires no reading effort, and is especially easily shared on social networks.

6.2.3   Tools of the Phygital Experiential Luxury Setting

The phygital experiential luxury environment is a context of consumption-integrated gateways set up by companies between different physical channels (offline) and digital (online) so that customers can pass from one to the other without any difficulties by guaranteeing consistency in the experiential journey from the physical to digital luxury context and vice-versa. For luxury businesses, it is essential to create effective, high-performance digital luxury experiences that are strongly rooted in consumers' daily habits both offline and online. Yet, designing thematic points of sale equipped with touchpads or other screens giving access to the brand's website, as is available to any other consumer at home, is only a minimalist solution that will only provide a small in-store phygital luxury experience.

The transformation of physical luxury stores involves the use of digital tools to support the customer throughout his/her experiential journey – and it starts well before the customer opens the door of the store. Luxury brands should then combine different tools and strategies to offer the ultimate customer experience and enhance the continuum between the real place and the virtual space and vice versa.

To create a satisfying and continuous phygital experience setting, luxury businesses can also use web tools that are available to them to deliver memorable online experiences. Web 3.0 is an Internet of connected objects in which aggregated data make more sense based on three essential elements: semantics, mobile objects, and connected objects. Web 3.0 marketing enables businesses to use Internet-connected objects, database-enabled devices, intelligent sensors, and an instant responsiveness to the real world. In marketing 3.0, there are four main elements: data, objects (connected hardware), social interactions, and software. Connected objects represent a fast-growing market in all areas of activity: sports, well-being, home equipment, work, etc. Among the main trends in connected objects that luxury brands can consider when creating a phygital luxury experience, there are two categories: cognitive connected objects and sensory connected objects.

- **Cognitive connected objects**. These objects that collect data about their users, analyze them, and provide them with the results are in great demand by consumers who want to know more about their own behavioral patterns, to control them, to share them, or to compare them with other users. Health and well-being are two sectors that are very attracted to this technology. Other examples of connected objects that can use analyzed data to make everyday life easier include devices that control the entrances and exits of a house according to the daily movements of the user as well as:
  - Connected objects worn by users that have multiple functions.
  - Connected objects that are practical and part of everyday consumer management. These objects are proposed in order to create an innovative solution that answers the functional needs of everyday life.
- **Sensory connected objects**. These objects are designed to detect the emotion that the user expresses when using the product or practicing a given activity. These objects have sensors for an emotional reading and offer options for adapting to the mood of the moment.

Furthermore, to create an online luxury experience, it is important to involve the user in the co-creation of the product or service. Interactivity and co-creation should be at the heart of the device for developing an effective and satisfying, functional and emotional, phygital luxury experience. There are several technologies that allow interactivity and collaboration with users. Among these technologies, four digital tools are needed to adapt the luxury experience to the phygital environment.

- **Augmented reality**. It is one of the technological tools that companies can use to optimize the phygital customer experience by combining real and virtual settings. In an augmented reality, virtual objects are presented in realistic form in a three-dimensional (3D) video.
- **3D printing**. It is a rapid prototyping technology that allows luxury companies to manufacture three-dimensional objects using a 3D printer, a digital file (often accessible free of charge and open sourced), and some materials depending on the size and composition of the product/object to be printed (plastic, metal, resin, etc.). 3D printing is becoming increasingly attractive to more and more luxury and fashion businesses as well as to anyone else who is curious to explore all the possibilities offered by 3D printing. The technology allows consumers to create and personalize objects such as smartphone cases, cups, figurines, jewelry, etc.

Mini-case 6.9

Lockheed Martin files patent to print diamonds
The American company Lockheed Martin, best known for its activities in the field of aeronautics or defense, presented in August 2016, a patent for the development of a 3D printer capable of producing synthetic diamond objects. The printer is based on the combination of two materials: a ceramic powder and a so-called "pre-ceramic" polymer. The latter has the property of turning into ceramic material when heated to high temperature.

- **Mobile technologies**. They are widely distributed and consumers are highly equipped with smartphones. This has contributed to the spread of mobile technology and its incorporation into the phygital customer experience. In terms of functional interactivity, smartphones offer the opportunity for users to obtain product information through QR (Quick Response) codes that allows consumers to be in both the real and the virtual world.
- **Geolocalization**. It is also another form of technology appreciated by companies and brands for its effective targeting. Geolocalization allows luxury brands to geographically locate and target the recipients of a marketing message on a smartphone-like mobile terminal or on a website.

6.3 Summary

This chapter has examined one of the big five strategies that luxury companies can implement to design successful and emotional luxury experiences through experiential setting design. In the light of this strategy, luxury businesses can incorporate both physical and digital spaces to enhance customer experience by considering the following values: sensory, emotions, intellect, functionality and convenience, and socialization. These dimensions should allow consumers to navigate in a very fluid way between in-store experiences and online ones. These values allow consumers to establish an association between two universes, in turn giving the consumer the same feelings and efficiency. Therefore, implementing experiential setting design by understanding and embedding tangible and intangible values in their design, luxury houses can engage and stimulate the consumer's mind and feelings on an advanced level that go beyond the convenient or aesthetics physical settings in luxury.

Luxury Staff Training

7

The human dimension is very important to customer experience in the luxury field. It guarantees the quality of service and the satisfaction of the customer. In fact, the quality of the customer's luxury experience is not only related to the characteristics of luxury goods (e.g., know-how, rarity, quality, etc.); it is also linked to the perspective of the company's departments (e.g., HR, marketing, sales, communication, etc.), which should all be focusing on delivering qualitative and satisfying luxury experiences. The human element is, thus, a critical factor that should be taken into consideration by luxury businesses to guarantee the success of their experiential offerings. Yet, the human dimension is not limited only to the points of sale; it is also part of a continuum that includes two experiential spheres: domestic (households) and extra-domestic (stores, hotels, restaurants). Several key success factors are needed to ensure the qualitative training of luxury employees who are in contact with customers during domestic and extra-domestic experiences.

For luxury managers, it is important to question the human and managerial characteristics that are part of a qualitative and satisfying customer experience. Several studies in the field of luxury and services highlight the dissatisfaction of customers, although product and quality standards are met. This emphasizes the importance for luxury managers to rethink the training of their employees who may be involved in both domestic and extra-domestic experiential settings. This chapter examines another strategy related to luxury employee training that is part of the big five strategies, which luxury businesses can implement to design successful luxury experience offerings. Also, in this chapter, I emphasize the importance of empathy as the main focus in luxury staff training to help them deliver valuable experiences to luxury customers, including both domestic and extra-domestic spheres.

© Springer Nature Switzerland AG 2019
W. Batat, *The New Luxury Experience*, Management for Professionals,
https://doi.org/10.1007/978-3-030-01671-5_7

7.1   The Human Value in Domestic and Extra-domestic Luxury Experiences

A luxury experience is global and mixes two main experiential spheres: extra-domestic (outdoors) and domestic (indoors). Although the quality of the service provided by luxury employees is often studied in extra-domestic settings, such as service quality in the retail sector, hotels, and restaurants, the domestic dimension, which should stay in step with the values and DNA of the luxury brand, is even more important when it comes to offering a global luxury experience indoors and outdoors. For example, the purchase of luxury furniture in a high-end furniture store is followed, beyond the store experience and the relationship with personal selling, by a home delivery service that is often supported by external service providers. These providers partnership with luxury brands and are responsible for delivery and home installation. If providers are not trained, the home-based experience is likely to be negative (e.g., indiscretion of the service provider, failure to meet delivery deadlines, lack of uniforms, etc.). This example highlights the issues related to the continuity of the customer experience from the extra-domestic sphere to the private home. For luxury brands, it is critical to focus on the customer experience well beyond the store and the product by training their partners in charge of delivery to offer service excellence that is consistent with the reputation and the DNA of the luxury brand.

Mini-case 7.1

The Luxury Collection: A baggage delivery service from the customer's home

The Luxury Collection offers a luggage handling service to its customers from their home. The service is available to the 65 luxury collection hotels around the world. This is a new "signature" service that offers guests staying in luxury hotels the "Luggage-Free Travel" or "Light Travel" service.

By partnering with Luggage Forward worldwide, The Luxury Collection offers a more personalized service. Customers can have their luggage delivered to the hotel of their choice in the 26 countries where The Luxury Collection is located. Personal items will be collected at the customer's home and delivered to his/her destination hotel for prices ranging from 2,000 to more than 10,000 USD.

Beyond the extra-domestic customer experience, several retailers have recently specialized in luxury home services to offer high-end, personalized home, and wellness services tailored to the needs of customers. The domesticity of the luxury experience is a sector that is growing more and more, especially in terms of house employee services (e.g., butler, personal assistant, cleaning staff, gardener, cook, babysitter, etc.) which are in great demand, since they can be subject to tax cuts, which encourages the hiring of domestic workers.

Nowadays, customers have expectations that go beyond taxation and the functional dimension of house employees. They look more for the "rare pearls" of high-end home-based services trained and placed by specialized recruitment agencies that take care of the personalized selection of staff according to the needs of each client (e.g., bilingual staff, discreet, mastering the floral art, at the service of the employer 24 hours a day, dedicated, multitasking, smiling, cultivated, with a sense of well-being, a good knowledge of the daily habits of the employer, etc.).

Mini-case 7.2

The butler luxury service experience in the United States

Due to British TV series and movies like Downton Abbey featuring butlers, a lot of people believe that the butler is a British philosophy. However, this is not the case. What is said to be true is that the French invented the butler and the Americans invented the *modern butler*. It is worth to mention that most successful butlers are Swiss with butlers from the United States and France coming second and third place. Also the best butler school in the world is located in the Netherlands. A butler usually earns a salary between $50,000 and $150,000 annually, plus benefits. Nevertheless, successful butlers earn up to $300,000 a year. Previous butlers were all male and somewhat older, but today women are working in the field, as are younger men. Nowadays opportunities for butlers are less than they have been in the past. The reason behind this is because the present wealthy individuals don't understand the need for professional help managing their property and their lives and don't want a lot of staff around them to keep their privacy.

The primary duty of a butler is to oversee the household staff, many times at more than one residence. This requires knowledge of high social practice in order to receive guests and supervise the reception of visitors. The modern butler can be a house manager, personal assistant, valet, chef, bodyguard, and a number of other positions in a household. Other responsibilities include things like organizing duties and schedules of domestic staff, scheduling and overseeing household maintenance, organizing parties and events, and performing light housekeeping duties and booking hotels, restaurants, etc. The modern butler could also be taking care of the household accounting and creating household budgets. Thus, the modern butler needs strong communication, organizational and management skills, and ability to multitask.

US agencies. Colonial Domestic Agency, International Institute of Modern Butlers, and MoniCare Nannies and Household Staffing are well-known US butler agencies with high staffing industry experience that provide wealthy families and celebrities with highly qualified and experienced domestic staff professionals that include housekeeper-cooks, executive housekeepers, laundresses, personal assistants, house managers, estate managers, chauffeurs, etc. These agencies make every effort to build strong relationships between candidates and families.

7.2   The Key Success Factors for Luxury Employees' Training

In the luxury sector, a well-trained and dedicated staff is vital to providing a memorable and satisfying customer experience. There are a number of key success factors (KSF) whose mastery determines the success of luxury experience offerings, thus marking a strong differentiation from the competitors. Identifying the KSF of an efficient training program for luxury employees seeking to offer the ultimate luxury experience allows managers to capture the personal motivations of employees that managers can rely on in the design of the training programs. These KSF bring together five core competencies that luxury employees should develop to guarantee a strong competitive advantage and thus the loyalty of satisfied customers who are happy with the professionalism of the staff as well as the relational aspects and the human qualities.

The five core competencies luxury managers should incorporate in their training programs that aim to deliver a satisfying customer experience are the following: *quality of training, management, corporate spirit, technical knowledge,* and *the emotional skills of luxury staff.*

7.2.1   Training Luxury Employees

Beyond the daily commercial applications, sales representatives should not only make the customer want to buy; they should also make him/her live a pleasant luxury experience. The training of luxury staff is, therefore, an essential component in the success of the experiential offering enhancing that leads to customers' loyalty. In business schools specializing in luxury marketing, sales, and retail, the courses offer extremely varied career opportunities in luxury: marketing and luxury strategy, sales, communication, digital, etc. Additionally, the majority of luxury graduate and undergraduate courses are internationally oriented for better adaptation to foreign customers. Students and professionals alike have two training opportunities:

- Broad-spectrum education that will allow them to enter the world of luxury as a whole;
- Specialization in one specific luxury sector, such as watchmaking, jewelry, gastronomy, luxury hotels, etc.

To differentiate themselves, schools and training institutions specializing in luxury offer rich and varied training courses for future luxury professionals, whether managers, marketers, product managers, or personal sellers, so as to acquire and develop specialized skills or more generalists. Yet, training a luxury staff should follow an approach based on three main skills: knowledge, know-how, and savoir-vivre (life/interpersonal skills). The advantage for future luxury employees, who will come in contact with clients or who are enrolled in training programs that include these three skills, is that they can learn to be prepared to face any situation and develop their own culture of luxury and its codes. They are also trained not only regarding luxury management techniques but also according to the codes of savoir-vivre and the way they should talk about products and how they are supposed to behave with different profiles of luxury customers. Staff members can also develop an understanding of the product by exploring how artisans and the makers of excellence manufactured it. They should also know how they could immerse the customer in the codes of luxury before, during, and after the purchase, even in the digital space or through communication.

Today, the challenge in training luxury staff is related to the personalities of individuals that could work in the luxury sector. An employee's personality is a critical factor that should be taken into account by luxury managers during their recruitment process. Indeed, a person who will embody the values of luxury (humility, respect, and listening) will be consistent with today's values of luxury, which revolve around modesty, especially after the economic crisis in 2008. As a matter of consequence, the luxury staff should remain in its place behind the client, the artisan, and the designer. To do so, the main focus in business schools should be on how to introduce students/future luxury professionals to the art of kindness and humility in a sector where materialism, ego, and cupidity are common.

Although training in schools provides luxury professionals with a rich learning approach that integrates many aspects, ranging from brand management to sales techniques, through crafts, design, and art, this kind of intellectual training is unfortunately limited to the traditional techniques of luxury marketing and only focuses on the functional needs of customers. Indeed, it does not identify all the dimensions related to the perception of luxury and the accumulation of experiences. It is also incompatible with the emotional, subjective, and ideological dimensions of customer experience in luxury. To complete actual training offers and train future luxury professionals with adequate skills, in terms of customer experience, there is a need for training programs that include an experiential perspective of luxury. This training program should focus on topics such as the development of empathy and emotional capital, experiential merchandising, the pyramid of experiential needs, co-creation, digital experiences, continuum and phygital experiential offerings, and alternative consumer insights in order to better understand customer experiences.

7.2.2   Management of Luxury Employees

The luxury staff is very important in providing a memorable and, above all, satisfying customer experience. Employees have a direct influence on the perception of the image of the luxury brand and the quality of the service. However, sometimes good training and appropriate management techniques are not enough. Indeed, the motivations of employees to work for a luxury company are of great importance regarding how they will represent the DNA and the values of the brand through the service delivered and the experience offered.

Of course, it is up to the manager to set up a selective and qualitative recruitment process in order to hire a dedicated and loyal staff that is congruent with the image of the luxury brand. However, sometimes, even if well-trained employees are recruited, their motivation and commitment can decline over time. This will directly affect the quality of the customer experience and the service delivery. In fact, the negative emotions of the employees can be transferred to the customer and, therefore, not only give him/her a negative image of the luxury brand but also generate a negative customer experience. In this case, staff well-being and appropriate management techniques through an individual follow-up of employees are essential to guaranteeing their loyalty to the brand and thus maintaining a consistent quality of the customer experience.

To ensure a satisfactory experience, luxury staff management processes should take into account five major elements: the manager's journey, image, and culture of the luxury brand, workplace atmosphere, quality of the service, and individual as well as collective objectives of the staff. These five dimensions are explained in Table 7.1.

7.2.3 Corporate Spirit

In order to reinforce the feeling of belonging or we-ness within a luxury brand among employees and to encourage them to carry the values of the brand and communicate them positively to customers, the corporate spirit, or the entrepreneurial spirit, becomes a fundamental element for motivating staff to deliver a satisfactory customer experience. The corporate spirit refers to the myths and values of the luxury brand that are highlighted in its internal (employees) and external (customers) discourse. The corporate spirit of a luxury brand includes the following elements:

• Personality of the creators/founders of the luxury brand. Founders often use their personalities and their experiences to create a unifying corporate culture. The set of values, beliefs, and culture of the founders should be acculturated by the employees who will be committed to adhere to the values of the brand and reflect them in their discourse and their storytelling to make customers dream.

Table 7.1 The five dimensions of luxury staff management

Professional experience	It allows the profile of the employee and his/her seniority to be defined
The image of the luxury house	It provides insights into the staff's vision of the company and the importance of corporate culture
Daily work	It is used to define the degree of involvement of staff and the working atmosphere within the structure
Service quality	It allows employees to know concretely how the quality materializes in the service and the customer experience
Personal and collective goals	It helps to determine and measure if business life and personal projects match

- History of the luxury brand. The corporate spirit is reflected in daily habits, behaviors, discourses, and modes of reasoning influenced by the cultural characteristics of the luxury brand, its specificity, its environment, and its management.
- Culture of the luxury brand evolves according to societal and environmental trends and should be passed on to new employees and gradually assimilated by the following ones as such.

Therefore, corporate spirit is a key element in designing a satisfying luxury experiential offering while ensuring the performance and productivity of the company by employees who feel good in their workplace, who are highly motivated, and who are loyal to the luxury brand.

7.2.4 Valuing and Preserving Employees' Knowledge of the Brand and Its Products

Traditionally, craftsmanship and technical know-how have added a strong value to sales pitches, which highlights the technical characteristics of the luxury good. Luxury employees involved in a customer experience should then master the discourse and develop cognitive skills related to the manufacturing process and the know-how of the luxury brand. The customer experience is not only limited to relational aspects or to the social setting in which the experience takes place; the customer also needs to acquire technical, commercial, and historical information on the following topics:

- Manufacturing process and the materials used;
- Artisans and designers who created/designed the product;
- Specificities of the brand's know-how;
- History of the brand and its origins;
- Positioning of the brand in relation to the competition;
- Geographical aspects and places of sale;
- Place of origin.

For luxury brands, employees in direct contact with customers have to be trained in sales techniques as well as craftsmanship and the history of art to allow them to convey relevant and rewarding discourses to clients who would feel reassured and valued. Nowadays, it is important for luxury brands to relocate their know-how by focusing more on crafts and the training of qualified staff. The challenge is to make craft training and artisan works attractive on all levels. The goal is to put in place well-trained professional resources who are at the disposal of a strategy focused on the improvement of relational and informational exchange and the offer of satisfactory customer experiences in luxury.

Mini-case 7.3

How do italians train artisans to protect the know-how of italian luxury brands?

A center of excellence has been created in Milan to ensure the training of a skilled workforce. The challenge for Italian luxury brands is to train apprentices, who should learn about the craft of Italian artisans and designers at schools, and to make craft trades attractive by recalling, for example, that the great Italian luxury designers started out as tailors or shoemakers. Andrea Illy, president of the Altagamma Foundation, which brings together all luxury companies "made in Italy," has launched a project that should lead to the creation of a training dedicated to the world of luxury.

In 2018, 500 students came out of this school of arts and crafts. The purpose is to make well-trained professional resources available to the strategic luxury sector of Italy. The project "The Polytechnic School of Italian know-how, a project for the reinforcement of technical and professional training" is already being studied by the Ministry of Education and the Ministry of Economic Development to relocate production and guarantee a qualitative training of staff.

7.2.5   Developing the Emotional Capital of Luxury Employees

Emotional capital refers to the ability of luxury staff to show empathy that contributes to generating a positive emotion in the client. Emotional work is an integral part of the customer experience and enhances the experience of a very rich and demanding international luxury clientele. The emotional capital of the staff has a significant impact on the quality of the luxury experience. The pleasurable dimension of emotional work in luxury has three main components that each professional should acquire and develop: enthusiasm and involvement, spontaneity and kindness, and acceptance of social inequalities by recognizing the rights of wealthy clients. Developing an emotional capital is particularly complicated when the physical fatigue and stress of the staff are high due to lack of sleep or standing for hours.

Therefore, the emotional work depends upon variables such as work organization, gender, staff profile, and customer expectations and moods. For example, the division of labor in a luxury hotel assigns to a certain profile of staff interacting with customers a variety of tasks depending on:

- Gender (e.g., women often occupy front desk functions or receptionist positions, while men are in charge of the concierge and may be valet or porter);
- Position (e.g., refers to employees who are rarely in direct contact with clients, such as cleaning staff in rooms and common areas).

7.3   Growing Employee-Level Empathy to Enhance Luxury Experience

Empathy is the ability to take the perspective of others, to understand their reasoning and their emotional state. For a luxury professional, more specifically, it is the ability to take the customer's point of view and put one's self in his/her place – a provision, which should go without saying but which is not so widespread, especially in the field of services. A good luxury experience is then based on the idea that with a strong empathy capital, luxury employees, who are in contact with customers, would think "customer-first" at both emotional (how does he/she feel today) and cognitive levels (what does he/she need according to his/her feelings today). This can be achievable from the moment employees are able to develop an adaptive empathy capital that helps them use their social and interpersonal intelligence to identify the profile, moods, aspirations, and expectations of the client's experiential moment.

Most of the time, empathy is referred to as "I feel your pain," a shared emotional state that goes beyond "I know how you feel." In other words, empathy is the ability of the individual to put him/herself in the other person's place, to understand his/her reasoning and his emotional state. Empathy is a multidimensional concept and involves both emotion and cognition. Applying empathy to designing customer experiences in luxury highlights the idea underscored in Greenson's definition (1960) that suggests that a company's employees should have the ability to put themselves in the shoes of their customers.

The capacity to put oneself in another person's position allows sellers to understand feelings of their customers or to imagine their emotional, psychological, and intellectual representations. Consequently, empathy can be studied as a different concept, such as altruism, projection, intersubjectivity, compassion, or identification. Since empathy is a complex phenomenon, this section will focus on the origins, definitions, and the evolution of the concept of empathy. It will also distinguish empathy from other closely related but confusing constructs in order to provide a marketing definition and an application for creating satisfying luxury experiences.

Empathy is not a mechanism in itself but a process of communication, the purpose of which is to specify the mechanism(s). Freud (1920) states that the process of empathy identification shows how to get into the feelings of the other without being emotionally involved. According to the iconic North American humanistic psychologist Carl Rogers (1980), empathy is about capturing, as accurately as possible, the internal references and emotional components of another person and understanding him/her as if she/he was that other person. In the phenomenological tradition, empathy represents the apprehension of the affective dimensions of others.

Rogers established a relationship between empathy and client experience by developing a permissive, person-centered psychotherapeutic relationship. Through a series of interviews, the customer gradually acquires an understanding of her/himself to a degree that makes him/her able to deal with the realities of life in a more constructive way, discovering, with relief, his/her own solutions to his/her problems. Then, Rogers theorizes his psychotherapeutic practice, which refers to empathy as a significant variable in the helping of relationships. In other words, empathy is a matter of internally perceiving the personal reactions and the essential feelings of the individual as they appear to him/her while communicating this understanding to him/her.

Furthermore, the concept of empathy should be distinguished from sympathy. Unlike sympathy, which refers to sharing a feeling or a belief allowed by the phenomenon of "affective contagion," empathy reflects the representation of the feelings, desires, and beliefs of others and thus does not simply address only conscious subjectivity. To be in sympathy with the other is to be concerned about his/her well-being. Empathy, thus, appears as a conscious mental simulation of the subjectivity of others. In other words, the mental simulation allows individuals to understand what another person thinks and feels in a present, past, or even anticipated situation (Decety 2004). However, despite widespread contributions in different disciplines, empathy is not a well-defined concept and is frequently confused with other notions.

7.3.1 How Does Empathy Work?

The empathy of people (e.g., salespeople, waiters, front desk personnel, and other companies' employees), who have direct relationships with customers, refers to a complex mental state in which different perceptual, cognitive, motivational, and emotional processes interact with the "others." Empathy is deeply embedded in the lived customer experience, and it is this shared experience that allows people, ranging from frontline sales staff to the managing director, to recognize customers not only as clients but as like-minded people who wish to be treated according to the logic, "I treat customers the way I would like to be treated."

Since the concept of empathy is by nature nomadic and unstable because of its continued migration from one discipline to another – formerly from aesthetics, philosophy, and psychology before finally ending up in marketing – based on a selection of dimensions, I propose a theoretical definition of empathy in customer experience marketing, which can be related to the following criteria:

- Empathy takes place in a state of consciousness;
- Empathy implies a relationship;
- Empathic understanding occurs at different levels of accuracy;
- Empathy has temporal dimensions limited to the present moment;
- Empathy requires energy that varies in intensity;
- Empathy implies objectivity;
- Empathy means validation of the experience;
- Empathy requires being free from a value judgment or evaluation.

Empathy is not an easy element of the luxury experiential offering to consider when attempting to creating memorable and satisfying customer experiences. Indeed, empathy is a complex element that involves several human, social, and environmental factors.

In his book *Empathetic Marketing: How to Satisfy the 6 Core Emotional Needs of Your Customers*, Mark Ingwer uncovers an empathic marketing framework that will help companies identify human needs (in terms of empathic consumption experiences) and apply this logic to marketing strategy, customer experience design, as well as communication tools and campaigns. To do so, Ingwer (2012) identified eight key dimensions, which are an integral part of Empathic marketing: the capacity to identify emotional needs behind decisions, the need for continuum, the need for control, the need for self-expression, the need for growth, the need for recognition, the need for belonging, and the need for care.

7.3.2 Developing the Empathy Capital of Luxury Employees

Empathy capital is important for luxury businesses and particularly for luxury experience design because it allows marketers and brand managers to truly understand and decode the hidden needs and emotions of the customers they are designing the experience for. As such, companies can design customer experiences that go beyond the three dimensions of the product or service (attractiveness, viability, and sustainability), by developing the empathy capital of their employees, from their engineers to their salespeople, and training them to develop and practice their empathy potential. It is, therefore, obvious that luxury professionals who demonstrate empathy provide better customer experiences with higher satisfaction.

The best approach to training luxury employees in developing their empathy skills is to make sure that their professionalized empathy is customer-centric, focused on customer well-being, helpful, intentional, self-conscious, self-inspiring, and maintainable. In order to help professionals develop their empathy capital, luxury managers can apply the McLaren's empathy model (2013), an innovative tool developed by Karla McLaren while working in the area of health experience, which makes the development of empathy capital achievable and all of the practices in customer experience empathy easily manageable.

By applying this model, luxury professionals and managers can learn how to develop and work with their empathy as well as learn how to become a knowledgeable and happy empathic market actor, such as a salesperson or service provider involved in the customer experience. Drawing on McLaren's model, empathy capital can be developed by focusing on six essential aspects of the empathy journey (Fig. 7.1).

As shown in Fig. 7.1, the six aspects of empathy build upon each other, and although emotion contagion tends to occur automatically, the other elements are more deliberate and can be advanced with the empathic skills one can learn and develop throughout life.

- Emotion contagion: before empathy can be implemented, consumers need to feel that an emotion is happening – or that an emotion is expected of the service provider or the salesperson. The entire process of empathy relies upon the capacity of the company's employees in contact with customers to feel and share emotions with them by developing emotional skills.

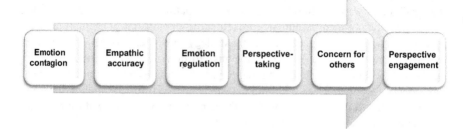

Fig. 7.1 Empathy journey

- Empathic accuracy: refers to the ability of employees, who are in contact with customers, to precisely identify and understand emotional states and intentions in themselves and in the customers.
- Emotion regulation: in order to be an active empathic responder, a company's employees should develop the ability to understand, regulate, and work with their own emotions; they have to be self-conscious of their own emotions in order to regulate them and be able to respond skillfully to the needs of the customers in the occurrence of strong emotions, rather than being overwhelmed by them.
- Perspective-taking is a competency that helps employees who are in contact with customers put themselves in the place of the customers and see situations through their own eyes in an attempt to sense the feelings, needs, and fears of the consumer.
- Concern for others: empathy is not enough to provide a satisfying customer experience; employees have to show their ability to care about their customers in a way that displays compassion and concern.
- Perspective engagement allows employees to make perspective decisions based on their empathy and to respond and act in a way that is in accordance with their empathy while offering solutions for customers. It includes the ability to feel and precisely identify the emotions of customers, regulate their own emotions, assume the perspective of customers, focus on them with care and concern, and then act in a skillful way based upon their perceptions.

Furthermore, McLaren's framework applied to empathy capital formation to improve customer experience can help luxury professionals to:

- Define strategies that create, support, and maintain empathy capital;
- Help professionals develop emotional skills and mindfulness training;
- Develop, practice, and apply the six aspects of empathy in designing appropriate customer experiences;
- Identify strategies to involve or disengage certain facets of empathy depending on customers' states and requirements;

- Understand the role of emotions either positive, negative, or both in the workplace and customer experience and its impact on empathy, communication, performance, customer satisfaction, and outcomes;
- Develop practical skills to encourage and support an emotionally well-synchronized customer experience.

7.4 Summary

In this chapter, I introduced one of the big five strategies: luxury staff training as a critical strategy that luxury houses should take into account when designing luxury experiences. Indeed, the idea is to shift the focus from cognitive and technical training to introduce empathic training approaches and management practices by knowing more about employees in order to help them deliver the ultimate luxury experience in domestic and extra-domestic settings.

Consumer Initiation into Luxury

8

Consumer education is about building the knowledge, skills, and attitudes that are vital to life in our societies in order to help consumers organize their daily lives in a responsible and civic way. In the luxury sector, the education of consumers, the initiation, and the information about luxury goods (products and services) are very critical. This education should be at the heart of the luxury experience offering. This chapter introduces consumer initiation to luxury as one of the big five strategies luxury houses should implement to empower their customers and make sure they will enjoy their luxury experiences. Consumer education and initiation regarding luxury refer to activities that provide consumers with knowledge and skills in the consumption of luxury goods (products and services). It aims to train consumers regarding different aspects of luxury, such as craftsmanship, good manners, history, know-how, creative arts, or developing skills to recognize counterfeit luxury goods.

8.1 Consumer Education for a Better Appreciation of the Luxury Experience

Promoting consumer education toward luxury is a way for luxury businesses to help their consumers construct and develop adequate skills as well as change their mentality and limited perception of luxury, which is often about the brand or the price. Focusing on consumer education that helps individuals acquire knowledge will, consequently, lead them to develop a better appreciation of their lived luxury experiences. Consumer initiation and education, with regard to luxury codes and norms, can also help luxury businesses retain their actual customers and attract new ones. Thus, an educational policy helps reinforce the consumer's awareness of the universe of luxury and thus his/her preparation to be immersed within enjoyable and satisfying experiences. Educating individuals who might be novice or have less knowledge or familiarity with certain luxury brands, products, and sectors and

© Springer Nature Switzerland AG 2019
W. Batat, *The New Luxury Experience*, Management for Professionals,
https://doi.org/10.1007/978-3-030-01671-5_8

introducing them to luxury could lead luxury businesses to improve their customer experiences at both levels: cognitive and emotional.

Furthermore, consumer education, with regard to luxury, also promotes responsible, modern, and dynamic luxury habits and consumption patterns that place the customer's quality of life and well-being at the forefront of his/her lived luxury experiences. In the field of luxury, consumer education and initiation can include three main categories:

- Luxury education refers to any activity or action whose main objective is to provide novice and regular consumers with elements enabling them to fully appreciate their luxury experiences by being informed, valued, critical, responsible, and socially engaged consumers.
- Luxury education is an ongoing process whose objective is to gradually provide consumers with a set of cognitive elements, procedures, and techniques that help them to develop their conscious and critical attitudes toward the world of luxury.
- Luxury education is an educational commitment to contribute to the overall development of young and adult consumers by transmitting concepts, proce-

---

Mini-case 8.1

Petrossian educating consumers on how to eat caviar

Petrossian, the excellent and most known name in caviar, has always empowered France to be a distinct caviar destination country. A family business of two brothers founded almost 100 years ago – currently owned by Armen Petrossian – supplies about 30% of the caviar in the world, sourced from different farms, including the United States, Italy, France, China, and others. As Petrossian turns out to be a major luxurious distributor, serving this fine delicacy at the most outstanding tables, people have come to realize that its success lies behind the fact that Petrossian family takes the time to nurture their caviars themselves. For them, it's essential to ensure that these farm-raised and sustainable pearls are matured enough to be sold at the right time, not before that, nor after. They tolerate on their sturgeons to age to give their caviar a more robust, subtle, and fine taste. But the most surprising thing about Petrossian's casually elegant shop and restaurant is that they do not only serve delicious, unusual, little fish eggs but also aim to emphasize the education dimensional to help their customers develop their palates and thus appreciate the taste of caviar.

This luxury corporation shares passionately its love of caviar to those who come with a learning attitude. Petrossian believes that money should not be a

(continued)

Mini-case 8.1 (continued)

barrier for people to taste caviar and to convince those who are afraid of trying it that it is a matter of taste and not cost.

During the Petrossian Caviar 301 class, the caviar experts enlighten the history and the journey of caviar to the attendees from its farming to shipping, including every possible nuance of fish eggs. While at the dinner table, Petrossian teaches its guests how to serve and taste caviar properly: types of utensils they should use and how to feel and crush the little eggs with their tongue for a better savory experience. Petrossian explains as well that all caviar tastes are different and none can be labeled as the "best caviar"; it is the most expensive only when it is the rarest. And the only way to judge the quality of the caviar is to use one's own senses and anyone should first try it before buying it.

dures, and attitudes to facilitate their immersion, discovery, and enjoyment of the world of luxury.

Consumer initiation and education regarding luxury should be an integral part of the consumption culture or subculture to which the consumer belongs. It should also respond to emerging issues, constraints, and personal dissatisfactions. Promoting consumer education regarding luxury is a way for luxury houses to assist and guide consumers in the process of discovery and initiation to luxury. In order to enhance the luxury experience, consumer education can focus on the following aspects:

- Feeling of well-being: getting to know luxury and feeling good with its universes, codes, and culture;
- Developing cognitive know-how: learning how to do, to consume, and to enjoy luxury goods and services;
- Promoting a way of life: learning to live together, learning to live with others, and learning to be with others.

Following this logic, education regarding luxury and its codes and values is an essential starting point for the development of specialized educational programs in the field of luxury that are adapted to consumers in different countries who have different approaches and definitions related to their own history of the rise of luxury (e.g., emerging countries that are discovering luxury brands but are unaware of the codes and values of the luxury world). The outcomes of consumer initiation and education in regard to luxury can be summarized according to three main objectives related to:

- Discovering and learning about the world of luxury and how this world works;
- Empowering consumers by informing them of counterfeit luxury items and training them to identify them;
- Providing consumers with a critical analysis of luxury.

Mini-case 8.2

A mobile application for identifying counterfeit luxury products

The luxury market is the most affected by counterfeiting, which either can be attractive to some consumers or be a source of confusion for others. By launching a mobile application, the startup Entrupy helps consumers identify and control, at the moment of the purchase, the origin of a luxury product.

The startup attempts to answer this major problem for fashion houses and their customers by allowing consumers to identify the origin of a Birkin bag or a Chanel 2.55 purchased online thanks to the use of an innovative algorithm system to compare millions of images in a few seconds. The user of Entrupy application can also take captures of certain fragments of the luxury product. According to the company, the system has an authentication accuracy greater than 96.4%. The service offered by Entrupy is also charged $10 per product authentication.

Furthermore, there are other fields such as wine tasting or perfumes where consumers need education and assistance to learn more about luxury and fully appreciate their experience and their discovery of the universe of the luxury brand. For example, niche perfumes and their workshops or discreet boutiques are a luxury domain in which consumers need education and initiation. The niche perfume market is the opposite of classic perfumery consumers used to experience or purchase. It is an exclusive venue both regarding of the reception area and decoration and in terms of the level of service and products designed by fragrance creators. In this haute perfumery universe, the act of the sale has a ceremonial and educational character that includes proactive listening for decoding and capturing the personality of the client and the perfume that matches with it. No more than three to five perfumes should be presented to the consumer so as not to saturate the olfactory capacity of the client.

In the niche perfume sector, consumer education and initiation are about advice, about taking time, and also about inviting creators to interact with customers. For example, consumers can experience literary caves where creators come to talk about their perfumes and exchange knowledge with them. The olfactory research with the client depends on whether the client gives him/herself sufficient time to experience the discovery process, as it may take more than an hour.

8.2   How to Initiate Consumers to Luxury

Consumer initiation and education in regard to luxury universes, products, brands, and codes can be achieved by applying different strategies (Fig. 8.1).

- **Events, workshop visits, and meetings with designers**. Luxury brands can educate and initiate their customers through the organization of outdoor events

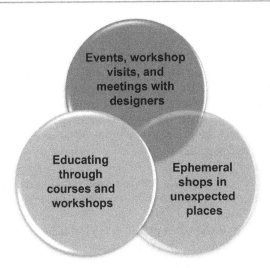

Fig. 8.1 Luxury houses' strategies for initiating consumers

and by opening their doors to the public. For example, Hermes opens its doors to the public and allows those interested to visit the craftsmen, discover their work, and ask them questions. Visitors can participate in recreational workshops to have fun and learn about fashion design. It is also possible to taste a selection of organic coffees alongside the artisans. Hermes set up an ephemeral bookshop where visitors can find and sell signed books on craftsmanship and crafts.

Other public initiatives can also be launched by luxury houses to guide customers in their discovery of their products and universe. For example, the cristal brand Baccarat launched an experiential concept, "Baccarat cristal room," a restaurant where consumers can experience the sensory elegance of drinking from Baccarat cristal glasses.

In the luxury retail sector, Galeries Lafayette's emblematic department store of the Parisian fashion organized a giant fashion show on the theme of fashion capitals to celebrate the first fashion week parades, thus, allowing its clients to experience their first fashion show. Furthermore, Galeries Lafayette offers its clients the chance to discover its history dating back to its foundation in 1893 until today, from the little shop of novelties on Lafayette Street to the flagship on Haussmann Boulevard. The visit is educational since it informs clients and visitors about the nineteenth-century commercial revolution that gave birth to department stores, the beginnings of Galeries Lafayette, and their evolution since 1894. The secrets of its construction are also unveiled, step by step, from the ground floor to the panoramic terrace and around the Neo-Byzantine dome inaugurated in 1912. The large hall, with the famous dome decorated with colorful stained glass windows and balconies in ironwork art, marks the beginning of the historical relationship between the company and artistic creation. Visitors are thus invited to take a new look at the history of Galeries Lafayette and the elements of its architecture that make it a monument of Art Nouveau in Paris admired by thousands of visitors for more than 120 years.

Other luxury brands can educate consumers about their craftsmanship allowing them to understand the mysteries of their manufacturing processes and admire the craftsmanship, the richness of their products, and the creations of contemporary artists by opening the doors of their manufactures to visitors and clients so they may experience what happens backstage and learn more about the artisan know-how and the techniques used to manufacture luxury goods. For example, Bernardaud porcelain and dinnerware (in business since 1863) launched a tour that shows in detail the different stages of manufacturing, from the raw material to the finished product. A demonstration and an introduction to the techniques of manufacturing and decoration accompany the course, which is embellished with exhibitions.

- **Ephemeral shops in unexpected places**. It is a technique to push the product to the customer and make it accessible, such as Hermes, which launched "Hermesmatic," a fun ephemeral luxury laundry machine that allows consumers to overdye the Hermes silk scarves. Hermesmatic offers a complimentary service where clients in different countries, such as France, Amsterdam, Austin, Munich, or Tokyo, can update their vintage scarves via washing machines and dip dying. Pop-up stores are also launched by luxury brands to attract new customers and raise their awareness of the brand and its products. It is also a way to allow customers to purchase the brand's products that are available, such as sneakers and leather wallets.

- **Educating through courses and workshops**. Learning about wine, caviar, delicate meals, etc. can be part of the educational program of luxury houses who can initiate their customers by assisting and guiding them within their first culinary or wine tasting experience. Indeed, people can also learn about wine and gastronomy by a simple interest in this universe. Similar to food and wine, a first experience of driving a sports car could be facilitated by setting up driving schools. For example, the official Porsche driving school allows current clients, future clients, and curious people to discover the exclusive Porsche concept, which combines pleasure, learning, and thrills, by having them participate in the international Porsche Track Experience program in many countries around the world (Germany, Italy, Spain, Japan, United States, England, etc.) where novice drivers can live their first Porsche driving experience. Supervised by Porsche professional drivers, participants have the opportunity to get behind the wheel of three different models: 718 Cayman S, 911 Carrera S, and 911 Carrera 4S. This allows expert and novice drivers to test and understand the differences between these different models.

8.3   Summary

This chapter presents one of the big five strategies that addresses the consumer's initiation into luxury culture, its universe, know-how, codes, and rituals in order to help luxury consumers fully immerse themselves and enjoy their luxury experience by understanding the feelings and benefits from each luxury product, experience, and service in different sectors. This chapter highlighted certain strategies that luxury businesses can implement through various educational programs to help reinforce the consumer's consciousness of the world of luxury and thus prepare him/her to live immersive, educational, and valuable luxury experiences.

Part III

Challenges for the Future of Luxury Experience

Alternative Market Research for Understanding Luxury Experience

9

It is frequently thought that science tells us how things function and that there is no more exhaustive a science than that of quantitative scholarships. Scientific works are quantitative in numerous ways, but every field of knowledge has a qualitative facet in which the individual's experience, subjectivity, perception, and skepticism function together with other philosophies to support the construction and experimentation of theories. Distinct from the quantitative method, which trusts direct aspects, and statistical modeling, the qualitative methods are mainly related to individuals' perceptions and definitions of their own world. While quantitative and qualitative methods have their own value, in this chapter, I decided to discuss alternative market research to better understand luxury experiences. These alternative methods are qualitative, immersive, and well adapted to study and analyze customer experience. By using immersive creative tools, allowing an exhaustive analysis of the luxury experience offline and online, and examining its subjective, paradoxical, symbolic, and emotional dimensions, luxury businesses can be able to innovate and design suitable experiences and create a competitive advantage. This chapter introduces experiential and e-experiential research methods as an alternative to studying luxury experiences.

9.1 Beyond Surveys, New Alternatives for Studying Luxury Experience

In contrast to quantitative research methods and surveys whose unique purpose is to measure variables related to the process of purchasing luxury goods at the point of sale, alternative methods are qualitative, immersive, and experiential in nature and offer more relevant consumer insights regarding luxury experiences. Table 9.1 summarizes the differences between qualitative and quantitative techniques.

Alternative market research includes two categories of data that can be analyzed: customer discourse (e.g., verbal expressions, text, etc.) and collected material

© Springer Nature Switzerland AG 2019
W. Batat, *The New Luxury Experience*, Management for Professionals,
https://doi.org/10.1007/978-3-030-01671-5_9

Table 9.1 Quantitative vs. qualitative

Element	Quantitative	Qualitative
Approach	Confirmatory according to a top-down strategy: the investigator tests the hypotheses by collecting data	Exploratory according to a bottom-up strategy: the investigator produces new hypotheses of the data collected
Study objective	Describe, explain, and anticipate	Explore, discover, and build
Focus	The study of behaviors under the control of certain variables	The study of consumption experiences in their natural environment
Report	A statistical report with correlations, comparisons, and statistically significant results	A narrative report illustrated with verbatim, photos, videos, and personal productions

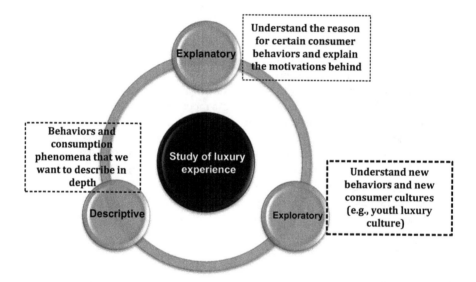

Fig. 9.1 Three main approaches to luxury experience

(e.g., images, photographs, drawings, video, etc.). Multiple techniques can be used by market researchers to meet specific objectives related to the study of luxury experiences in different sectors (gourmet restaurant, luxury store, online shopping, hospitality, etc.). Therefore, three methodological perspectives can be followed to better understand the tacit and explicit dimensions of the luxury experience: descriptive, explanatory, and exploratory (Fig. 9.1). Although these three approaches are relevant to the study of the luxury experience and its characteristics, the exploratory approach should be considered ideal because of its adequacy in dealing with the in-depth analysis of the tacit dimensions and meanings related to the lived luxury experience.

Immersive and exploratory techniques allow luxury businesses to better anticipate the motivations and attitudes of different consumer profiles in terms of desired and expected experiences. Exploratory techniques using immersion in studying the customer luxury experience are considered an essential methodology for collecting relevant data on the emotions of customers during their experiences of purchasing or consuming luxury goods (products and services). By being closer to their reality, social market researchers can capture the personal motivations of consumers who can express subjective opinions and emotions as well as their functional and symbolic needs related to their luxury experiences.

Exploratory methods help marketing researchers better understand the reality of luxury consumption practices since they can study the consumer according to his/her own experience and his/her own definition of what he/she means by a satisfactory luxury experience from his/her own perspective. Exploratory and immersive studies, thus, allow luxury companies to see the world through the eyes of the consumer and include all dimensions of the experience, whether it is objective or subjective, rational or irrational, emotional or functional, tangible or intangible, etc. In contrast to quantitative studies, qualitative exploratory tools highlight issues that the surveys tend to quantify by using questionnaires to collect data. Therefore, exploratory qualitative techniques should be used to better examine the luxury experience by helping market researchers to:

- Identify the reasons for consumers' choices and behaviors with regard to luxury;
- Study consumer groups, such as VIP consumers, who are difficult to access through a questionnaire;
- Study representations of the world of luxury, needs, perceptions, life courses, etc.
- Study the codes and norms in luxury consumer cultures and subcultures;
- Determine the typologies of the luxury experience, why they exist, and how they exist, instead of quantifying them;
- Identify new luxury experiences and adapt them to online experiences;
- Describe particular cases of luxury experiences, luxury domains, or individuals;
- Analyze the meanings of luxury that consumers in different cultures and subcultures attribute to it;
- Analyze the dynamics of social interactions in the different luxury experiences that often elude marketing managers because they are expressed in a tacit way.

Furthermore, by applying exploratory methods, market researchers do not need to recruit a large number of participants, as is the case in quantitative studies. In fact, the number of participants may vary from one to a few dozen people; however, the issue of representativeness and reliability of results is no less important and requires that particular attention is given to the composition of the group studied. The more the group represents the total population of consumers in its diversity, the more relevant the data will be. Although the limitations of qualitative methods are, essentially, due to their "subjective" and "interpretive" nature, they are, nevertheless, essential in the study of physical and digital luxury experiences and their tacit and explicit dimensions.

The qualitative exploratory techniques have the advantage of allowing data to be cross-referenced by re-embedding customer behaviors and experiences in the field of luxury in a well-defined cultural context. The immersive exploratory tool is also the most appropriate for the study of experiences and consumer cultures in highly experiential luxury spheres, such as gastronomic restaurants or luxury hotels. Indeed, exploratory and immersive tools help market researchers analyze and understand the codes and norms of luxury cultures as well as consumer's perceptions, behaviors, and attitudes toward luxury. The exploratory study is, thus, a source of inspiration for luxury professionals who are looking for new ideas to retain the heterogeneous market of luxury consumers with values, consumer experiences, and a definition of luxury.

In luxury marketing, the use of qualitative exploratory studies is linked to the evolution of luxury, behavior, and consumption trends of luxury, which can be explained by the following reasons:

- The exploratory tool allows retailers and luxury brands to better understand the challenges of the transformations engendered by the sociocultural and technological context and the importance of emotions and consumer cultures in the analysis of the customer experience and its dimensions.
- Exploratory studies are the only tools that allow marketing managers, who would like to design a suitable luxury experience, to use a wide range of techniques: the study of motivations, in-depth interviews (individual, dual, and group), projective techniques, documentary analysis, etc.
- The use of different methodological tools provides an in-depth analysis of the luxury experience and its dimensions and thus facilitates the decision-making process.
- The qualitative tool allows companies to gather the maximum of elements that can help the decision-maker to better understand the desired luxury experiences according to the perceptions of the customers.
- The exploratory methods help decision-makers understand the subtle behaviors and symbolic dimensions that are integral to customer experience. These symbolic dimensions play an important role in the adoption or rejection of certain luxury goods and brands.

Mini-case 9.1

The exploratory study of personal experience and its impact on the perception of luxury brand fragrances
Context and objectives of the study. An essential element of the luxury experience is its personal nature. Thus, two people will not feel and perceive a given experience in the same way. This is partly because of their own personality and also because of their own story. Thus, the experience provided by a brand cannot be apprehended independently of the personal experience that will profoundly modify the interaction with the brand. This is what marketing

(continued)

Mini-case 9.1 (continued)

researchers, Ardelet and colleagues (2015), pointed out by demonstrating that the association of a brand with personal memories is a determining factor in the preference for the brand.

The exploratory study and selected luxury brands. The study was conducted with clients aged 20–50 years. The objective was to test new fragrances developed for the brands Nina Ricci, Lancôme, and Chanel. The researchers gave the women who entered the cosmetic and perfume shop samples asking them how they would describe the perfumes with the question "What makes you think this perfume?" The respondent did not know which sample was associated with which brand of perfume so that the image of the brand did not skew sensory perceptions. At the end of this phase in the store, participants were free to take samples home if they agreed to be contacted by phone a week later. The Chanel, Nina Ricci, and Lancôme brands' heritage perceptions were also measured among the study participants separate from the odor test. After having smelled a perfume, the respondents reported experiencing very intimate memories associated with certain smells, "This perfume reminds me of the one worn by my grandmother," or very general impressions, not related to particular events, such as "It smells like grass." In order to highlight the importance of personal experience, the analysis also identified associations that referred to personal stories, which can also be called "self-referencing narratives." To facilitate this precise distinction between the personal comments and the generic comments, the descriptions were then divided into two segments to distinguish those "referring to one's personal history" and those "remaining generic."

What are the main results? Participants who mentioned specific people, places, or events and, therefore, generated narrative self-referencing by "feeling" a scent. On the other hand, among those who simply loved the fragrance without mentioning personal experience, few people wanted to keep the product. Thus, the ability of a fragrance to evoke memories or personal life events increases the likelihood that a customer will choose the fragrance. A second lesson learned from this study is related to the brand's heritage, that is, its roots, its key characters, its values, its know-how, its regional ramifications, and so forth. The results show that a strong brand legacy boosts associations' impacts on personal stories. When the brand's legacy was perceived as strong by the clients, the researchers found that narrative self-referencing had an even greater impact on preferences for these products. The brand's legacy is what makes it special and tells its story, of course, but it also plays the role of a bonding agent between the personal stories of consumers and a given brand.

What are the marketing implications of the exploratory study? The story we remember when experiencing a brand creates value for itself and the brand. The results of this study demonstrate the importance of the intimate

(continued)

Mini-case 9.1 (continued)

bond that is created between a consumer and a brand to ensure the preference, as well as the maintenance, of the relationship over the long term. It is, therefore, imperative for luxury brands to find the means to find a footing in the life of each consumer by creating a constant dialogue between the history of the brand and the personal memories of each. The difficulty lies in providing reassurance through connecting elements with the consumer while continuing to surprise him/her in an attempt to strike a subtle balance between familiarity and innovation. For this, the brand should be very familiar with both its heritage and its customers in order to build bridges between the two. Brand managers should also be able to take risks by proposing new stories. A good reference would be the example of the Chanel brand. Indeed, Chanel offers videos on its website illustrating the story of Coco Chanel. By highlighting the strength of character and courage of Gabrielle Chanel, the brand creates a link with the public, who can recall some difficulties in their own life's journey and how they came out of past situations. On a different note, Guerlain Shalimar perfume campaign takes the viewer into an exotic and magical world peopled with princes and princesses. The many women who had a childhood cradled in fairy tales will generate personal associations with the brand.

9.2   Experiential Market Research

Experiential research methods employ a range of immersive and qualitative methodological tools for advancing scientific awareness in the social sciences. There are areas and themes inclusive of all the topics of customer experience that have the potential to lead meaningful understandings, results, and insights of consumers by using an experiential research method, such as ethnography. The main experiential research method by which information about consumers, their experiences, and the meanings they assign to their consumption practices and brands can be obtained include four qualitative techniques, as shown in Fig. 9.2.

9.2.1   Projective Techniques

When a scholar is leading an in-depth interview or conducting a survey through the use of questionnaires as a tool, he/she might face difficulties in the form of language obstacles, a communication gap with the respondent.

- The researcher might come across illiterate respondents, especially in social research and in rural areas.
- Researchers may also face social barriers, whereby respondents are too uncomfortable to talk about a subject.

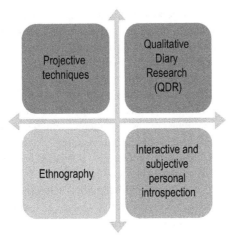

Fig. 9.2 Experiential methods of luxury experience

Other psychological obstacles might also occur when consumers feel uncomfortable recalling special events or feelings. Therefore, they might try to avoid certain questions or answers. In order to overcome such difficulties encountered during an interview process, the researcher might substitute the use of a questionnaire for projective techniques. In the marketing field, Haire's research (1950) on consumers' perception of Nescafé instant coffee's new product image was the pioneer in projective technique research. This research had been conducted at a time when instant coffee was considered a product of innovation and when most households still used traditional drip coffee.

Following Haire, many researchers in the marketing field (e.g., Hill 1968) used replications and extensions to test the usefulness of the projective method in different consumption fields. Other researchers have addressed the use of projective techniques to emphasize the following subjects:

- The need for marketers to make a connection with consumers (e.g., Day 1989);
- The need to evaluate the measurement competences of lifestyle typologies (e.g., Lastovicka et al. 1990);
- The need for projective approaches in examining the meaning of gift giving (e.g., McGrath et al. 1993).

The advantage of projective techniques is to get individuals to express feelings that they would otherwise not express verbally. In order to obtain a response from the respondent without asking a direct question, the researcher will create a situation where the respondent projects his/her feelings on to some other person or object. For instance, a researcher might ask respondents to comment on a situation represented as a cartoon and ask them to describe what the cartoon characters think. Alternatively, they could be provided with a list describing an individual's choice of tourist destinations and ask respondents to describe the person who is likely to have formulated this choice.

In consumer research, projective techniques are a method for researchers to overcome oral communication obstacles and discover characteristics of consumer experience that respondents may find challenging to voice. Researchers are then able to investigate people's feelings, thoughts, and experiences and encourage respondents to discuss personal issues or motives that the respondent may not be aware of and without them feeling threatened by the direct line of questioning (Haire 1950). These techniques are used to overcome the obstacles inherent in explicit consumer attitude measures. Respondents, whether consciously or unconsciously, are inclined to provide answers that are socially acceptable when placed in the role of the subject in a research experiment. If this technique is used properly, it will help researchers circumvent the "common social barriers that inhibit the respondents' expression of attitudes and behaviors" (Steinman 2009:2). As in psychology, we can identify four main projective techniques: association, elements to be completed, construction, and expression.

- In association techniques, a stimulus is presented to a participant who is asked to reveal the first thing that goes through his/her mind. The association of words is the best known of these techniques. It consists of presenting a list of words, one by one, that the participant should answer using the first word that comes to mind. Interesting words, called test words, are scattered throughout the list, which also contains neutral words to hide the purpose of the study. Thus, in the example of a restaurant experience, some of the test words could be food, quality, location, service, and price. The association technique allows respondents to reveal deep feelings about their consumption and purchase experiences. Responses are analyzed by calculating the occurrence with which a word is specified as an answer, the time that intervenes before the answer, and the number of people who do not reply at all to a test word in a reasonable time. The schema and details of a participant's responses are used to determine an individual's hidden attitudes or feelings about the subject being studied.
- Elements to be completed. With this technique, the respondent should find the end of an incomplete sentence or story. The sentences to be completed are similar to word associations. Respondents are offered sentences whose end is missing and which they must finish. They are usually asked to use the first word or phrase that comes to mind. Completing sentences can provide more information about the consumer's feelings than word associations. However, this kind of techniques is not so hidden, and respondents can guess what it is. In the technique of stories to be completed, respondents are offered a part of a story, sufficient to draw attention to a particular subject but without any hint as to the nature of the story's ending. They are encouraged to conclude it with their own words. The end of the story as told by the participants will reveal their hidden feelings and emotions.
- Construction techniques are similar to completed sentence techniques. Participants are asked to construct a response in the form of history, dialogue, or description. The story proposed by the researcher is less developed than with the previous technique. The two main construction techniques are the response to an image and the comics test.

- Image response technique. The origin of this technique can be traced back to the Thematic Apperception Test (TAT), which shows a series of images of ordinary or unusual events. In some of these images, people or objects are clearly represented, while in other images, they are relatively blurred. The respondent is asked to tell stories about these images. The interpretation he/she makes gives indications of his/her personality. For example, an individual can be characterized as impulsive, creative, unimaginative, and so forth.
- Comics test refers to comic characters that are presented in a particular situation related to the problem. Respondents are asked to indicate what a character might say in response to the comments of another character. This helps to identify respondents' feelings, opinions, and attitudes about the situation. Comic tests are easier to pass and analyze than picture response techniques.

• Expression techniques. In these techniques, a verbal or visual situation is presented to the respondents. They are then asked to describe the feelings and attitudes of others about this situation. Respondents do not express their own feelings or attitudes but those of others. The two major techniques of expression are role-playing and third-person technique.

- Role-playing. Respondents should play the role or adopt the behavior of someone else. The researcher assumes that respondents will project their own feelings into the role. These can then be detected by analyzing the responses.
- Third-party technique refers to a verbal or visual situation that is presented to the respondent. He/she is then asked to describe the opinions and attitudes of a third person rather than directly expressing his/her own opinions and attitudes. This person can be a friend, a neighbor, a colleague, or a caricature of a person. The researcher assumes again that the respondent will reveal their own opinions and attitudes by describing the reactions of a third person (speaking on behalf of another person reduces social pressure). Thus, the role-play technique assumes that the individual sees his/her creative spontaneity stifled by the constraints imposed by social life and by physical and mental habits. The role-play will free the individual by making him play the role of another.

Projective techniques can then provide verbal or visual stimuli through their indirection and encourage respondents to reveal their unconscious feelings and attitudes without being aware that they are doing so. Therefore, projective techniques, as a tool to examine customer experience, are fundamental to researchers for capturing the meanings and dimensions related to consumption practices. They are mainly used for answering the "how," "why," and "what" questions that arise in consumer behaviors. Thus, projective techniques can provide a deeper understanding of what consumers truly think and feel about their consumption and shopping experiences.

Although projective techniques are indirect approaches that seek to reveal the opinions, motivations, feelings, attitudes, or even the values of the consumers within their own experiences, this type of technique is used very little in marketing but has significant advantages in certain situations. Unlike focus groups or in-depth interviews, the purpose of the projective technique is not known to the individuals in the sample studied. When using a projective technique, participants are asked to analyze the behavior of others, not theirs. This method allows companies to bring out, indirectly, the emotions of the participants. The method is enhanced even more so when the staged situation is vague and ambiguous. Thanks to this technique, luxury companies will be able to collect deep and interesting data about the tacit meanings and habits of consumers' experiences.

9.2.2   Qualitative Diary Research (QDR)

Qualitative Diary Research (QDR) is an innovative way to capture rich insights into customers' experiences, their processes, relationships, settings, products, and rituals (e.g., Patterson 2005). A diary is a personal record of daily events, observations, and thoughts that inform us about the way individuals see and talk about their everyday life. We can then argue that QDR is particularly suited to exploring complex aspects (functional, social, emotional, spiritual, ideological, etc.) of individuals' ordinary and extraordinary experiences from their own perspective. So far, very few studies have been carried out using qualitative diaries as the main method of investigating consumption experiences, although the first study was carried out in the early 1940s (e.g., Allport 1942).

Some authors, such as Arnould (1998), argue that diaries could add previously unexplored dimensions to consumer research methods. In fact, the use of consumer diaries as an alternative methodology in marketing could yield promising directions in the field of customer experience studies; however, few studies have taken advantage of a diary-centered approach even though this approach, in particular, allows researchers, as stated by Patterson (2005), to capture a "thick description" of the complexities and the dynamics of the customer experience.

QDR is an individual documentation of everyday events, observations, thoughts, and feelings that is used as a self-reported tool by individuals to report and explore ongoing experiences with their tacit (hidden meanings) and explicit (behaviors) dimensions. The use of QDR allows customer experience researchers to accomplish three main objectives:

- Diary method captures little experiences of everyday life that fill most of an individual's working time and occupy the vast majority of his/her conscious attention.
- Diary research is a suitable tool to reveal experiences and thoughts of consumers, which are often hidden since events are recorded in their natural environment.
- Everyday diaries offer the opportunity for marketing and consumer researchers to study social, psychological, and physiological processes within everyday situations.

Qualitative Diary Research takes place immediately after the event in its natural and spontaneous context. As Gould (1991) acknowledged, this method can have a retrospective shortfall and could potentially be overwhelmed with biases by the limited ability of participants to recall their experience (Wallendorf and Brucks 1993). In the consumption field, QDR is also used as a methodology for understanding why young people send each other text messages (e.g., Batat 2014). Another study conducted by Patterson (2005) used real diaries as an alternative methodology to explore relationships between products and consumers. Other consumer researchers, such as Wohlfeil and Whelan (2012), used diary techniques to explore the life of a movie actress's fan from his/her own perspective.

9.2.3 Ethnography

Ethnography is an exploratory, interactive, and immersive methodology that enables marketers, ethnographers, and researchers to understand the social interactions between consumers and market actors as well as the internal interactions within each consumption culture. The aim of ethnography is to analyze the symbolic and emotional dimensions of consumption experiences, behaviors, and practices of consumers from their own point of view. Ethnography allows luxury companies to:

- Go beyond the cognitive and rational vision of consumer behaviors by adopting a symbolic and sociocultural perspective.
- Study how consumers build and develop attitudes toward brands and products in their consumption culture and how the latter contributes to the formation of consumers' attitudes and consumption patterns.
- Use visual and verbal data through the recording of behaviors in real consumption situations.
- Allow researchers to stay in the natural surroundings of the group they are studying. It is up to the ethnographer to make efforts to "become invisible" and "indispensable" within the group.

For luxury companies, ethnography is a source of innovation because it provides a deep knowledge of their customers, which can help marketers identify, categorize, and analyze cultures, subcultures, countercultures, and microcultures of luxury consumption. In these different cultures, marketers will be able to identify typologies of behaviors according to shared norms among consumers who belong to the same consumption culture and thus better adapt their offerings as well as marketing and communication campaigns.

Given the sociocultural dimension of consumption, the use of ethnographic techniques appears to be the most appropriate tool in understanding the customer experience. In fact, ethnography is used to uncover, interpret, and understand the consumer's perspective shaped by his/her sociocultural environment. The study of customer experience through ethnography requires immersive and longitudinal methods for working with, rather than on, consumers and for discovering meaning in, rather than imposing meaning on, consumer behaviors (e.g., Eckert 1988).

According to McCraken (1988), ethnography allows researchers to access customer experience dimensions imbued with social meaning that is otherwise tacit and made in day-to-day consumption practices, and thus researchers can gain a thick description of experiences from the perspective of consumers to attain an understanding of the consumer's view in context. In order to develop a better understanding of customer experiences and uncover the explicit and tacit meanings, Batat (2015) suggests that researchers can familiarize themselves with the consumption culture of the group they are studying and thus collect rich data by following three main stages: socialization, collaboration, and auto-confrontation.

- Socialization. In the socialization stage, researchers can use observation and informal conversations to work with participants. This stage can be extended over a period of 3 or 6 months and allows researchers to be fully immersed within the consumption culture of the informants. Participating in formal and informal conversations and social activities among consumers, observing their behaviors and reactions, and informally interviewing as many individuals as possible can help researchers accomplish the socialization task. As the researcher becomes more involved and the group members start to trust him/her and consider him/her a member of the group, sharing the same interests and, in turn, regarding him/her less as an outsider researcher, data collection becomes more systematic and easy to conduct. This phase allows the researcher to access deep insights into consumer consumption culture and meanings that cannot be obtained by any other means.
- Collaboration. In the collaboration stage, researchers can conduct a participatory study using a model with principals of Participatory Action Research (PAR) similar to that proposed by Ozanne and Saatcioglu (2008). The researcher can invite participants to engage in collective and individual in-depth interviews and workshops on consumption experiences.
- Auto-confrontation. In this stage, the researcher can ask participants to comment on primary results describing their own consumption experiences and others experiences.

The three stages and the path of exploration can lead the researcher to build a full picture of consumers' perceptions and definitions of their own experiences that are shaped by a particular luxury consumption culture within a marketplace in which they interact with other market actors (e.g., institutions, industry, other consumers, etc.). Furthermore, luxury companies and ethnographers can have the choice between two ethnographic approaches: multi-site and "quick and dirty." Figure 9.3 summarizes the differences between these two approaches.

Therefore, using ethnography (multi-site and "quick and dirty") allows the ethnographer to delve deeply into a consumer's meanings as perceived within the particular subculture in which the experience takes place. Various methods can be used to bring the ethnographer and/or the company close to day-to-day consumer consumption experiences and meanings. Among the existing tools that luxury businesses can use when conducting an ethnographic study, I can mention the following: observation, photographs, and narratives.

"Multi-site" ethnography	**"Quick & dirty" ethnography**
• It consists of following in parallel several fields, several groups of consumers, several consumption practices in different consumption cultures • This technique is facilitated by the frequent back and forth between the analysis of the data and the field • It is necessary to retain participants to ensure their engagement in the study	• It is an accelerated method in step with the changes and rapid shifts in the contemporary society • It is more fragmented, faster, and more fluid • This technique is important when it comes to studying the launch of innovations for example

Fig. 9.3 Multi-site vs. "quick and dirty"

- **Observation**. Observational research is traditionally associated with an ethnographic and anthropological approaches. Observation methods can be a good tool for obtaining information about consumer experiences. This method is used for recording behaviors, objects, and events. Informal observations are extensively used for observing customer buying patterns and the impact of advertisements on buying products or services. The observation technique is usually used in conjunction with other research techniques. A specialized form of observation called participation observation occurs when a researcher joins a group for an extended period of time and observes the behaviors of the group members (e.g., Easterby-Smith et al. 2002). Adapted from anthropology, this type of research is growing in popularity, especially in situations where the researcher needs an honest and behind the scenes peek into consumers' lives (e.g., Churchill and Iacobucci 2005).

Mini-case 9.2

Observing the experience in a luxury store

Context of the study. How do luxury brands invest the codes of the sacred to make these places a heritage site? To study this phenomenon, Dion and Borraz (2015) conducted research based on in-store observations and interviews with managers and sellers in luxury sectors to explore the way in which luxury houses embellish the heritage store. The two researchers focused on the luxury industry to understand the management of heritage brands since

(continued)

Mini-case 9.2 (continued)

heritage is crucial for many luxury brands and brings an element of authenticity and uniqueness.

Methodology. To analyze heritage stores, researchers adopted an inductive approach, an emergent and interactive research process rooted in ongoing engagement in the field of retail. Their analysis is built on continuous comparisons between the data collected through field observations and interviews with experts, inductive analysis of data, and the scrutiny of these data through a number of conceptual lenses. The data collection began with the observation of 45 luxury stores in Paris, which were selected by location. Researchers visited all the luxury fashion and jewelry stores located in the Triangle d'Or, the historic headquarters for luxury shopping outlets in Paris bordered by the Champs Elysées and the Avenues George V and Montaigne. The length of each visit varied from 15 to 45 min depending on the size of the store. Systematic observations were carried out using an observational grid that was organized around three dimensions: the substantive staging of the point of sale (design, materials used, decorative elements, music, fragrances, lighting, colors, and street frontage); evaluation of the point of sale (inductive appreciation of the atmosphere and retail design elements); and the impressions made by the store and its staff. Then researchers established several store categorizations (e.g., by brand, country of origin, street, store design style, artistic director, etc.). They also interviewed 17 experts in the luxury retail. The objective was to obtain different perspectives on heritage stores by interviewing people in marketing and retailing departments.

Results. The main results of the observational research of luxury stores and the way brands manage their heritage show that by transposing the characteristics of the sacred to luxury stores, these sacred places are integrated into the mythical stories of the brand and are at the heart of the ritual practices of the brand.

1. *Mythical stories*. The sacred is based on myths, founding stories that members of societies have passed down from generation to generation since the earliest times. Myths seek to give meaning to origins, existence, and the future. The mythical stories create dedicated spaces that become an absolute point of reference, a "center of the world." Thus, French luxury houses build many myths around their history and, more specifically, around historic stores. They seek to mythologize these places, which are at the heart of their identity and their history.
2. *Rituals*. The sacred does not become institutionalized through mythical narrative alone; it also becomes institutionalized through ritual practices.

(continued)

Mini-case 9.2 (continued)

Classically, the ritual practice was restricted to the domain of the sacred. The rites go beyond the narrative to the extent that one proceeds here to an action of the sacred, an operationalization of the sacred. Fashion shows are undoubtedly the most important collective rituals of the luxury industry and represent a major symbolic and marketing event for brands. The iconic features of the luxury stores are often replicated in fashion shows – such as when in 2009, Channel scrolled through its models in front of a reproduction of the façade of the Cambon Street store. The following year, the parade was organized around a gigantic reproduction of a sculpture of a lion in the apartment of Coco Chanel, rue Cambon. Thus, the luxury houses invested the codes of the sacred to make sacred the historical stores, which are at the heart of their identities, in order to maintain the dream and to avoid trivialization of the brand. To that end, luxury brands manipulated the symbolic structures of the sacred through the establishment of a set of mythical stories and ritual practices. Thus, it appears that the sacralization of a store is the result of an intimate link between a brand, a place, personalities, a heritage, and a story.

Luxury brands use several devices to mark the footprint of creators and founders. One or more portraits of the founder-creator are often found, as is in this case, for example, in the lobby of Dior avenue Montaigne or Cartier rue de la Paix. Using the same logic of mythologizing the brand's places around the founding creator in the Cartier store, rue de la Paix. Here, the idea was to artificially recreate the store as it could have been when Louis Cartier moved to rue de la Paix in the late nineteenth century. It was not a question of creating a pastiche of the old-fashioned store but of drawing inspiration from past design to create Cartier's historic store from Cartier's archives. The architects plunged into the archives of the house to imagine the shop that Louis Cartier would have dreamed. In particular, they worked a lot around the garland style woodwork that was so dear to Louis Cartier. The aura of Louis Cartier is everywhere. His portrait greets visitors at the top of the stairs. To reinforce the myth of the place, Cartier has created, on the occasion of the 150th anniversary of the brand, 13 sets of fine jewelry and an exclusive collection of watches and jewels, called XIII, inspired by the symbolism of the place and its history, in honor of the address of 13 rue de la Paix. These stores then become iconic elements for the brand. They are introduced into the mythical stories of the brand and are disseminated through media and other outlets.

- Observational research may usefully be guided by a framework such as PERCEIVE that stands for (spatial) Proximity, (facial) Expressions, Relative orientation (in space), Contact (physical), Eyes, Individual gestures, Voice (vocal gestures), and Existence of adapters (small mood accommodating behaviors). Such a framework draws explicit attention to participants, interactions, routines, rituals, temporal elements, and the setting and elements of a small social organization. This framework points to the importance of nonverbal communication. The advantage of this observation technique is that this method does not rely on the willingness of the respondent to cooperate and provide information, which means that researchers can discover behavior patterns that a respondent is not necessarily aware of. This information can be recorded by observation only, such as the facial expression of a consumer while examining a new product. However, by using the observation method, one cannot observe the consumer's beliefs, feelings, awareness, etc. By replacing humans with mechanical devices, such as video cameras, the accuracy of observation increases and observer bias is reduced and so are the observational costs.

  The immersion in the consumption culture of the informants allows observers to collect data from several sources:
  - Direct observation in the field by sharing the life and consumption activities of people at work, with friends, on holiday, at home, at the supermarket, with their families, etc.
  - Comprehensive in-depth interviews through occasional field conversations and formal and informal exchanges related to consumption practices.
  - The analysis of personal "diary, blogs, and social media" documents in which informants reveal in their own language their point of view about their consumption practices and the world around them.

- **Photographs**. Taking photographs is a way of involving participants in the data collection process. In fact, having participants in the field who are offered the possibility of expressing their practices of consumption through photographs taken by them which represents the consumption objects and practices that constitute their universe allows researchers to get access to a visual representation of their consumption cultures.

- **Narratives**. This technique refers to the life story and tales of people as a qualitative method that originated in the social sciences and can be used in marketing to understand individuals, their consumption experiences, and practices that are socially constructed within a particular consumption culture. The narrative discourse of consumers provides knowledge about their sociocultural sphere and their interactions with other people, companies, parents, and other social agents.

9.2.4 Interactive and Subjective Personal Introspection

The method of data collection through interactive introspection is closely related to action research and was introduced to the social sciences by Rambo-Ronai (1992) in a sociological study of exotic/lap dancers. In this method, the researcher engaged in an interactive dialogue with other informants who shared their private experiences and insider knowledge. In marketing, Holbrook (1997) introduced subjective personal introspection (SPI) more than 25 years ago as a research methodology that has an extreme form of participant observation. For Gould (2012), there are two approaches that marketing and consumer researchers can use to explore consumer experiences:

- The first approach refers to the use of introspection by taking into account multiple researcher perspectives.

Mini-case 9.3

Ethnography: A tool for creating luxury brand storytelling

Context and objectives of the study. This study is a clear evidence that today, many brands launch into storytelling for reasons of fashion and/or necessity, without having clear theoretical and methodological references. Even the most emblematic brands in storytelling have recently shown that telling a story is anything but an easy job. For instance, the last television episodes of the N°5 Chanel or Louis Vuitton's "Invitations to Travel" fail to exploit the potential of storytelling. As a result, the synthesis of studies by researchers like Visconti (2016) and, of course, those of other researchers underline a minimum of principles to refer to for the creation of a more effective and conscious brand storytelling.

Methodology and field of study. This research is based on research in the field of ethnography applied to marketing. The researcher collected storytelling created by the most famous luxury brands from a variety of industries: jewelry, cosmetics, design, fragrances, luxury department stores, luxury hotels, fashion, high-end food, and restaurants. From a methodological perspective, the qualitative data were themed according to the principles applied in the field of interpretative studies.

The main results of the study. The results of this research differentiate three major levels: (1) the storymaking, which represents the design phase of a brand story (what elements to bring together in the story, what principle to refer to in order to write a more effective story, where to find narrative sources for a brand); (2) storytelling, which involves the phase of proposing a story (who to target, which media to use, which storytellers, what effect do we want

(continued)

Mini-case 9.3 (continued)

to achieve through a story, etc.); and (3) the "story-receiving," which assesses the effects of a story on its audience (what does the narrative need for such an audience, what form of persuasion is obtained, etc.). In addition, this research also allowed the researcher to propose pointed answers such as, for a more powerful storymaking, it is necessary to bring together four elements: (1) characters to identify with; (2) a story that is imaginable; (3) a crescendo in the story; and (4) a moral, which allows one to learn and memorize the meaning of history. The results of this ethnography show that many of the luxury brands are deficient in the construction of their storytelling.

In the fragrance industry, for example, it is quite rare to encounter a real story, the majority of brand communications being reduced to clichés of seduction, daring, and freedom. One can, however, find an excellent example of storytelling about a fragrance in the episode of Coco Mademoiselle titled "It's a man's man's man's world." All elements of a story are brought together and produce their effect on the viewer.

- The second approach, however, uses a personal perspective, in other words, the way the researcher can tell a story in his/her own way (it implies looking inward at oneself) (e.g., Batat and Wohlfeil 2009).

  According to Holbrook (1997), SPI is an experiential, private self-reflection on the joys and sorrows related to consumption found in one's own everyday participation in the human condition. This is an extreme form of participant observation that focuses on impressionistic narrative accounts of the writer's very own personal life experiences from the privileged position of an insider, who is providing primary data. Thus, Gould (2012) states that unlike any other research methodology in qualitative research, the researcher often takes on the dual role of both researcher and informant.

  One of the major advantages of this research method is its possibility to allow researchers to observe unlimited, 24-h access into an insider's everyday lived experiences with the research phenomenon without having to wrestle with ethical concerns regarding the informant's privacy. Furthermore, SPI enables the researcher to explore the subjective nature of human feelings, daydreams, sensations, and streams of consciousness related to consumption, which could not be identified with traditional qualitative research methods. There are four different approaches to collecting introspection data, as stated by Wallendorf and Brucks (1993) in their review of auto-ethnographic literature: researcher introspection, interactive introspection, guided introspection, and syncretic introspection.

- **Researcher self-introspection**. This auto-ethnographic technique is the most controversial introspective data collection approach. It was introduced to consumer research by Holbrook (1986) and advanced by Gould (1991). The research context is about the researcher's private life experiences; therefore, he/she acts as the expert and sole informant in a sample of one study. The latest study using researcher introspection was conducted by Wohfeil and Whelan (2012) in "Saved! By Jena Malone." This portrayed an introspective study of a consumer's fan relationship with a film actress in "Pride and Prejudice." In this study, the first author, who is a fan, explored celebrity fandom as a holistic, lived experience from a fan's insider perspective. The lead author (Wohfeil) used SPI to provide insights into his private fan relationship with the actress Jena Malone.
- **Interactive introspection**. This technique has been used in recent works focusing on interactive introspection through a narrative transportation approach. In their research on film experience perception, Batat and Wohfeil (2009) used interactive introspection to examine consumers' movie enjoyment. In so doing, the two authors wrote, exchanged, compared, and interpreted retrospective essays of their personal movie consumption experiences with special attention given to the film "Into the Wild" (US 2007), which they both watched at the same time.
- **Guided introspection**. This data collection approach is becoming increasingly popular in market research practice as an alternative to traditional in-depth interviews and focus groups, as it is relatively easy, convenient, and cost-efficient. Informants are asked to write a detailed introspective essay on their personal lived experiences with regard to a phenomenon of interest (Brown 1998). This approach has been used in research by Brown (1998) in "Romancing the Market: Sex, Shopping and Subjective Personal Introspection." This type of data collection method can provide some potential for marketing and consumer research.
- **Syncretic introspection**. It is essentially a mixed method approach that involves a combination of the other three introspective methods: researcher self-introspection, interactive, and guided introspection. It was suggested by Wallendorf and Brucks (1993) as a way to introduce more scientific rigor into introspective research, but it has not been applied in any study so far.

9.2.5 Netnography and Mobile Self-Ethnography

Marketing research methods are regularly renewed to adapt to emerging consumer behaviors while capturing the opportunities offered by information technologies, the Internet, and social media. Conventional face-to-face interviewing and in situ observation techniques are thus enriched by the use of online qualitative data available on the Internet, particularly on discussion forums and social networks. This is how netnography appeared in the late 1990s and how mobile ethnography/self-ethnography arose later in the early 2010s.

- **Netnography**. It refers to an online immersion technique on social media and specialized blogs to analyze the discourses and exchanges between people on the Internet. As the world is changing, netnography, or online ethnography, certainly can be and has been applied to research questions concerning many social researchers' interests, from consumption experiences to game playing and disabled groups. In the marketing and consumer field, Robert Kozinets was the first researcher who introduced, in 1997, the use of netnography as a tool to learn more about consumption practices. The goal of netnography is not only to understand, but also to share the common passion that drives community members online and offline. This method takes the classic steps of ethnography and adapts them to the study of behaviors and online communities. In order to conduct a netnography study, the investigator/researcher should follow the four main stages described by its founder, Robert Kozinets (2002, 2010, 2015):

  - Step 1: entry. The first step of netnography is to make an "entry," wherein the interviewer should prepare the groundwork before selecting the community to study and beginning its analysis. First, it is important to set a clear goal and question, then, an identification on the online communities which corresponds to the defined objective. This approach is used to filter the groups that are most relevant to the objective. It is therefore essential to carefully gather as much information as possible about the chosen community and its participants.
  - Step 2: data collection. Several types of netnography data should be integrated during the collection process. There are data available within the virtual community in the form of texts written by the members of the group and other data related the external elements of communication with subjects, such as voice, silences, etc. Other data are also considered, such as the data produced by the researcher: notes, reflections, and remarks written by the researcher during the observation process. In the case where the researcher adopts a participatory attitude, contact can be established with the members for the purpose of making individual interviews or starting a new discussion.
  - Step 3: data analysis and interpretation. This step is for analyzing messages using a message classification system to identify off-topic messages. Then, the researcher performs an analysis using the constant comparative method. During this process, data are encoded with variables that reflect the behavior of the participants. The researcher should adopt an "emic" approach to achieve a profound level of understanding of culture. Then, a so-called "ethical" approach is necessary in order to conceptualize the results.
  - Step 4: validation by participants and ethics of the process. Netnography is a method that facilitates data validation by involving the participating members. The members of the virtual community can be contacted and the results of the netnography research presented to them for the purpose of obtaining their comments and being transparent. Feedback is important because it allows members to qualify the results and improve their understanding.

This new form of ethnography is also popular in the study of worldwide, online, or virtual communities. From the relatively humble beginnings of individuals' web pages, blogs have now gained considerable popularity as a form of individual self-expression and an alternative to large media depictions of the news. As an offshoot of the personal web page, the blog remains acutely and deeply personal. The self-report and laboratory limitations of surveys and experiments are patently unable to reveal the rich cultural worlds that are being created and experienced through online communications and systems.

More recently, other sources of information such as consumer rating sites (for accommodation, destinations, etc.) have also provided a very useful source of information. Netnography relies on the collection of qualitative and quantitative data on the Internet that are generated by online communities. Like ethnography, netnography is interested in the study of brand communities on the Internet. The construction of a netnography approach can appeal to several methodological tools: online interviews, participant observation on the Internet, and a narrative account of consumer practices.

Netnography is, therefore, an adaptation of the qualitative and quantitative methods often used to study consumer cultures and experiences in a real context in order to match them with an online context. In general, netnography can be conducted through participant or non-participant observations. Therefore, the advantage of using the Internet for exploratory studies, such as netnography, is to allow people to express themselves freely without fear of judgment. This allows luxury companies to collect more personal information because of the lack of physical maintenance.

- **Mobile self-ethnography**. Mobile ethnography now allows companies to ensure easy and low-cost implementation for "in situ" approaches. In these approaches to self-ethnography, the observer-investigator is replaced by a portable device (smartphone or minicamera) that accompanies the consumer or the buyer in all the moments of his/her daily life. Ethnography is part of the qualitative study techniques for which observation is the major element of the survey. The observation is made "in situ" (where the product/service is consumed/used or purchased). Unlike focus groups or in-depth interviews, ethnography leaves the field of study open, widening the scope to elements that appear a priori outside the field of study for the product or for the brand, including conversations/discussions about all other aspects of respondents' lives: their values, beliefs, motivations, and behaviors. Ethnography, thus, allows to further investigate the lives of consumers/users and to pave the way for opportunities that could not have been identified by another study protocol. Understanding the cultural environment of consumers/users helps luxury businesses to capture unconscious reactions to the brand or product and thus better understand the relationship consumers have with the luxury product or brand. Thus, methodological tools must evolve to include more observational stances in order to adapt to the "new consumer," who is experienced in marketing techniques and who is rapidly evolving in his/her expectations and behaviors.

Thanks to new technologies and their rapid adoption by consumers, mobile ethnography now allows easy implementation complemented by the reduced costs of "in situ" approaches. Such a collection methodology leads participants to record their experiences via their mobile phones, without the presence of a researcher, by transmitting the data on a platform in a format of their choice, whether it is video, photo, text, or audio. Participants have the flexibility to discuss their motivations and provide insights while researchers can re-launch and guide participants to gain new insights. The device can easily take place in multiple locations over the course of a day or weeks, reducing the need for travel. Content is hosted and analyzed from an online platform where the project is managed, enabling real-time interaction with participants.

9.3   Summary

Unlike quantitative research methods that aim to measure variables related to the purchasing process, experiential (projective techniques, Qualitative Diary Research, ethnography, and subjective and personal introspection) and e-experiential research methods, such as netnography and mobile self-ethnography, are, by their nature, exploratory and provide avenues for reflection in order to better understand luxury experiences and the paradoxical behavior of luxury consumers within a particular luxury consumption culture. The immersive and exploratory aspects of these alternative methodologies allow luxury businesses to better anticipate the motivations and attitudes of consumers regarding the expected luxury experiences.

How Millennials and Post-millennials Are Reshaping Luxury

10

Millennial and post-millennial consumers are a particularly strategic target for luxury industry and services. Indeed, not only does it represent a significant weight for luxury, but it is also a deeply globalized consumer segment, which is a major asset for international luxury brands. Raised in an environment of political, ecological, and socioeconomic crises, the young consumer, meanwhile, is lacking values. Swapping from one channel to another or from one brand to another, he/she seeks advice from virtual communities and searches the web for a way to consolidate his/her choices by instantly sharing his/her buying experiences or his/her personal relationships with luxury brands.

If the consumption habits of this new generation (accessibility, fleetingness, and the importance of the experience) do not seem at first sight compatible with the values embodied by traditional luxury (rarity, transgenerational, and the cult of the object), the objective of this chapter is to demonstrate through the examination of luxury brands' practices that congruence does indeed exist between the luxury industries and the expectations of millennials and post-millennials. From then on, some questions arise: What are the expectations of millennials and post-millennials in relation to their consumption of luxury goods? What are their values and is there a possible overlap with those embodied by luxury brands? Do millennials and the luxury sector really need each other and if so, what are their mutual contributions? Which luxury brands are consciously seeking to speak to this specific generation, and how do they do it? Dedicated "love brands" of some luxury brands (Christian Louboutin, Michael Kors, Balmain, etc.) address and attach themselves to millennials and post-millennials without knowing them, while others, more traditional luxury brands (Hermes, Tiffany's, etc.) offer them strong reassuring references in a world full of uncertainty. The question is, therefore, whether luxury can, ultimately, be welcomed into the lives of the youth generation and if, in turn, the young customer can be a way for luxury to get off its pedestal, to desacralize itself, and to question its positioning and offers.

© Springer Nature Switzerland AG 2019
W. Batat, *The New Luxury Experience*, Management for Professionals,
https://doi.org/10.1007/978-3-030-01671-5_10

10.1   Who Are Millennials and Post-millennials, and What Are Their Expectations of Luxury?

As this generation is sometimes connected simultaneously to upward of five screens (TV, mobile, desktop, laptop, and MP3) and while the previous generation uses only two, this current youth generation is distinguished above all by its overconsumption of the Internet and social media as well as by its ability to switch from one medium, one distribution channel, or one brand to another. Definitely, omnichannel, millennials and post-millennials place image and aesthetics at the heart of their luxury buying experience, an experience that only makes sense if it is dubbed so by their peers and their community and shared through stories or online games in which they are staged with the brand.

From the desire to buy a product or a luxury service to its achievement through the act of purchase, the behavior of millennials and post-millennials is profoundly different from that of traditional luxury customers. For this youth generation, the dream of luxury is transmitted by its virtual community, while for other types of customers, the desire for luxury is fed by the endorsers who wear it. During the act of purchase, youth generations are constantly connected to others. After the purchase, these young people are staged with the luxury product to intensify its pleasure within their community; the traditional client sees the luxury product as a means of social valorization and confronts his/her choices with the other customers or sellers of the store.

10.1.1 Swapping Generation

Overall, millennials and post-millennial consumers have a compulsive buying behavior that is less reasoned and less faithful than the previous generations. Hedonists, they favor experiences with luxury goods, and their desire or pleasure in the moment guides their buying preferences according to a customer journey that is increasingly complex to understand for luxury businesses.

- **Millennials and post-millennials are omnichannel and swappers from one luxury consumer location to another**. These young people are referred to as omnichannel buyers. They explore, compare, and become experts in luxury products and brands through the numerous platforms that make information immediately available. They make their purchase decision online according to their desires of the moment and they choose their place of purchase. They also expect a pleasurable purchase and need to be immersed within an enjoyable and experiential setting, ranging from physical stores to e-commerce websites and other multi-brand websites, through promotional and secondhand websites in which the luxury codes are perfectly embraced. The millennials and post-millennials are then hedonistic consumers who select their point of sales according to what they consider as being the most convenient channel, which responds to their immediate need. Yet, the Internet remains the first luxury meeting spot for youth generations who push luxury brands to offer cheaper products in their stores. For some categories of luxury products, such as cosmetics, makeup, or fashion and accessories, the web channel is preferred over physical shops by young people, and the majority of these young consumers prefer to buy their clothes online. Similarly, for more masstige brands that are consumed by younger generations (Burberry, Longchamp, Michael Kors), the weight of the web, in terms of purchases, is more significant. However, the luxury store is still part of millennials' and post-millennials' consumer journey. Despite their overrepresentation on the web, these young consumers remain attached to the luxury store, but their motivations for visiting stores have evolved, and luxury houses are now reconfiguring their offline/physical outlets to meet the new expectations of these generations.

Mini-case 10.1

Karl Lagerfeld reconnecting millennials and post-millennials with luxury stores

The Karl Lagerfeld boutique places the user experience at the heart of its digitalization practices by offering the same facilities as those offered by the web with permanent access to advice from the community. Thus, iPads or tweet mirrors are made available to the young customer in the fitting rooms so that he/she takes a picture and shares his/her fittings with his/her community. Wearers of clothing are also interactive, which allows young customers to get away from the seller's advice in order to obtain the desired information (price, stock, and product characteristics).

The possibility of delivering purchases, which are made on the brand's website, to the store does not represent an important lever for millennials. The luxury store has to transform and rethink its retail strategy to connect more millennial and post-millennial shoppers and offer them a "user experience" that includes the following elements:

- Their subsequent multichannel consumer journey (on the web);
- Connections and contacts with their virtual community;
- Access to the backstage or the secrets of the luxury brand.

For luxury brands, the use of iBeacons to personalize the customer journey (e.g., Barney's in Chelsea); Google glass for replicating, at home, the experience of trying on makeup in-store (e.g., Yves Saint Laurent); virtual reality headsets (e.g., Dior Eyes) for giving backstage access to fashion shows, etc. can help luxury houses capture and retain youth. In fact, altogether, these innovative digital devices allow luxury houses to gradually reconnect to their youth targets with its traditional places of consumption (stores). Thus, whatever channel is used by millennials, it should be considered in the light of the web. Indeed, the idea is that there should be no break in the brand narrative throughout the different points of contact that these highly connected, young consumers use in their daily consumption habits.

- **Millennials and post-millennials as switchers of luxury brands**. They are switchers from one place of consumption to another and from one screen to the next. Young people also have no qualms about switching from one brand to another. Indeed, this generation would like to embrace everything. In fashion or jewelry, as in haute cuisine, millennials and post-millennials go from fast food to Michelin-starred restaurants and from basic accessories to luxury jewelry. Millennials and post-millennials have a multitude of interests, including sharing their experiences with and about their favorite brands. This particular hybrid generation combines inspirations: it is able to eat burgers like truffles, to combine H&M with Kenzo, and to attend the Opera as in Festival. They embrace fashion and design, sports, restaurants and exhibitions, jewelry, and so forth.
- **Millennials and post-millennials switch from one luxury brand value to another**. For this generation that refuses to bend to the contingencies of society and, in particular, luxury, for fear of having its own identity hindered, cultural boundaries are no longer necessary. Therefore, the values embodied by luxury brands can be endorsed by internationally renowned actors and actresses, such as Marion Cotillard for Dior, by a rock star from Metallica for Brioni, by a transsexual makeup artist, or even by a street graffiti artist. By using young street artists previously unknown to the public (London makeup artist, Parisian musician, etc.) in its latest advertising campaign, H&M, by Kenzo, the Swedish brand responds to this confusion of values desired by the younger generations and blurs the boundaries between exclusive luxury and luxury for all. In the same manner, brands such as Burberry, Gucci, and Vivienne Westwood have decided to merge all of their men's and women's collections from 2016, as a response to this generation that is socially liberated and in favor of "marriage for all."

Mini-case 10.2

How does Rolex target millennials and post-millennials?

Rolex is targeting millennials and post-millennials through different approaches:

1. *Celebrity Branding and Sports Marketing*. We are living in an era where most celebrities are becoming role models to younger generations. Most of the high-profile athletes, (Tiger Woods, Roger Federer), high-profile celebrities (Kevin Hart, Ellen DeGeneres), and high-profile singers (Rihanna, Justin Timberlake), all wear Rolex. Ads are being placed on magazines and billboards followed by younger generations. In addition, Rolex is present in most prestigious events where young people attend, like golf, football, tennis, and motorsports tournaments.

2. ***Online Marketing***. Watch sales for young men have dropped around 30% in the past several years. Rolex immediately created a way to reach the younger audience and hence, focused on social media. The younger generations are highly active on the Internet, and they are mostly influenced by advertisements as well as by their friends' posts on social media. That is why Rolex has created links on its official website to social media sites, such as YouTube, Facebook, Instagram, and Twitter, where the target market can visit and make the best choices. Also, the brand recently focused on social listening and comments to determine what kind of watch interests the target audience. It created a section on its website "Every Rolex Tells a Story," which was a success, and discussed the distinctive features of watches in a more fascinating way to attract young consumers.

3. ***Educating the Target Market***. Since the majority of Rolex customers are 35 years and older and since, nowadays, the generation is more interested in cell phones and don't yet appreciate the value of a watch, Rolex came up with an objective in its strategy to educate the younger market on the value of watches and grab their attention. Rolex succeeded in persuading the young generation to believe in its luxurious product and hence, use it as a tool to appear classy and feel great by showing it off to their friends since it is often difficult to afford one at that age.

10.1.2 Show-off Generation

In their mode of communication, millennials and post-millennials are usually more attentive to images than texts. According to OpinionWay study (June 2016), 53% of youth first pay attention to photos on a brand's website (against 44% for the entire population surveyed) and then to the graphs (24%). On the other hand, they prefer pictures that arouse emotion (52%), above all, rather than reflection or dream. Therefore, any visual staging that sends them a strong and instant emotional message is relayed spontaneously by this generation who decides to seize it and share it with peers. Aesthetics, emotion, and experience with the brand, all these insights only make sense when young people can share them with their communities by placing themselves under the spotlight. As a result, luxury houses should rethink their communication policy and feeding social media not only with institutional content (events, advertising campaigns, new collections, news related to the use of muses) but also with interactive information for their young fans (commercial offers, questions and answers, advice, tutorials, etc.).

- **Millennials and post-millennials favor aesthetics to communicate about luxury**. A perfect response to the expectations of this generation is the photo-sharing platform, Instagram (300 million users in 2015), which is the preferred platform within the framework of the expression of the relationship between youth and luxury. Indeed, after the food sector, luxury is the second most traded subject on Instagram with 2.6 million images shared monthly around the world. The most represented themes concern jewelry and watchmaking (44%), shoes (36%), leather goods (15%), and clothes (5%). Also, luxury brands are using this platform because it places aesthetic, image, photographs, and videos at the heart of the lived luxury experience.

Mini-case 10.3

Balmain, as a response to the insta-aesthetic generation

The ultra-publicizing of Balmain's artistic director, Olivier Rousteing, has largely contributed to the awakening and success of this sleeping beauty, and its purchase by the fund Qatari Mayhoola for 500 million euros (15 times its EBITDA) is the proof. As soon as he took office, the 25-year-old artistic director began posting selfies that put him on stage from morning till night with his celebrity friends, like Kim Kardashian, or during his travels. He is a 2.0 creator with more than a million followers on Instagram from generation Y who speaks to millennials and post-millennials who are the prescribers of his brand.

- **Millennials and post-millennials value authenticity and exclusivity**. Far from unrealistic aesthetics offered on the Instagram media, the Snapchat application (60% of whose users are under 25 years old) currently holds 150 million assets each day (and as many Snapshots sent). It is the first social network used by youth prior to Instagram and Facebook to share their emotions with their brands, but for the moment, luxury businesses have only modestly invested in this platform. The ephemeral dimension associated with the "raw" and voluntarily untouched nature of the shared photos does not seem to be in line with the codes of the main traditional luxury logic. On the other hand, some outsiders, like Burberry or Valentino, recently understood the interest of this place of exchange, which privileges the spontaneity of the "beautiful moments," the exclusivity, and the instantaneousness of the contents proposed for users, to the traditional retouched glossy aesthetic. Burberry's spring-summer collection was first revealed to Snapchat users around the world, who had access to runway images, backstage events, and visual collections before their demonstration. Users then relayed the resulting information on all social networks, creating a much bigger buzz than any other media. The Snapchat effect, whose shared images mix staging, chance, and strong emotional power, has also motivated other millennial and post-millennial platforms, such as Instagram, to change its format to benefit from more natural, authentic visuals, even those punctuated by flaws.

- **Millennials and post-millennials use games to connect with luxury brands**. An effective re-enchantment of everyday life through the incorporation of imaginary elements into the real world needs strong emotional experiences focusing on the image rather than texts. Youth also need games to feed their relationships and connect with their selected luxury brands. Therefore, inspired by the joint success of video games, the explosion of social media, and collective actions within this youth generation, some luxury brands understand the need for gamification to engage this target and steer it toward their products and services: smartphone applications (quizzes, virtual fitting, etc.) or quizzes followed and shared through social media became very popular among luxury businesses. It is about finding ways to engage and retain long-term teenage consumers and bringing luxury brands and young people together around a sporting, playful, or simply entertaining event inspired by the success of augmented reality games that allow young consumers to immerse themselves virtually in the universe created by the luxury brand. Thanks to this new immersive experience game, the luxury brand has a more active audience, fully impregnated with its narrative and codes that allow it to engage its audience for a longer term.

Mini-case 10.4

L'Oreal introduces enhanced gamification in luxury

In partnership with Image Metrics, L'Oreal has opened the path to luxury in augmented reality and gamification with this generation thanks to its "Makeup Genius" application, downloaded by nearly 20 million users worldwide since its launch in May 2014.

In 2016, a new license on its makeup ranges consolidates its expertise in the field of virtual cosmetics. This new license with Image Metrics allows the cosmetic brand to explore new possibilities, to be even more connected to its consumers. The application is a facial recognition system designed to apply virtual makeup in real time to see the effects of a product on a customer's face and help facilitate the purchase decision.

Faced with this young generation, for whom every purchase is a fully social act, luxury brands are transforming into real relational intermediaries with evocative images or symbolic hashtags, moderators of communities, providers of cultural content, entertainment, and advice of any kind. Luxury brands disseminate images or texts on the virtual networks more and more distant from their products in favor of the values that they wish to embody in order to create personal and intimate relations with their young targets.

Mini-case 10.5

Jimmy Choo promote playful experiences to target the youth generations

To ensure the commitment of millennials and post-millennials, Jimmy Choo has created a real buzz on social networks by partnering with Foursquare, on the occasion of the launch of its new collection of trainers shoes. More than 4,000 young people participated in the treasure hunt of finding a pair of shoes across the streets of London after finding clues on Twitter. Result: 285,000 mentions of the brand on Facebook, more than 4,000 tweets, and 250 blogs covering the event. Even in-store sales increased by 33% following the release of this game with the brand in London "The Evening Standard."

10.1.3 Share Generation

Millennials and post-millennials constantly need the approval of their peers to legitimize their purchases or justify their choices. Also, they always take advice before their purchases and share their experiences of buying with their peers. On the other hand, this generation, marked by collaborative economy, such as Airbnb, is more interested than ever in rental or secondhand luxury items. To give a second life, young people understand that it is in the exchange that they enrich and nourish their own existence.

- **Millennials and post-millennials search experiences**. For these young people, the luxury experience is not individualistic; it is collective and only makes sense when it radiates beyond its place of consumption. Social shopping is the favored buying method of this generation that uses tweet mirrors and other interactive displays available in the shops to instantly export its look on social media and solicit the opinion of friends before buying the product of interest. Purchases are increasingly connected, and despite the strong reputation attached to luxury brands, the products and services in this universe are related to feedback from their customers. To respond to these specificities, certain luxury brand websites have also created social media consultation buttons next to the products on their e-commerce site.

Mini-case 10.6

Gucci as part of youth consumption culture

Gucci's primary target market has always been high income, high status, middle-aged businessmen and women. However, in the late 1990s, the brand included a trendy feature in addition to its more mature line, which was designed to appeal to a younger audience. Generations Y and Z are already the main growth engine in the luxury goods market. In 2017, 55% of Gucci's sales came from customers under 35 years old. Gucci attracts young people by implementing the following strategies:

1. *Digital integration*: social media, followed by young customers, has been an important source for Gucci not only for understanding the spending pattern of consumers in their 20s but also for communicating with the group. This generation expects quick responses due to growing up with mobile devices and access to real-time responses, which has made them impatient. They expect quick replies when reaching out to a customer service representative through social media or when posting online content that can be easily shared and shows positive consumer feedback. Gucci succeeded in its industry-leading Internet strategies and managed to integrate digital connection in the company. So, due to the attention-grabbing designs and the fascinating pictures on Instagram, e-commerce for Gucci has more than doubled in the first quarter of 2018.

2. *Product diversity*: Gucci operates in 450 stores across the globe including franchise stores, duty-free boutiques, and leading department stores. In addition to repositioning its brand to appeal to a wider audience, Gucci also tailored its lines of products to ensure they perfectly matched the tastes of their customers. To do this, the brand performed in-depth market research about its client base in order to establish their ambitions, tastes, and needs. As such, the brand was able to create products that matched the exact needs of its clients. Due to strong demand for the new Gucci image, the company is building the Gucci Art Lab to produce leather goods and shoes. In every collection, Gucci is aware of the fashion needs that appeal to a young consumer. From belts to T-shirts, boots to blazers, or slogan hoodies to Gucci's fur-lined slippers, it is offering young people what they want rather than telling them what they need. Gucci, in turn, was able to win the youth vote.

3. *Celebrity marketing*: in order to get rid of outmoded ideas that were holding the brand back, Gucci now dresses up-to-date style icons that understand youth, like Harry Styles, Rihanna, Blake Lively, the Kardashians, the Hadid sisters, and LeBron James. Elton John was also an inspiration for many fashions shown at Gucci's spring/summer 2018 show. Almost all the high-profile athletes, actors, musicians, and models dress in Gucci during big events, and many famous songs, nowadays, like "Gucci Gang," focus on the luxury brand and spread its reputable image to the young generation.

- **Millennials and post-millennials need the recognition of their peers to legitimize their choices of luxury brands.** These young people learn about new brands through their friends, loved ones, siblings, and fashion blogs, and they use magazines and other traditional media less than their predecessors to learn about luxury brands. Therefore, their peers, the people who resemble them by their mode of communication or because they are part of their virtual community, are their main referents and even serve as an entry key to the purchase of certain luxury products and services. The opinions of bloggers, popular celebrities, and those of regular consumers sometimes have more weight than the heritage or the discourse of the luxury brand.

  - Bloggers are the first influencers for youth. The Italian blogger and founder of The Blond Salad, Chiara Ferragni, has as many subscribers as Barack Obama (6.5 million Instagram followers and 500,000 unique visitors per month in 2015), owns its own e-commerce website (www.shop.theblondsalad.com), is as famous as Anna Wintour, and offers a wide range of products in her name. In fashion, as in beauty (the "beautystas"), the advice and various tutorials of the community of bloggers are real levers for the purchase of youth generations. Furthermore, bloggers overall do not hesitate to monetize their influential power to luxury brands (The Blond Salad generates two million USD in annual revenue thanks to the advertising banners present on its blog and its partnerships with Louis Vuitton and Burberry) or simply use their style and their pen to influence their readers on the "love brands" and "it-bag" of the moment.

  - Luxury endorsers remain the reference model for youth. This generation is also very sensitive to luxury brand endorsers and their lifestyles. They use them and choose them as a standard bearer more subtly than in a traditional advertising campaign. Indeed, the number of subscribers the celebrity becomes the only objective measurement criterion of his or her fame. Movie stars of the past are being replaced by young references in the world of music, fashion, or sport that use, as widely as possible, the same means of communication as millennials and post-millennials. For example, many stars with a large online following, such as Cristiano Ronaldo (more than 100 million likes on Facebook), David Guetta (55 million), Cara Delevingne (12 million on Instagram), or Kim Kardashian, are the new spokespersons for watch brands or fashion. When Kim Kardashian posted a picture of herself with her new Louboutin shoes on Instagram, the increase in demand for the model she wears was immediate. The idea is that "instagirl" bridges the gap between fashion (or luxury), entertainment, and social media. Indeed, to provide a real guarantee, the endorsement should be a continuum for feeding the capital of the brand. It is the scenario of its relationship with the brand transmitted on social networks that is fundamental. For example, when Ronaldo tweets on a meeting with tag Heuer, it is worth a fortune. The key to entering a relationship is the emotional availability of the ambassador as well as his/her consistency and sympathy for the brand. The activity of an ambassador on social media has much more credibility with young people than if it is the brand that expresses itself.

- Youth generations favor the opinion of their peers. If 50% of them feel it is easier to communicate with others via the virtual, they can also express the need for feedback from their close community. It is through sharing that the good, whether purchased or not, is of great importance. Since the community is an experienced receiver, it is natural that some brands use their members as endorsers for the duration of an advertising campaign.

Mini-case 10.7

Clergerie girls: Today's it-girls

Luxury houses, such as Robert Clergerie's, do not hesitate to use mere customers as muses, who become true ambassadresses, a "testimonial" for the brand. Launched in 2016, the "Clergerie Girls" advertising campaign brings to center stage simple young consumers who share their experiences with the brand and their lifestyle in their community.

- **Generation "me too" and luxury**. More anxious, less protected, and more in search of landmarks than their big brothers and sisters, millennials and post-millennials are largely connected to their parents and have a mimetic behavior of purchase. Most of them buy the same brands of clothing as their predecessors do, like Gap, Polo, Tommy Hilfiger, etc. Furthermore, these young people use the same fashion items as their parents, hence the success in France of fashion and lingerie brands, such as Comptoir des Cotonniers, initiator of the mother-daughter tandem in its communication campaigns, or Petit Bateau Marinières and swimwear Vilebrequin, or Darjeeling, which offers coordinated products for mother (or father) and daughter (or son). Beyond the property and the maximization of the underlying economic interest, this "sharing" generation seeks in this specific purchase act to create a transgenerational social bond. It is an "extension of self" on the side of the parent, where it is a necessity to claim one's status as an independent "small adult" while creating strong emotional bonds with one's family on the youth's side. This buying behavior finally gives meaning to their act of purchase while giving it an additional guarantee. This habit of consumption is visible both for fashion products as well as for more statutory products, such as watches.

Mini-case 10.8

Patek Philippe, the watch brand that is passed on generation after generation

As a watch manufacturer, Patek Philippe creates timepieces that are among the most desirable in the world. It is a desirability fueled by the brand's "generation" advertising campaigns: "We are never quite the owner of a Patek watch, it is the watch who chooses you and asks you to keep it for generations to come," reminds the slogan.

- **"Luxury and couch-surfing" generation**. Every action that makes up the youth generation's life is now accessible in the form of sharing, renting, bartering, or lending through special platforms and websites. Therefore, luxury is organized to respond to this new collaborative economy, the phenomenon of "couch-surfing." If luxury is eternal, the youth generation gives it a second life by encouraging it to be at its disposal through these new places of exchange. From then on, this generation reaches luxury when it wants and at the rate it wants, and thus the price variable becomes secondary.
- **"Secondhand" generation**. As for promotional websites in the post-Internet years, luxury brands have been slow to recognize the referencing of their second-hand products on secondhand websites. Today, faced with a generation that no longer perceives these divisions as discriminating for the brand, luxury goes so far as to endorse these already worn products to turn them into vintage products. Some outsider brands do not hesitate to develop exclusive partnerships with websites such as Vestiaire Collective. Even luxury designers like Jean-Charles de Castelbajac have created limited editions distributed exclusively on these websites and Gucci partners with Christies to legitimize authenticity of its used products sold by the auction house "Gucci collectors." Luxury houses create for themselves a vintage luxury dimension as a need to claim their status as a generational brand over which time has no hold.

10.2 What Do Millennials and Post-millennials Want from Luxury?

The emphasis on experience and emotion, as well as the need to express one's identity, makes youth generation consumers' expectations particularly well-matched with luxury brand responses. The importance of values, such as immediacy, that millennials and post-millennials assign to their consumption of luxury seems to create a gap between the long-term approach in luxury and today's youth generation expectations in regard to time. Furthermore, the need for excitement, adventure, and the desire for immediate satisfaction make it complex for luxury brands to match the expectation of this generation by emphasizing the temporal aspect of creating and delivering luxury goods (products and services).

10.2.1 Millennials and Post-millennials Want Luxury Experiences, Emotion, and Self-Esteem

Experience, emotion, and exclusivity are the foundation of the luxury universe that contribute to seducing millennials and post-millennials who are in search of products and services that can affirm their identity in their community.

- **The luxury experience before the luxury product**. For millennials and post-millennials, a luxury experience is more important than the object itself. The youth generation refers to something immaterial, which cannot be damaged with time. It remains engraved in the memory of these young people and enriches their life. On the other hand, the luxury experience of millennials and post-millennials continuously needs to be transmitted and lived – even by its community. For them, luxury does not have the same meaning as for previous generations. In fact, the objective of luxury is no longer to accumulate material wealth but to experience immaterial wealth. While in the twentieth century, the consumption of luxury responded to a need for heritage accumulation, such as donating properties and luxury items to one's descendants (a reference to the necessary durability of luxury), for youth generations, the purchases of luxury do not meet the same need for possession and transition to next generations. Thus, the consumption of luxury tends to move products that are anchored in the long term, such as watchmaking products, to one-shot or immaterial services, such as travel, hotels, starred restaurants, etc. It is less important to possess luxury and more important to use and share it. For millennials and post-millennials, luxury is, first, an experience (e.g., traveling, eating something good, feeling the wind in their hair). In the catering sector, in particular, the chefs have clearly understood the importance of the experience and have gone to great lengths to retain their customers in the concept of gourmet meals whose obsolescence is intrinsically planned.

Mini-case 10.9

The case of Pierre Gagnaire, "the suspended time"

Since the advent of chefs in haute cuisine, starred restaurants have become places of worship and temples of luxury in which rituals are held and ceremonies are orchestrated by the butler and signed by the cook. Therefore, it takes on average 3 h to enjoy a gourmet meal, from the moment the customer arrives at the restaurant until the moment he/she pays the bill.

The staging at the restaurant and the importance given to the duration of consumption contribute to the nourishment of the memory of the gastronomic experience, a luxury experience, a dream shared by all the clients. Nowadays, chefs not only create meals, but they develop themes, an atmosphere, a feeling. These gastronomic experiences are more emotional and almost touching for their clientele who believe that it is important to be given a few moments of emotion during their dining experience.

- **The "wow" effect**. For millennials and post-millennials, the idea behind the "wow" effect is to get what others have not been able to get or to receive from the brand an exclusive supplement of experience. For luxury houses, whose brand content is acknowledged through ancestral know-how, renowned customers, historical markers, creators, and so forth, the "wow" effect is an integral part of their ceremony, and the attention paid to their privileged young customers is particularly exclusive. Therefore, the youth generation's aspirations for exclusive experiences are perfectly in line with luxury brands' invitations for distinction.

Mini-case 10.10

An example of "wow" effect at Chaumet

How can we create an unbreakable bond with a brand's VIP customers if it is not by making them discover a space that is usually closed to the public? In the first floor of its flagship store located in Place Vendôme, Chaumet offers to its customers an experiential discovery of a real private museum staged by the renowned architect Jean-Michel Willemotte (historical objects including the Eugenie tiara, Empress, was manufactured by Chaumet). Customers enter the legacy of the brand in a very exclusive way. For the luckiest of them, there will be the discovery of a prestigious guest in the living room with parquet floors classified in points of Hungary: the grand piano of Frédéric Chopin on which the composer created his last mazurka opus 68 n°4. Through this experiential journey, Chaumet has achieved the "wow" effect expected by its clientele who felt privileged and considered.

- **Self-esteem (or identity extension) rather than social aspiration**. Although in a state of permanent demonstration, the youth generation is, however, far from being bling-bling and defines luxury as not being an end in itself. These millennials and post-millennials do not perceive luxury as a way to enhance social value but rather as a solution to promote their identity. Thus, young people prefer statutory and symbolic objects (watches and jewels being cited first among luxury objects in Japan, second in France, and third in the United States) as well as technological objects and it-bags, which remain an ineluctably ephemeral fashion product.

Mini-case 10.11

A return to discrete luxury in China

Since 2011, the actions taken by China (anti-gifts and ostentatious banquets) for senior officials combined with the economic difficulties of Russia have led to a return to discrete luxury. Far from bright logos and brands with strong social aspirations, young Chinese consumers (25–35 years), in particular, now seek to express their personality in ways that go beyond the mere display of money or social status. Nowadays, in China, success is not synonymous of financial wealth. When China is discreet, the luxury world reacts accordingly and revises its offer by transforming the packaging of its products so that it is more authentic, less ostentatious, and refocused on its image craft or core business and know-how (e.g., Guerlain and the art of perfume, etc.).

10.2.2   Relationship to Time and Immediacy of Millennials and Post-millennials

The relationship to time as a reference to the past (e.g., nostalgia and search for authenticity) and the present (e.g., instantaneity) is no longer the same for the current youth generation and seems not very compatible with the fundamentals of luxury. In services, also, it is all about getting it right now. For example, most hair care brands, such as L'Oreal Professional, encourage hairdressing salons that use their products to make themselves visible on immediate appointment sites, such as the British site Haircvt, which has developed its offer to Paris recently.

Considered a place of memory, the luxury brand perpetuates traditional know-how transmitted from generation to generation while manufacturing its products. Thus, because it is a myth, time has no hold on luxury, and it becomes imperishable and eternal. Yet, there is often a need to stop, to "suspend" time (Reference to the Hermes Complications watch, "the suspended time" which allows the customer to stop the needle of his/her timepiece and restart it without the watch falling behind). The temporal dimension is intrinsically linked to luxury goods and does not seem to be taken into consideration for the youth generation for whom only the present moment seems to count.

- **Instantaneity and fluidity**. For millennials and post-millennials, the access to luxury items and their purchase time should be limited (e.g., Amazon Premium demonstrates this permanent need for the younger generation to obtain objects at the very moment when it expresses the desire). The youth generation privileges immediacy and speed in its consumption in order to have the feeling of optimizing its time and its life. Thus, to save time, millennials and post-millennials prefer luxury brands that help them save time through their presence on social media (for information), an e-commerce website (for the online purchase and home delivery), geolocation (to find the place of purchase more easily), offering in-store services (to avoid queues), or late closing hours.

  Extreme luxury is simplicity for the customer. On the other hand, if the notion of experience remains important for millennials and post-millennials, the interruption of the related time is not well-suited to their usual consumption practices. More than ever, "multitasking," thanks to mobile phones and their continuous use, is becoming very popular among youth generations that have indeed embraced a culture of the moment, a culture nourished by interactive and instant platforms, such as the Snapchat app. Yet, intensive interaction does not facilitate being fully immersed in luxury experiences. Furthermore, luxury brands can offer a response adapted to this FOMO "fear of missing out" generation which is anxious about the idea of missing something. Therefore, a pop-up store could be an answer to this fear and to the immediate need of millennials and post-millennials.

Mini-case 10.12

Prada's strategy to attract the youth generation

Prada connects with young clientele through online sales and flexible pricing. The brand tends to increase its online variety of products, especially its shoes. Prada also expands advertising through social media by introducing new items at lower prices for the young, teenage customers. Taking into consideration that the millennial and post-millennial generation has grown up in a rapidly developing digital world, social media is critical as a marketing strategy used to connect to the younger generation of consumers with luxury brands and among them.

Through the development of digital media, advertising has had to adapt and change as well in order to accommodate a new, more transparent world. As a result, brands such as Prada aim to be as authentic as possible in displaying their goals and their desire to communicate with and relate to their clientele. Because of this change in advertising methods, the luxury brand should also incorporate a story in regard to every product offered in order to enhance the appeal of the brand to its younger customers. Once the products have a satisfying backstory and aesthetic, Prada can move quickly to constantly create and display new products in order to keep up with the customers' desire for new and exciting products.

- **Desire for change**. Millennials and post-millennials see themselves as chameleons, able to move to the other end of the world, to reinvent themselves, or to change jobs. With the continuous changes in their lives, these young consumers constantly need to change their buying habits. Indeed, the timelessness intrinsically linked to luxury can become degrading for this generation, which is more unfaithful in its mode of consumption and is in search of continual change rather than looking for investment purchases. Therefore, the notion of "eternal luxury" is questioned, and some recent initiatives of watch brands reveal a slight examination of their fundamentals. The watchmaking and jeweler brands are gradually investing in the territory of connected watches and bracelets (Hermes in collaboration with Apple, TAG Heuer, Frédérique Constant, Swarovski) or collaborate promptly with other luxury and fashion brands (Jaeger-LeCoultre and Christian Louboutin).
- **The need for sensations and strong emotions**. The lifetime of a product or service has no hold on millennials and post-millennials. It is the generation of "emoticon" that expresses, permanently, its emotions or its mood of the moment on different social media and platforms with great simplicity, immediacy, and openness. Also, these young people have high levels of risk-taking and "thrill-seeking." They seek intense and new experiences that bring immediate sensation and pleasure, hence the success of energy drinks or extreme sports for example. Some initiatives of luxury brands tend to overlap the desires of thrill-seeking

adventurers: Chanel association with muses (Gigi Hadid, former reality TV star) or Dior (Rocky, a singer with a sulfurous past). The creation of extreme sports products or the creative inspirations of certain brands or products is a reflection of the uncontrollable nature of life that is so acknowledged by younger generations.

10.2.3 Luxury as a Means to Identity Construction for Youth Generations

In need of experience and assertiveness, luxury brands offer a part of the answer to millennials and post-millennials who are in search of preservation and distinction in relation to their community. Therefore, if the eternal character of luxury does not seem to have a grip on youth generations, the recent initiatives of some luxury brands reveal that the aspirations of this young generation can question the fundamentals of luxury.

- **Luxury as a means of self-preservation**. Having lived through the greatest recession since the crisis of 1929, the younger generation is haunted by astronomical suicide rates and mental health challenges. According to the Centers for Disease Control and Prevention, suicide was the third leading cause of death among young people between the ages of 10 and 24 in the United States in 2014 (Social Media Concerns of Teen Suicide Contagion, USA Today, May 2014). The youth generation considers the act of consumption as a means to exist and survive. Similarly, these youth are concerned by environmental crises and feel compelled by a moral obligation to preserve their planet by joining humanitarian associations even for short periods. Therefore, they expect brands that are emblematic of luxury to be not only irreproachable in their actions but that they lead the way by being the flag bearer of values, an act in which young consumers could see a reflection of themselves. Thus, when the brand Moncler is blamed on social media because it mistreats the geese in its process of manufacturing jackets, the sales of this luxury brand were strongly impacted. In contrast, luxury houses, such as Guerlain, Chaumet, or Hermes, take into account environmental or cultural preservation to position their image on the territories of predilection of this generation. Among luxury initiatives set to meet the need for self-preservation, we can cite the following:
    - Preserving raw materials: launched by Guerlain, the web series "The exploration of the imperial orchid by Michelle Yeung" presents the story of the birth of the Orchidée Impériale range of products and focuses on the actions of preservation of orchids of Yunnan.
    - Recycle products: with its "Petit H" initiative, Hermes reuses scrap leather to design new clothing creations.
    - Defending an artistic heritage: Chaumet's artistic collaborations and the links between luxury and art contribute to this need for preservation. The ephemeral Chaumet museum, which opened its doors as a "pop up store" and brings

together the timelessness of art and luxury and instantaneity of the youth generation, seeks to share its high-end jewelry with visitors as we pass on a part of history and French heritage.

- Preserving ancestral know-how: immersing customers in LVMH Group workshops during its "Particular Days." The luxury brand defends a heritage craft and reveals its behind the scenes to the public.

• **Luxury as a means to exist and distinguish oneself**. The youth generation is continuously searching for experiences or products that give it a "happy few" status. Luxury can be a way of distinguishing oneself from the moment when it grants, for example, privileges. These exclusive contacts can take the form of invitations to private events organized by the luxury brand, immersions within the heritage of the brand to uncover the secret of its history, or limited edition products and unique tailored items. These are the initiatives of brands, such as Fendi, which allow its young customers to customize their bags with the help of "Fendirumi," a kind of little fur monster evocative of the universe of Pokemon, thus making the customized bag unique.

- Being unique thanks to luxury. This race for exclusivity is also reflected in the youth generation's quest for singularity to distinguish itself by the bizarre or even the imperfect. For example, Balenciaga did not hesitate to use, on its last two shows, the American star with her iconic toothless face, Zumi Rosow. Similarly, Kenzo, Calvin Klein, and Proenza Schouler scroll between openmouthed model Sarah Lin, who stood out with her dental device "rings," accessory suggestive of adolescence.

- Discovering products or exclusive places. Saturated with media information, the youth generation seeks to identify and differentiate itself by appropriating niche products that are exclusive to narrative codes and visually strong. This generation values the confidential nature of some luxury goods. In the cosmetics and perfume sector, if the bestsellers in Europe still remain Lancôme, Chanel, and Dior, multinational groups, such as L'Oreal (Proenza Schouler), Puig (Penhaligon's and Craftsman Parfumeur), and Estée Lauder (Frédérique Malle, The Lab, By Killian), have recently acquired niche brands in order to conquer these new customer targets.

- Confidential places appeal to young customers. Private circles, confidential bars, exclusive places, and secret places in which members or clients find themselves among peers have multiplied in recent years and are very popular among millennials and post-millennials. These circles go beyond the simple club concept. Exclusion produces inclusion and powerful links between those who are entrenched in it. The exclusive nature of these clubs generates mystery because no one really knows what is going on there. Indeed, there is no more searching, no more waiting, no more hope, and no more society if there is no mystery. All individuals aspire to a secret world, including millennials and post-millennials.

- **Luxury as a break**. The race for luxury to catch youth generations has had its day, and some luxury brands are taking the opposite approach to stop time and refocus the consumer on the basics. The return of "slow made" movement in luxury advocates for the respectful creation of know-how and the environment as well as respect for the time required for a job well done. It also advocates the right price: a price that would be justified not only by the brand or logo pinned by the luxury house on the product but, above all, by the time spent researching the design of the product, its manufacture, and its materials. Responding to real desire to slow down the pace to serve their customers more effectively, fashion brands, such as Tom Ford, Gucci, Vivienne Westwood, and Burberry, have announced, in 2016, the redesign of ranges, a limitation of the number of shows, a merger of collections men-women, and an immediate availability of their novelties in their network of outlets (the "Show now, buy now" collection of the last Burberry show in September 2016 challenges the concept of distancing luxury). Products are immediately available to the consumer. The new Burberry collection also plans to focus on its craftsmen and promote "Made in Great Britain" through a collaboration with The New Craftsmen (after the Burberry collections show, the work of the craftsmen who participated in the development of these collections was exhibited in a dedicated space during an exhibition in September 2016), as a return to the roots of luxury. Clarification of the offer, improvement of the quality, optimization of the rate of service, and highlighting the origins of manufacturing, all signify that slow luxury is on the way and the weak signals carried by the youth generation that contributed to this return to the true values of the luxury.
- **Millennials and post-millennials are at the center of luxury**. The virtual world, occupied by the younger generations and their social networks, has normalized the relationship between luxury brands and consumers. The difficulty for luxury is to preserve the distance with its consumers while allowing them access behind the scenes. This may require a decentralization of the luxury brand, which will be forced by the dialogue with its customers, to speak less of its products and to offer more unique, emotional, authentic, and exclusive experiences to its customers, especially younger ones.

10.3   Do Luxury Brands Speak to Millennials and Post-millennials?

The actions of luxury brands to target the youth generation directly and exclusively seem to still be scarcely visible. However, the behaviors and attitudes of millennials and post-millennials toward luxury and their strong ability to influence other luxury consumers tend to challenge the practices of luxury houses. Even the statutory, institutional luxury brands that see "love brands" sprout up question themselves and agree to "play" with their codes and their stories to interact with the youth generation that includes their actual and future clients.

Mini-case 10.13

Louis Vuitton's approach to seducing young consumers

The luxury industry faces changes as a response to the shifts in the customer behaviors toward a more digital, experimental, and social preference. Louis Vuitton has a strong social media presence and has adopted successful marketing strategies that efficiently target the millennial and post-millennials (young) generation. Millennials and post-millennials today prefer spending money on their lifestyles, positive experiences, and social media currency instead of tangible and physical products themselves, thus, Louis Vuitton, with its omnichannel strategy, makes the young generation's experience a positive lifestyle.

Louis Vuitton is considered a worldwide powerhouse since it has celebrities collaboration in their marketing regularly. For instance, Louis Vuitton has involved in its spring campaign a character from a video game called "Final Fantasy" with pink hair. This character has millions of international loyal gaming fans. The brand has also a variety of products lying in a range between $100 and several thousands of dollars. Moreover, Louis Vuitton has been hiring young and talented designers to appeal to the young generation of buyers. Additionally, to attract youth targets, Louis Vuitton sponsors important sporting events, such as motorsports and yachting.

10.3.1 Luxury Brands that Have Understood Youth Generations

To become "popular" and thus exist among this generation, luxury brands have to become a "love brand." It is necessary to capture what the youth generation means by "love brand" and how luxury brands can be transformed into "love brands." Depending on the sector, the strategies used by luxury to become love brand houses are not the same.

While some might focus on the product by offering a wide range of products on their websites and making a very targeted and shallow offer in the shop by defining a wide range of prices on the website, others apply place strategies by proposing few shops placed on unusual arteries for luxury – or on promotion through media investment where customers are the flag bearers and influencers of the brand.

- **In the volume industries (perfumes and fashion accessories)**, owning a designer product is essential to stand out as a "love brand." In this way, it is the brand that manages to impose itself in a very natural mode in the minds of consumers. For example, Louboutin has more than 8.5 million fans on Instagram without investing a cent for that. To become a "love brand," Louboutin has always sought to preserve its status as a designer brand by protecting the creative genius of its artistic director from any constraints related to the market. At Louboutin, there is no marketing plan. It is a sincere brand and its creator is authentic, and everyone knows that the products are made in Italy in the brand's factories. In terms of distribution, the shoe brand Louboutin scrupulously selects its outlets and has only four stores in China when statutory brands like Cartier have more than a hundred. Therefore, the Louboutin experience is always unique because each store references the shoes that it wishes, and thus, the customer is always surprised to discover an offer that evolves according to the meeting places with the brand. Only 50% of the offer is a reflection of the wish of the creator (his/her "love products"); the rest is selected by the store manager according to the tastes of the customers and their personal desires. Paradoxically, the website Louboutin is the only place where we can find the entire collection (three times more products than the website of Jimmy Choo) because it is the only place where the customers seek an effective experience that combines the practicality, availability, and speed of delivery of products. The digital experience is little exploited at the moment because it does not wish to be simply an accessory without branded content; some luxury brand pop up store trials in September 2016 introduced the sharing of the experience of the visitor by being photographed with the iconic designer of the house as a chic portrait of fair, and as a return to the world of mountebank of Christian Louboutin.

In niche perfumery, the same desire for distinction is felt, and the only category that is growing strongly in a sluggish sector is that of designer perfumes. Millennials and post-millennials are ready to pay more for a rare perfume, with a strong personality, distributed in more confidential shops. At the same time, brands such as Burberry use youth generation insights to stand out: Worn by Kate Moss and Cara Delavigne or the "my Burberry" advertising campaign (in 2014), which focused on the fact that perfume bottles could be customized with the initials of its owner.

- **When the supply is plethoric, the idea is to inspire confidence**. For luxury brands, there should be a very transparent side in their relationship with their customers. The luxury brands realize that trust is very difficult to obtain from the younger generation. This generation is surrounded by brands and advertisements in everyday life, and it wants transparency and proximity. If the youth generation is influenced by the opinions of its predecessors, it is far from devoid of personality and also seeks to forge its own point of view on brands. Thus, the preferences of youth generations are for those luxury brands that are honest, ethical, authentic, and true. With this young consumer, the brand cannot lie and should inspire confidence with the products it offers (origin, innovation, know-how).

In fact, millennials and post-millennials have strong values linked to sharing and to business ethics; luxury brands should then be honest and humble. For example, in the cosmetics sector, the entry of the youth generation becomes apparent in the product category of makeup, because it is the most attractive in price and is visual and provides tutorials, videos, and communication tools favored by these young consumers. These young people invent uses or gestures that belong to them alone; it is by this means that the youth generation appropriates the product with confidence and transparency with the brand. With Lancôme (including the customizable lipstick "Juicy Shaker") and the recent acquisition of the brand Urban Decay (which speaks to professionals), the group L'Oreal manages to seduce youth generations. With products worn by peers that are customizable and/or used and endorsed by professionals, this is how to win the trust of millennials and post-millennials.

Mini-case 10.14

The "Studio by Petit VIP" Barrière hotel group, a service specifically developed for millennials and post-millennials

In order to renew its offer for younger generations, the Barrière hotel group has signed a partnership with Petit VIP, an expert in high quality childcare that develops a fun-educational, intergenerational, multicultural, and emotional spaces. The content is focused on an artistic and environmental sensibility. At the Hotel Barrière Normandy and the Majestic de Cannes, in particular, launched in June 2016, this offer provides children with a dedicated butler service ("kids concierge"), various activities in the arts, comics, cinema, entertainment, sports, and a specific catering format that promotes fun, gastronomy, and homemade meals.

- **In the service industry, it is the quest for authenticity that comes first**. In the realm of the immaterial, it is the immersive experience of services that makes the difference. Thus, the R&D department of the Marriott hotel chain in Charlotte (the United States) has identified that in contrast to generation X, for whom the consistency of services offered from one Marriott to another was unavoidable, the youth generation preferred a local and distinctive experience that immerses these young guests in the local culture. From then on, in the Marriott of the city of Charlotte, it was decided that the hotel would integrate some local touches by asking local chefs and entrepreneurs to invest in the hotels. For example, instead of the standard Starbucks, an independent coffee shop is now located in the corner of the hotel lobby.

10.3.2 Luxury Brand Comparison Is Key Among Millennials and Post-millennials

The traditional luxury brand remains a reference for this generation that is in need of landmarks. The place of traditional and ancestral luxury brands, such as Louis Vuitton, Chanel, Dior, Tiffany, or Rolex, remains predominant among this generation.

- **When luxury brands play with their identity codes to seduce youth generations**. Tiffany's "#lovenotlike" campaign launched by the brand's new digital director, Diana Hong-Elsey, in August 2016, did not hesitate to play with the more than 100-year-old identity codes of the famous jewelry brand. Through the choice of young models, the creation of an exclusive Snapchat icon, and the use of Kim Kardashian's sister, Tiffany & Co delegates to the younger generation the right to appropriate its codes and have fun with its logo and its visual identity. Similarly, the brand Guerlain was able to speak to younger generations simply by launching its perfume "La Petite Robe Noire," which was number one in perfume sales in France for the 9 weeks following its launch. Incarnated by no muse, this little black dress is an icon in fashion and luxury, and Louis Vuitton has largely used the silhouette of this universal symbol of Parisian coquetry and feminine freedom by making it dance in a pictorial world within which everyone can meet "Behind this perfumed little black dress, hides a Parisian dreamed with a personality that is a bit insolent and mutineer."

- **The luxury brand is not enough in itself, bonding with peers remains important.** The youth generation spends much less time than the average population watching television (it replaces those moments with emails and social networks). As a result, this generation is less available to assimilate advertising messages. This is true for even the most traditional luxury brands in beauty. For example, the influence of YouTubers is the only key for young consumers who subscribe to at least ten channels on YouTube. The only brands that could be successful are those which understand that this generation values the opinions of its peers. These YouTubers do not take themselves seriously; they are funny and film their beauty tips in their bedroom. They are similar to those to their viewers and are part of the same "family." Some of their videos are averaging more than 500,000 views, indicative of an audience that is unreachable by television advertising campaigns or other traditional media used by the statutory luxury brands.

- **Use of storytelling as a social link.** The youth generation transcribes, more readily, its illustrated story about its last luxury trip rather than its recent purchase of a luxury product. The idea is to share a story with its peers (if it's not shareable, it did not happen), and this is what some luxury brands rely on to translate their narrative codes. Very present in lingerie and perfumes, the brand Calvin Klein uses evocative "hashtags" in its advertising campaigns that encourage millennials and post-millennials to use products to tell stories among their communities. The idea is to declare on Instagram what we do when wearing Calvin Klein ("I make money in #myCalvins," "I am free in #myCalvins," "I seduce in #myCalvins," etc.). The Pandora jewelry brand also uses the emotional aspect to play and connect with the youth generation on Mother's Day. In its "the art of you" communication campaign, the brand offers stories of mothers and daughters around its products and asks its community to tell their own stories and to share them with their communities on social media.

Mini-case 10.15

Pandora, a jewelry brand that makes sense to millennials and post-millennials

Launched on the occasion of Mother's Day, the new communication campaign of the American brand Pandora has placed emotion at the heart of its storytelling. Pandora is barely present in advertising, but the brand has aroused a keen interest among youth who have understood that one does not stand out by the jewelry that is worn; its value lies on the one who gave it to you. Pandora does not position itself as a traditional luxury brand; it is exclusive because of its emotional anchoring that surrounds its products.

10.4   Summary

The youth generation (millennials and post-millennials) has a number of features that encourage luxury to challenge itself. However, there is no guarantee that these young people's consumption habits will continue in the future or will be the same when the youth generation is old enough to consume more than perfumes and fashion accessories. Nevertheless, in this chapter, I showed that capitalizing on the youth generation allows luxury brands to expose their products differently, to transmit their codes with more naturalness and ease, and to diffuse their story in a distinctive way. Indeed, having stronger expectations, millennials and post-millennials tend to redefine the codes of luxury toward exclusive luxury, transparent, authentic, experiential, emotional, and shareable moments.

Is Luxury Experience Compatible with CSR?

11

In the spirit of many, luxury and sustainable development are especially opposed. Indeed, where sustainable development often advocates sobriety and simplicity, luxury refers rather to the image of abundance and complexity. Yet, the world of luxury is not necessarily antithetical to that of sustainable development. Looking more closely, luxury is also (and perhaps above all) quality products that are timeless, transmittable, and sustainable over time and developed from know-how excellence. In a way, luxury is, therefore, an alternative to the logic of disposable and programmed obsolescence, which is in contrast to the overconsumption that characterizes our societies and their ecological issues. There are bridges between sustainable development and luxury. To produce additional bridges in a more sustainable way, one can draw inspiration from luxury and its ability to create quality products that are resistant and elegant but functional. And luxury can also be enriched with sustainable development ideas to produce better-rationalized costs, secure supplies, and take advantage of the circular economy.

In addition, consumers are increasingly attracted to sustainable development trends. And this is good because the luxury industry is seizing these trends: more and more brands and designers are now combining "luxury" with "sustainable and responsible" development. This chapter explores the sustainable practices of luxury houses and the corporate social responsibility (CSR) strategies they implement to create sustainable and engaged luxury experiences. In this chapter, I emphasize the compatibility of ethical/sustainable and luxury consumption from a luxury house's perspective as well as the consumer's point of view. This dual perspective provides an understanding of ethical/sustainable luxury production and consumption with guidance on how to promote ethical/sustainable luxury businesses to achieve green and social luxury.

© Springer Nature Switzerland AG 2019
W. Batat, *The New Luxury Experience*, Management for Professionals,
https://doi.org/10.1007/978-3-030-01671-5_11

11.1   Luxury Experience and CSR

In recent years, corporate social responsibility (CSR) has become a strategic issue for businesses and a topic of study for researchers in different disciplines. CSR invites luxury houses and brands to rethink their strategies in the broader perspective of their relations with society as well as the environment in terms of sustainable development. Under the institutional and social pressure, the majority of luxury companies are now setting up a range of actions and strategies oriented toward social responsibility with the initial aim of responding to a problem of image vis-à-vis stakeholders and their customers.

Therefore, the definition of CSR relies on two core ideas according to which luxury companies have responsibilities that go beyond the pursuit of profit and the respect of the law that involves not only shareholders, but all parties related to the company's activities. Several conceptual frameworks have been defined by scholars to explore the relationships companies have with these new actors. Among them, Sobczak and Berthoin Antal (2010) identified three main approaches: contractual theory, institutional theory, and stakeholder theory. This last theory has become, today, an essential reference for practitioners when we talk about the operationalization of CSR in the luxury sector.

Mini-case 11.1

Rolex CSR through awards for enterprise

Rolex is a company that stands behind sustainability, and because of that, in 1976, the watch brand offered a sustainability award program that honors individual acts of courage and kindness. It was created to encourage sustainability by expanding knowledge and improving life. These individual acts improve human lives and preserve cultural heritage as well as protect the nature and environment.

The five areas that Rolex Awards support are the environment, science and health, technology, cultural heritage, and exploration. This program boosts improvements in corporate social responsibility through various forms of creative ideas turned into reality and also promotes the idea that Rolex has the ability to be environmentally responsible and act in a sustainable manner.

The stakeholder theory applied to the implementation of CSR refers to the identification of different stakeholders and the collection of their expectations. The foundations of this CSR approach are based on the logic of a "stakeholder orientation" of the company's strategy and are considered an extension of the "market/customer orientation" (Kohli and Jaworski 1990; Narver and Slater 1990). This CSR approach takes into account the expectations of different actors and re-entrench the company in society. Yet, overall, it should be noted that CSR remains eminently complex and unclear not only for the practitioner but also, and especially, for the consumer who is exposed to many messages carrying societal commitments whose relevance is not obvious to verify. It, therefore, seems important to examine how consumers perceive the concept of CSR in its entirety and how they assess the social responsibility practices implemented by luxury houses while checking to see if this perception influences the reputation of luxury brands.

11.1.1 What Is CSR?

The CSR is not a new concept; it dates back to the late nineteenth century in the United States and has been in the process of being reconfigured for 15 years in a context where traditional modes of regulation are being questioned. This renewal is characterized by a growing internalization of CSR in management practices and by the rise of new markets of social responsibility. Yet, CSR is often confused with sustainable development. This is because sustainable development offers a pragmatic approach to CSR. It is then easier for organizations to refer to them in order to define their CSR actions.

Although the concept of CSR is fully recognized in academia, the absence of a consensual definition does not facilitate its implementation. Indeed, since the first work published by Bowen (1953), CSR has generated a vast current of studies and led to different conceptions inherited from distinct historical and cultural contexts. Additionally, the hybrid definition of the concept combined with that of sustainable development is far from being shared in all cultural settings. Researchers have identified three distinct conceptions of CSR: the first inherited from paternalism, the second strategic and utilitarian, and a third conception related to the concept of sustainability. In line with previous works, recent studies identify four approaches indicating that the dynamics of CSR are part of a disputed field:

- The first perspective gives primacy to the shareholder and is based on the idea that if markets are efficient, societal well-being will result.
- The second perspective refers to the "voluntarism of the stakeholders," highlighting the profitability and the "business case" of CSR, that is to say, the perfect reconciliation of the objectives of the triple bottom line (people, planet, and profit).
- The third perspective, based on co-regulation, relies on a process of institutionalization of CSR and on a potential conflict of actors.
- The fourth perspective is part of the mainstream of global public goods, with solidarity and sustainable development being the main values of this scenario.

Nowadays, many works in management science often refer to the utilitarian rationality of CSR and the organizational process that results from it. Both academia and practitioners have focused on the relationships between CSR and business performance (e.g., Barnett 2007; Orlitzky et al. 2003). More specifically, as

Siltaoja (2006) points out, the question of the societal legitimacy of the company and the competitive advantages results from socially responsible actions. In addition to exploring the links between financial performance and societal performance, the interactions between CSR and corporate reputation have been the subject of many recent works, including the luxury field.

According to these works, the reputation of an organization comes from the assembly of all the images that have been built as time goes on among different audiences. It may or may not result from the company's stated strategy and is based on a series of experiences with the company and past and present actions. Thus, the time factor is the main distinguishing element of the notions of reputation and corporate image. Indeed, reputations are relatively stable and durable and are distilled over time from multiple images (Rindova 1997). A company's reputation is similar to how the organization is perceived by all its stakeholders and its ability to create value compared to its competitors. Therefore, a company's reputation is a "multi-stakeholder" concept because it encompasses all the perceptions received and generated by them, including the consumers' perceptions. Despite the growing interest in CSR and corporate reputation, interactions between these two concepts do not seem to be clearly identified.

- For some authors, CSR is considered an antecedent of the good reputation of the company. Therefore, the implementation of a strategic CSR approach, the standardization of CSR within the company, the proliferation of philanthropic donations, or the dialogue with stakeholders facilitate the building of a CSR strategy and thus a good reputation for the company.
- For others, CSR is viewed as an intrinsic attribute or dimension of reputation. Following this logic, Fombrun (1996, 1998, 2005) establishes the construction of a company's reputation based on six criteria: financial performance, product quality, employee treatment, community involvement, environmental actions, and organizational performance.

Exploring CSR in the luxury field leads us then to consider a form of complementarity regarding these two concepts taken from the stakeholder/consumer perspective: each of the two notions (antecedent or attribute) can be considered as two sides of the same concept.

11.1.2 Is CSR a Function of Marketing?

Marketing literature has incorporated the dimensions of CSR for a long time but with a fragmented approach oriented toward the social requirements of the function of marketing (e.g., Kotler and Lee 2005; Kotler and Levy 1969) or toward the ethical decision-making of managers (e.g., Hunt and Vitell 1986), emphasizing the essential role of the cultural and social environment or the need for adapted organizational processes. These numerous works laid the conceptual foundations for a CSR approach to marketing but without exploring the corporate responsibilities of the firm as a global entity. Many studies also focus on limited dimensions of this construct, reinforcing the idea of fragmentation, for example, corporate environmental marketing or marketing related to great causes (e.g., Varadarajan and Menon 1988). This work establishes itself as the first step toward internal integration of the values of responsibility but focuses little on the deepening of the relations with the customers and the markets and on the holistic consideration of the concept.

The current CSR in its overall conceptual perspective is taken into account in marketing work (e.g., Maignan and Ferrel 2004, 2005). It appears as a response adapted to the increased complexity of markets and exchange processes. This conceptualization was reflected in 2004 when the AMA (American Marketing Association) integrated the concept of stakeholders in the definition of marketing by specifying its role as "a set of processes to create, communicate, and deliver value to customers and customer relationship management so that the whole organization and the stakeholders benefit from it."

The marketing function is then identified as a lever for disseminating the CSR strategy to the entire organization and stakeholders, in particular, by collecting feedback from them and orchestrating communication on CSR initiatives. This perception of marketing through the prism of CSR is not trivialized and still needs to be further developed. It, nonetheless, identifies particular strategic approaches with two emerging corporate typologies:

- One developing ad hoc responsible marketing strategies, which often take place in entrepreneurial or market-creating contexts. In this case, the marketing approach is aligned with the company's strategy and responds to the social, ethical, fair, or global environmental projects.
- Another is the development of action plans targeted at certain brands or products, which are often fragmentary, one-dimensional, or isolated, but which may also be the first step in a CSR approach. The objective is to develop a product offer or a communication tied to this trend, without overhauling all decisions and action plans, for example, the designing of a green product range, appending a societal label on a brand, creating an advertising campaign highlighting environmental claims, or developing humanitarian sponsorship.

In practice, the successive scandals of the last two decades highlighting the social irresponsibility of certain popular brands, such as Nike, Gap, or Exxon as well as some luxury brands using endangered species in their product manufacturing, have been accompanied by a deterioration of the reputational capital of these companies. In order to consolidate or strengthen their reputation, luxury brands have reactively or more proactively initiated CSR initiatives under the pressure of stakeholders by applying a consumer-centric approach and providing customers with a sustainable as well as a socially responsible luxury experience.

Mini-case 11.2

Gucci, the first luxury house to introduce CSR

Gucci was one of the first companies in the luxury industry to voluntarily initiate a corporate social responsibility certification process for its entire production cycle. According to the brand, this certification stands for values such as business ethics, respect for human rights, workers' health and safety, and equal opportunities.

1. *Animal and environment-friendly*. Luxury brands have become a natural target of animal rights activists and environmental campaigners due to their fur coats and crocodile bags. However, when it comes to precious skins and furs, Gucci brand products come from 100% "verified captive-breeding operations or from wild, sustainably managed populations," where suppliers employ accepted animal welfare practices. Additionally, the Gucci Eyeweb collection, known as the two bio-based glasses, focuses environmental issues and is made naturally from castor-oil seeds. Gucci is also taking steps toward making its packaging more environmentally friendly by sending packages to a dedicated center where it may be recycled to make new products.

2. *Philanthropy*. Gucci is particularly active in philanthropy relating to women's issues and girl's education. Gucci has donated more than $10 million to UNICEF during an 8-year partnership through a mix of charitable donations, which aim to provide access to quality education for millions of children in partnership with women, such as Beyoncé, Salma Hayek, Halle Berry, and Jennifer Lopez. Gucci also supports the Kering Corporate Foundation for Women's Dignity and Rights, which fights violence against women and promotes their empowerment by supporting community-based projects and encouraging employee involvement to sustain women's causes around the world.

3. *Contribution to socioeconomic development*. Gucci is committed to promoting, protecting, and improving the quality of life and the socioeconomic development of local, national, and international communities by supporting the creation of opportunities for the growth and development of craftsmanship skills and by promoting the development of local industries, knowledge transference, and the development of local professionals.

4. *Employment standards and relationships with stakeholders*. Gucci promotes employment standards that respect workers' rights, trade union agreements, and the principles of safeguards for workers in the Gucci system, effectively guaranteeing the exercise of freedom of association and the right to collective bargaining. Gucci rejects all forms of child labor, forced labor, and discrimination, ensuring that all workers have the same opportunities in terms of employment and career development. In addition, Gucci is committed to developing and pursuing a dialogue with its stakeholders based on fairness and transparency in the belief that they represent a key asset of the company, which should be promoted and developed.

11.1.3 Considering CSR Through the "Stakeholder/Consumer Experience" Approach

The integration of the stakeholder theory into the customer experience approach emphasizes the idea that marketing strategies should essentially be built on one stakeholder: the customer, by focusing more on his/her expectations, satisfaction, and loyalty. Companies should also take a global perspective while focusing on the customer to avoid customer myopia which is generated by a single goal in mind: the client with an exclusion of other stakeholders, a narrow definition of the customer and his/her needs, and the lack of consideration of the societal context of the company that requires taking into account all stakeholders. This attitude, which is considered myopia, led marketers to study the clients under the lens of the buyer's or consumer's unique behaviors and traits, forgetting that the consumer could be, at the same time, an employee, a citizen, member of an association, shareholder, or simply one who feels part of a "global village" (e.g., Smith et al. 2010).

At the same time, stakeholders other than consumers, such as members of associations, NGOs, scientific experts, and local authorities, have generally been ignored or simply considered by marketing managers as adversaries (e.g., Spar and La Mure 2003). Today, several studies are moving toward a more complete definition of the stakeholder profile to guide marketing strategies, distinguishing different groups of customers and their experiences according to their importance for the company along with the types of competitors. More direct approaches involve the client in a collaborative approach by evoking the idea of a client-partner relationship. Furthermore, many studies attempt to decipher consumer behavior by relating it to terms such as citizenship through the currents of ecological consumption, socially responsible, or ethical behaviors. These works deepen the notions of a consumer-citizen, ethical consumer, and socially responsible consumer dimension but remain focused on a utilitarian approach aimed at distinguishing new consumer profiles, consumption patterns, and purchasing behaviors. However, they also allow justifying a more global reflection on the intrusion of collective, social, and societal facets in the experience that a customer has with the company.

While recognizing customer experience orientation as a key concept in marketing strategy, researchers have positioned customers as the strategic stakeholder, thus omnipotent, which allows brands to create a shared value. Therefore, the adoption of the "stakeholder/consumer experience" theory invites the company not to focus solely on two types of stakeholders, i.e., customers and members of journeys and networks, but to be open to a multitude of actors that are directly or indirectly involved in the overall consumption experience. This includes more global notions, such as stakeholder communities, stakeholder norms, and the power of stakeholders. While much of the current thinking holds that actors are distinct and mutually exclusive, boundaries can become easily porous.

This perspective allows us to highlight the potential tensions and synergies generated by the networks of individuals and the interconnections between them within a particular sociocultural setting. This urges consumer researchers and businesses to commit to more comprehensive CSR and stakeholder guidance with a greater focus on the whole customer experience from a holistic perspective, which will be beyond the mere transactional relationship between an individual buyer and a supplier of goods and services.

11.2   Designing CSR Luxury Experiences

In early 2000, large luxury groups, such as LVMH, Pernod Ricard, and Rothschild Bank, joined the United Nations Global Compact for Development and Responsible Economic Growth. A couple of years after, in 2006, the WWF (World Wide Fund for Nature) published the report "Deeper Luxury," which was based on the survey of ten luxury companies that emphasized the contradictions of the luxury sector, which should be compatible with the principles of CSR and sustainable development.

Mini-case 11.3

Prada's implementation of CSR policies

As part of its corporate social responsibility, Prada puts an emphasis on respecting people by paying close attention to the professional satisfaction of its employees and by understanding the changes in the society and in the market. Prada has also committed itself to the environment by reducing its environmental impact and relying more on energy efficiency, use of renewable energy, and reduction of waste and paper.

Among the cases of luxury brands that embraced CSR and implemented it through different approaches, products, communication campaigns, and strategies, we can cite the following examples:

- The case of Hermes and the launch of its new Chinese brand Shang Xia to support local craftsmanship in China while offering a modern reinterpretation of authentic know-how.
- Loewe Madrid, (LVMH Group) with its new ambassador, Pénélope Cruz, who is a member of PETA (NGO that focuses on animals' welfare), organizes for its designers responsible creation workshops to enhance the fact that ecology goes together with creativity. These workshops display new ecological materials, explaining the recycling of fur and the reuse of leather scrap or the use of local materials.
- For brands such as Stella McCartney, Calvin Klein, Vivienne Westwood, Ralph Lauren, Tommy Hilfiger, or Adolfo Dominguez, the introduction of CSR practices is supported by the decision to ban all kinds of animal fur from their collections.

- Gucci launched in March 2013 a new line of glamorous and responsible handbags, proving that it is possible to make leather products while having positive impact on the environment, farmers, and their communities and without mistreating animals: the leather used, which comes from breeding farms in the Amazon, has been certified "Rainforest Alliance," which aims to preserve biodiversity and ensure the employees' well-being and gives local people decent working conditions and means of sustenance by transforming agricultural practices.
- For the Italian brand Fendi, the creation of Carmina Campus, a line of precious handbags made from recycled materials, was also used to support families in Africa.
- Saint Laurent, through its artistic designer Stefano Pilati, presented a capsule collection titled New Vintage III, new creations that have been made of unused textiles from previous collections. Saint Laurent initiated a new concept of sustainable creation and recycling which is at the heart of its creative process, to reinterpret the classics of the luxury house.
- In luxury hotels and palaces, CSR and sustainable thinking are also considered. For example, in Bristol, many actions have been taken, such as using a thermal dehydrator that processes kitchen waste (including at three-star restaurants) to get reusable water from washing the floor and the dry matter, the remnants of which becomes a fertilizer – all further reducing waste. As such, Fouquet's Barrière has also become the first five-star Paris hotel to have been awarded the triple certification related to the three pillars of a sustainable strategy: ISO 9001 (quality), ISO 14001 (environment), and SA 8000 (social). Furthermore, other international palaces, such as China's Shangri-La, also integrated social and environmental aspects into its organizational culture targeting both employees and customers.
- In jewelry, the luxury house Cartier is one of the founding members and the first certified member of RJC (Responsible Jewelry Council) that focuses on mining, metal production, and precious minerals. Although it is a noble gesture, this is primarily to protect the reputation of the jewelery and ensure the durability of its supply chain.

Therefore, associations such as ECRA (Ethical Consumer Research Association) have required luxury houses to be at the same level as mainstream brands in terms of transparency and commitment. For example, Greenpeace launched a luxury fashion challenge with its "Fashion Duel" campaign that focuses on sustainable and social aspects related to three segments of the luxury fashion chain supply: leather, wrapping paper, and textile production. Why should one care about CSR in luxury? Is CSR only used to protect the reputation of luxury brands or does it have other social and ethical implications?

The use of CSR in the luxury sector refers to two main approaches that support and justify the positive impact of CSR on luxury houses' profits. While the first approach establishes a positive link between CSR and profit by an increase in total productivity factors, the second justifies this positive link between CSR and profit by the gains in terms of image and brand reputation (e.g., Preston and O'Bannon 1997). Almost all studies emphasize an ambiguous relationship between two factors: social responsibility and performance (e.g., Salzmann et al. 2005). Yet, some authors indicate that there is no direct link between immediate profit and CSR. Though, CSR could serve as a shock absorber in the event of a negative shock for the company, in particular, shock that affects its reputation. CSR is, therefore, seen here as a defense against reputational risk. This would explain difficulties in finding a direct link between profit and CSR, this link being, in fact, very indirect and not immediate. In the luxury sector, CSR would be linked to the safeguarding of profit in the long term. Yet, there are some paradoxes related to luxury and CSR that make the implementation of a sustainable strategy complex and expensive.

11.2.1 The Paradoxes of Luxury and Sustainable Development

If luxury is described as unique, innovative, inscribed in the long-term, cultivating beauty and excellence, thanks to its ancestral know-how, it can also be described as elitist, superfluous, excessive – there would be no lean luxury – ever accused of indecency. The question that logically arises when it comes to combining sustainable development and luxury is that of the impossible marriage of these two universes, which in theory are the antipodes of one another. Indeed, among the elements that oppose luxury's sustainable development, we can cite the following:

- Luxury is defined as the opposite of necessity, whereas sustainable development focuses on the essentials.
- Luxury is only about the intrinsic quality of its products, whereas sustainable development thinking is only related to social and environmental quality.
- Sustainable development is a recent paradigm, but luxury is ancestral.
- Sustainable development questions and provokes the transparency, while luxury cultivates its secrets.
- Sustainable development explains everything, whereas luxury is mysterious, so magical, and that is how it makes consumer dream.

But can luxury houses sell dreams and beauty by destroying the planet? Can they relocate to reduce costs when profits are huge? Can luxury be transparent while cultivating its secrets? There are many luxury brands that not only believe in this unlikely marriage but also carry it in their DNA. Luxury items last a long time and are transmitted among generations. They consume in the long run fewer resources than more disposable products. Is it not Hermes, the quintessence of luxury that affirms it? Luxury is also what we repair. The ecological issue, for example, one of the three pillars of sustainable development along with the economic and social pillars, may be the result of the consumption of products with short life cycles, such as fashionable clothing and impulsive consumption stimulated by low prices beyond the moral commitment that we are entitled to expect or demand from a sector where cost is not a question. Luxury meets, in essence, the stakes of preservation of resources and know-how advocated by sustainable development.

According to François-Henri Pinault, the CEO of Kering, the impetus for sustainable luxury should come from companies that have to make green products the new standard. It is then obvious and inevitable that sustainable development will be part of the future of luxury rather than waiting for consumers to develop sustainable and social development responsibility on their own. Even though, if nowadays, the consideration of sustainable development by the luxury industry is not yet a reason for investment or loyalty, its non-consideration can eventually become a motive for its rejection by consumers. In light of this, even historic luxury brands could, indeed, have their territory taken by emerging alternative luxury brands with the desired sustainable vocation. Thus, no matter how motivated luxury brands are to engage in sustainable development, whether ethical or cynical, sincere or strategic, the essential thing remains consistent: the right answer is that they should give to a world in crisis and respond to emerging consumer trends.

Testimonial 11.1

Karen Olivo, Founder and CEO at LUC8K Ltd: The sustainable luxury experience of LUC8K luxury leather bags and accessories

1. How does LUC8K enhance and reinvent customer experience?

LUC8K is for "lifestyle-aficionados" that know what they want: We release sustainable luxury products that customers connect to and will be around for years to come. We are all about storytelling. The LUC8K brand experience is all about traveling, suspense, and action. Sustainable lifestyle is new luxury. "Self-made," "self-assertive," and "selective" are the key. Self-expression is part of LUC8K. We are not into trends. We set them and so do our customers who are seeking for brands that are socially responsible and environmentally conscious. Our mind-set is to target customers who buy their own style and who enjoy to customize their luxury leather accessory.

We tap the digital opportunity as direct-to-consumer brand and sell primarily through our luc8k.com website online. The Internet enables us to tell interesting and multi-faced stories with digital content as well as social-media-friendly visuals. Our distinctive voice is to build the relationship with our customers right at the start: At LUC8K you make your "own" luxury leather bag and accessory! In that sense LUC8K is not just a product you buy, but rather a digitally enabled experience that makes you actively participate in the brand.

(continued)

Testimonial 11.1 (continued)

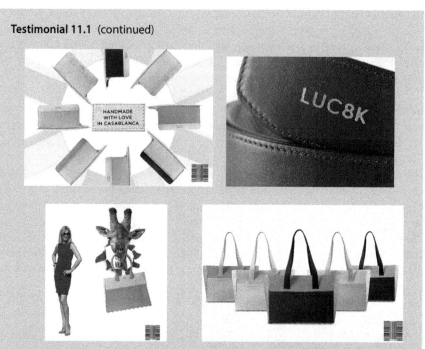

At LUC8K we create value that connects: In addition to providing bespoke luxury and reliable quality, LUC8K has cemented itself as a fun brand with great personality thanks largely to the use of its mascot, Sophie. The 15-foot giraffe is depicted traveling the globe with her LUC8K bags and accessories, showcasing the products as well as the company's charm that consumers of all backgrounds can identify with. That sense of resonating with the audience is additionally shown by the fact that all buyers are treated as ambassadors of the company. After all, by designing a handbag or accessory, the customer has played an active role in the company's continued journey.

2. How can you define LUC8K luxury experience?

The LUC8K luxury experience is a private and personal experience for customers, both when choosing, making, and wearing their own product. LUC8K offers sustainable luxury goods that inspire, stimulate, and excite those who create and wear them. Wearing a LUC8K makes you stand out of the crowd. A LUC8K bag is a unique outward statement of a woman's mindset and lifestyle. The customized LUC8K look includes clear and clean lines and a combination of functionality, quality, and craftsmanship.

(continued)

Testimonial 11.1 (continued)

LUC8K experience is everything from the handmade product to the door-to-door experience. Taking full advantages of the efficiencies of international supply and manufacturing chains to produce the leather goods using sustainable practices throughout the process, right down to the packaging that the products are mailed in, are aspects of the luxury brand experience. In truth, though, the luxury handmade handbags speak for themselves. The bespoke creations are crafted with care in Casablanca, Morocco, using the finest leathers. Not only is each product unique and designed with incredible attention to detail, but they also allow buyers to participate in creating a leather handbag that meet their specific tastes.

In addition to choosing colors, clients of the brand choose a unique four-digit code, which appears alongside the logo. LUC8K's decision to add that four-digit code serves as another element that underpins the brand's attention to detail, practicality, and ability to establish its place in the bespoke fashion market. Apart from adding that sense of personalization, the brand logo itself is stylized to replicate the idea of airport baggage codes. Moreover, the four letters of the ICAO airport code added to the four-digit personal lucky number selected by the user creates the number "8" of the LUC8K brand logo. Eight is our lucky number because turned to its side it symbolizes infinity and symbiosis – the process of achieving harmony within a community of individuals. This symbol serves as a testament toward our desire to work with our customers and seamlessly bring your dream products to life. Turned sideways 8 is the symbol for infinity ∞ LUC8K's signature belt buckle design. LUC8K customer experience is passion. We inspire new combinations based on the passion found within our sustainable lifestyle community.

3. How does LUC8K use experience offline and online to help reach luxury shoppers?

Humans cannot be automated like social media algorithms. Society and values will become a form of information and intelligence described as emotions that will affect everything from purchasing decisions to how we influence others. Offline experience such as delivery service is hard to control. We can influence them by choosing the right outside partners. However, as in the very basic nature of how LUC8K started, transparency is key to our customer experience. Our delivery partners offer tracking and safe to open the door delivery service, but let's face it the moments outside of our immediate control unfortunately can cause friction.

(continued)

Testimonial 11.1 (continued)

Our shoppers experience luxury primarily digital. Word-of-mouth recommendations and what people talk to people about us is that what matters. Pop-up stores and selected retail will act as sensorial touchpoints, as unfortunately you can't touch the Internet. We use primarily online experience to thrive on the basis of storytelling. We don't sell a product. We sell a service that has a story to tell. Our customers discover LUC8K on their terms, by staying online.

4. **How do you define the digital strategy and UX of LUC8K on mobile phone? Do you use digital devices in store to enhance customer experience? How?**

Our website is responsive, easy to use on mobile. We do not use an app since customers would need to download an app and this puts customers off, as they have many apps on their phone already. So our website is built responsive to be viewed on any mobile device out there, from tablets to phones. In store we use tablets that display an offline version of our entire collection that can be customized. That being said, most of the customers walk out with a pre-customized LUC8K that are part of our limited collection we offer on demand with selected retail only. That's the on-the-dot purchase feeling the Internet can't provide.

5. **How can digital and sustainability help you to create the true luxury experience targeting millennials?**

The #whomademyclothes is the latest kin-of-fashion revolution *hashtag* expressing the demand for #sustainablefashion. Millennials are a state of mind, not just an age group. Their customer behavior influences across generations and is greatly influencing consumer habits of future generations, too. Basically, they want to save the planet! Our LUC8K digital strategy however runs counter to prevailing industry trends. LUC8K customers influence sustainable luxury by building trust with a large group of sustainable luxury influential individuals who build a community of sustainable lifestyle lovers that seek value for their money.

LUC8K experience is about sustainable luxury and authentic content. We are a niche brand with major ambitions! We act in a sustainable way, and we stimulate our community by taking them along with Sophie our mascot who travels the world, exhibiting her style, having fun, and pontificating on sustainability and other issues. LUC8K democratizes luxury. LUC8K is not a

(continued)

Testimonial 11.1 (continued)

statement bag of your earning power. LUC8K is an expression of social independence. Customization becomes accessible through the Internet, and your personal luxury lifestyle shopping affordable. With bags and accessories starting at around $70, the LUC8K price tag isn't nearly as exclusive as the products themselves. Even at higher end of the scale, around $2,000, items are appropriately priced given the quality and attention to detail.

Hiring "influencers" with a heavy "followership" and "likes" on social media to increase perception is not part of our strategy nor vision. On a long run, we believe that paid engagement from individuals with large social audience will lose their influence as they dilute the real purpose of influencing a community to the positive when driven by commercial reasons. LUC8K has come a long way since opening its digital doors in 2016, providing men and women around the world with the personalized luxury that they deserve. With the latest collection of colors and design options, we take that sustainable luxury to a new level, and the journey has just begun.

11.2.2 The Reputation of Luxury and CSR

Certainly, the reputation of luxury houses is considered an intangible asset that is often attached to the prestige of the brand. In the luxury sector, this asset can reach extremely high values. For example, the Louis Vuitton brand was valued at $33.6 billion by Forbes in 2018. Furthermore, a CSR policy can help luxury brands control the level of sales in the event of a reputation crisis. This control has a cost since it is necessary to conduct actions or even global strategies to establish the legitimacy of actions in CSR. This cost is considered as a cover that the firm should pay to protect itself against a possible deterioration of its reputation (intangible asset) and, therefore, of its future sales.

The hedging behavior will also vary according to the starting value of the intangible asset: the firms holding the trademarks, such as luxury houses, which should be more sensitive to the need for coverage because their intangible value is greater. Thus, firms whose intangible assets, reputation, have the most value, such as luxury brands, are willing to pay more to cover these assets. In the same way, if the risk increases, the price of the hedge against this risk also increases. It is logical that firms are ready to pay the price of the increase. So, how do companies in the luxury sector implement CSR policies to protect their reputations and gain benefit out of it?

We can agree that luxury is qualitative and belongs to the repertoire of hedonism beyond that of functionality. It is a multisensory experience that is not consumed but is lived in relation to a social and cultural context, has a strong creative content (craftsmanship and/or artistic), and is characterized by a dual dimension, which is both aesthetic and ethical. More than any other sector, luxury produces cultural symbols and expresses what is most socially desirable.

As a consequence, nothing in the process of social stratification opposes CSR in regard to luxury where progress is judged by certain elements regarded as essential for most of society, including the prohibition of child labor and the protection of the environment. Furthermore, luxury houses should position themselves in the perspective of CSR from an ethical point of view beyond the paradox and the model of the future driven by luxury. To understand how companies build the link between luxury and CSR, there is a need to examine the process of reputation building of luxury brands in terms of CSR and how it evolves over time.

11.3   The Evolution of the CSR Policies to Offer Luxury Experiences

The rise of the concept of sustainable development can be traced back to 1972 at the conference of the United Nations in Stockholm under the term "ecodevelopment." In 1992, at the Rio Summit, 182 states together develop a common agenda for sustainable development. During this period, only LVMH, L'Oreal, and AccorHotels Groups adopted practices related to sustainable development. Commitments focused on preserving the natural environment in sectors that are sensitive to environmental issues: wines and spirits, tourism, and cosmetics. Actions and programs targeted the entire value chain.

Yet, the consumer was not involved, as is the case in the consumer goods sector. Employees and suppliers were the training targets considered for developing new skills and responding adequately to new requirements. In 2007, the luxury sector committed to a social and environmental responsibility approach with the aim of meeting the expectations of the various stakeholders of the company: employees, customers, suppliers, and civil society. The entire supply chain was organized to meet CSR criteria and limit the environmental impact of distribution, stores, and infrastructure as well as to increase consumer awareness through responsible products and practices.

Unlike LVMH, the strategy adopted focuses on both environmental and social objectives; the CSR approach consists of raising awareness and motivating the different entities of the group through training, skills development, and social dialogue. The process involves implementing working groups to recruit and involve different levels and organizational actors of the company. In addition, the other major French luxury brands, such as Hermes and Chanel, have adopted a progressive approach starting with the transformation of a part of their value chain. In the jewelry sector, Cartier (Richemont group) was in favor of the traceability of diamonds and precious materials used in the manufacture of jewelry but did not exercise a strict control of provenances. In this respect, NGOs remain very strict on the gold and diamond sectors and consider the commitments insufficient in view of the social and environmental impacts of this activity. Alongside the big luxury groups, young designers entering the luxury sector are engaging in strategies integrating sustainable development into the DNA of their brands and in the overall design of the value chain of their sector.

The case of LVMH is specific in terms of undertaking sustainable development. This leading luxury group is very diverse and must respond to many different issues. It is an asset for its developmental strategy to be socially responsible. Indeed, LVMH among other luxury businesses was part of the Carbon Disclosure Project and committed to greenhouse gas (GHG) emission reduction plans that included quantified targets and communications on this subject, thus encompassing different aspects to the implementation of the CSR approach.

The analysis of discourses and practices of luxury businesses offers an understanding of how they are constructing a CSR reputation around three main actions. First, the legitimization of CSR actions is a prerequisite for building a reputation. The two concepts are related but distinct: a chronology is generally observed in the deployment of actions in CSR to achieve a hierarchy of modes of legitimization from pragmatic, then cognitive, acceptability to the moral legitimacy of actions in CSR. Thus, the commitment of luxury brands to a CSR approach is generally justified by economic arguments and the rationality of management; training, charters, and codes are then aimed at anchoring CSR in the culture of the company. Second, luxury businesses can develop a communication campaign about their moral commitments to society. The luxury houses are, thus, much more cautious in the use of discourses emphasizing CSR. Third, greenwashing would be for luxury houses much more at risk in terms of image risk and reputation than brands from other sectors.

Therefore, before building any reputation based on a CSR approach, there is a need for luxury brands to master, internally, the process of its implementation and thus ensure the effectiveness of its integration into the value chain as well as into its performance. The credibility and legitimacy of the action do not depend only on downstream marketing luxury companies; they should also evolve from protection to value creation. CSR should be used as a tool for luxury businesses that is more than a search for the protection of the reputation. It should represent a willful transformation of all or part of the enterprise value chain; this is especially the case of luxury brands whose sector is integrated.

Mini-case 11.4

Chopard, the journey to sustainable luxury

The journey started with the launch of the Green Carpet Collection at Cannes Film Festival in the year 2013. The Fair mined gold was what this new high jewelry collection relied on, leading to a new era both for Chopard and the entire sector. In partnership with the Eco-Age, the main focus of the journey concentrated on issues like respectful sourcing and traceability of raw materials which will help in setting new standards for jewelry and watchmaking. The journey started with a relationship with the Alliance for Responsible Mining (ARM) NGO, which aims at improving the lives of artisanal gold miners who work in small communities by supplying education, training, and social welfare.

The first luxury watch and jewelry company supported the mining communities to get the fair mined certification which will help miners get fair deals during the sale of golds. A segregation process was initiated in Geneva workshops to ensure the traceability of the fair mined gold. The High Jewellery Green Carpet Collections are created through dedicated processes and according to the Green Carpet Challenge Benchmarking. The reason why the creations are special is that they have a story to tell which have attracted many actresses like Marion Cotillard.

11.4   Summary

This chapter focuses on the sustainable dimension of luxury experience and the corporate social responsibility (CSR) policies that luxury houses should implement to adapt themselves to challenges in sustainability and thus create green luxury. Since luxury brands carry cultural symbols and create social distinction, it is interesting to note that they should first master the fabric of CSR prior to being able to communicate a responsible external image. However, their image does not entirely belong to them, and particularly stakeholders, NGOs, and ethical rating agencies have had a great influence in accelerating commitments and the necessary voice of luxury players. This chapter shows that the reputation of luxury brands is the result of the process of manufacturing both internally (through discourses and techniques) and externally (through communication) under the influence of other environmental stakeholders (price, ethical rating, rankings, NGOs, etc.)

Conclusion

This book aims to propose a new definition of luxury with a focus on the experiential aspect of luxury consumption. In this book, I contribute to the new definition of luxury and the transformation of the paradigm from luxury as object to luxury as experience.

The various chapters in this book have offered a deep analysis of luxury experiences and how luxury businesses can design and create the ultimate luxury experience, one that is efficient, profitable, and emotional. The book provides a better understanding of the experiential approach applied to different sectors in the luxury field by offering a strategic framework that can be implemented by luxury houses to design suitable experiences that match the tangible and intangible needs of their customers and thus differentiate themselves through the use of the big five experiential luxury strategies:

- Capturing luxury customer values;
- Experiential branding of luxury;
- Experiential setting design;
- Consumer initiation into luxury;
- Luxury staff training.

For luxury brands, the understanding and the implementation of successful experiential strategies based on the consideration of these five big strategies need to be thought-out and shaped within an evolving context that is characterized by future challenges and new emerging sociocultural consumption trends in the luxury sector.

© Springer Nature Switzerland AG 2019
W. Batat, *The New Luxury Experience*, Management for Professionals,
https://doi.org/10.1007/978-3-030-01671-5

References

Alleérès D (2003) Luxe, stratégies marketing. Economica, première édition 1997, Paris

Allport GW (1942) The use of personal documents in psychological science. Social Science Research Council, New York

Ardelet C, Slavich B, De Kerviler G (2015) Self-referencing narratives to predict consumers' preferences in the luxury industry: A longitudinal study. J Business Research 68(9):2037–2044

Arnould EJ (1998) Daring consumer-orientated ethnography. In: Representing consumers, voices, views and vision. Routledge, London

Barnett M (2007) Stakeholder influence capacity and the variability of financial returns to corporate social responsibility. Acad Manag Rev 32(3):794–816

Batat W (2014) How do adolescents define their own competencies in the consumption field? A portrait approach. Rech Appl Mark 29(1):25–54

Batat W (2015) Changing places and identity construction: Subjective introspection into researcher's personal destination experiences. Int J Cult Tour Hosp Res 9(4):379–387

Batat W (2019) Experiential marketing: Consumer behavior, customer experience, and the 7Es. Routledge, London

Batat W, Wohlfeil M (2009) Getting lost into the wild: Understanding consumers' movie enjoyment through a narrative transportation approach. Adv Consum Res 36:372–377

Baudrillard J (1983) Simulations. Semiotext(e), Los Angeles

Bearden WO, Etzel MJ (1982) Reference group influence on product and brand purchase decisions. J Consum Res 9:183–194

Belk R (1988) Possessions and the extended self. J Consum Res 15(2):139–168

Berry JW (1994) Acculturation and psychological adaptation. In: Bouvry AM, van de Vijver FJR, Schmitz P (eds) Journeys into cross-cultural psychology. Swets and Zeitlinger, Lisse, pp 89–125

Bourdieu P (1979) La distinction: Critique sociale du jugement. Editions de Minuit, Paris

Bowen HR (1953) Social responsibility of the businessman. Harper & Brothers, New York

Brentano F (1973) Psychology from an empirical standpoint. Routledge and Kegan Paul, London

Brown S (1998) Romancing the Market Sex, Shopping and Subjective Personal Introspection. J Mark Manag 14(7):783–798

Campbell J (1949) The Hero with a Thousand Faces. 1st edition, Bollingen Foundation. 2nd edition, Princeton University Press. 3rd edition, New World Library, 2008.

Capron M, Quairel F (2008) L'hybridation des concepts de responsabilité sociale d'entreprise et de développement durable: quels enjeux? Colloque Le développement durable, 20 ans après, Lille, November

Castarède J (2003) Le luxe, Que sais-je? troisième edition (1992), Paris

© Springer Nature Switzerland AG 2019
W. Batat, *The New Luxury Experience*, Management for Professionals,
https://doi.org/10.1007/978-3-030-01671-5

Castadère J (2007) Histoire du luxe en France, des origins à nos jours. Eyrolles, Paris

Castelli AT (2016) The new revolution will be physical, not digital. Advertising age. Available at: http://adage.com/article/digitalnext/revolution-physical-digital/302734/. Accessed 20 June 2017

Castera E, De La Vega O, Douet A, Peénicaud E (2003) Marketing de luxe, existe-t- il un consommateur universel? Marketing international, maîrise des Sciences et Techniques de Commerce International, University de Pau et des pays de l'Adour

Chaffey D, Ellis-Chadwick F (2012) Digital marketing: Strategy, implementation and practice. Pearson, Harlow

Churchill GA, Iacobucci D (eds) (2005) Marketing research: Methodological foundations. South-Western/Thomson Learning, Mason

Day E (1989) Share of heart: What is it and how can it be measured. J Consum Mark 6(1):5–12

Decety J (2004) L'empathie est-elle une simulation mentale de la subjectivité D'Autrui. In: Berthoz A, Jorland G (eds) L'Empathie. Odile Jacob, Paris, pp 53–88

Denegri Knott J, Molesworth M (2010) Digital virtual consumption: Concepts and practices. Consum Mark Cult 13(2):109–113

Dewey J (1964) Why reflective thinking must be an educational aim. John Dewey on Education: Selected Writings, Chicago, pp 210–228

Dion D, Borraz S (2015) Managing heritage brands: A study of the sacralization of heritage stores in the luxury industry. J Retail Consum Serv 22:77–84

Drell L (2014) The experience economy. The American marketing association. Available at: https://www.ama.org/publications/MarketingInsights/Pages/The-Experience-Economy. Accessed 24 June 2016

Dubois B, Duquesne P (1993) The market for luxury goods, income versus culture. Eur J Mark 27(1):35–44

Dubois B, Laurent G (1996) Le luxe par delà les frontières: Une étude exploratoire dans douze pays. Décisions Marketing 9:35–43

Dubois B, Paternault C (1993) Le luxe en Europe: Produits semblables, mais consommateurs très différents. Communication-CB News 328:78–79

Dubois B, Laurent G, Czellar S (2001) Consumer rapport to luxury: Analysing complex and ambivalent attitudes. Les Cahiers de Recherche du Groupe HEC 736:1–56

Easterby-Smith M, Thorpe R, Lowe A (2002) Management research: An introduction. In: London Churchill GA, Iacobucci D (eds) (2005) Marketing research: Methodological foundations. South-Western/Thomson Learning, Mason

Eckert P (1988) Adolescent social structure and the spread of linguistic change. Lang Soc 17(2):183–207

Emigh J (1996) Masked performance: The play of self and other in ritual and theatre. University of Pennsylvania Press, Philadelphia

Firat AF, Sherry JF, Venkatesh A (1994) Postmodernism, marketing and the consumer. Int J Res Mark 11(4):311–316

Firat FA, Nikhilesh D, Venkatesh A (1995) Marketing in a postmodern world. Eur J Mark 29(1):40–56

Fombrun CJ (1996) Reputation: Realizing value from the corporate image. Harvard Business School press, Boston

Fombrun C (1998) Indices of corporate reputation: An analysis of media rankings and social monitor ratings. Corp Reput Rev 1(4):327–340

Fombrun CJ (2005) Building corporate reputation through CSR initiatives: Evolving standards. Corp Reput Rev 8(1):7–11

Freud S (1920) Psychologie des masses et analyse du moi, in Oeuvres completes. Quadrige/PUF, Paris

Frochot I, Batat W (2013) Marketing and designing the tourist experience. Goodfellow Publishers, Oxford, London

Gilmore JH, Pine JB (2002) Customer experience places: The new offering frontier. Strateg Leadersh 30(4):4–11

Gould SJ (1991) The self-manipulation of my pervasive, perceived vital energy through product use: An introspective-praxis perspective. J Consum Res 18(2):194–207

Gould SJ (2012) The emergence of consumer introspection theory (CIT): Introduction to a JBR special issue. J Bus Res 65(4):453–460

Greenson RR (1960) Empathy and its vicissitudes. Int J Psychoanal 41:418–424

Grigorian V, Peterson FE (2014) Designing luxury experience. European business review, Berlin, pp 46–50

Haas CR (1988) Pratique de la publicité. Dunod, Paris

Haire M (1950) Projective techniques in marketing research. J Mark 14(5):649–656

Hill CR (1968) Haire's classic instant coffee study–18 years later. Journal Q 45(3):466–472

Hoffman D, Novak T (2009) Flow online: Lessons learned and future prospects. J Interact Mark 23(1):23–34

Holbrook MB (1986) I'm Hip: An autobiographical account of some musical consumption experiences. Adv Consum Res 13(1):614–618

Holbrook MB (1994) The nature of customer value: An axiology of services in the consumption experience. In: Service quality: New directions in theory and practice. Sage, Thousand Oaks, pp 21–71

Holbrook MB (1997) Borders, creativity, and the State of the Art at the leading edge. J Macromark 17(2):96–112

Holbrook MB, Hirschman EC (1982) The experiential aspects of consumption: Consumer fantasies, feelings, and fun. J Consum Res 9(2):132–140

Holt DB (2004) How brands become icons. Harvard Business School Press, Cambridge

Howard JA, Jagdish SN (1969) The theory of buyer behavior. Wiley, New York

Hunt SD, Vitell S (1986) A general theory of marketing ethics. J Macro Mark 6(1):5–16

Husserl E (1931) Ideas: General introduction to a pure phenomenology. George. Allen & Unwin Ltd, London

Ingwer M (2012) Empathetic marketing: How to satisfy the 6 core emotional needs of your customers. Palgrave Macmillan, Basingstoke

Kapferer JN (2008) The new strategic brand management. Kogan Page, London

Kapferer JN, Bastien V (2015) Luxe oblige. Eyrolles, Paris

Kedzior R (2015) Digital materiality – a phenomenological exploration. In: Diehl K, Yoon C (eds) NA – advances in consumer research volume 43. Association for Consumer Research, Duluth, pp 275–281

Kleinginna PR, Kleinginna AM (1981) A categorized list of motivation definitions, with a suggestion for a consensual definition. Motiv Emot 5(3):263–291

Kohli AK, Jaworski BJ (1990) Market orientation: The constructs, research propositions and managerial implications. J Mark 54:1–18

Kotler P (1986) Principles of marketing. Prentice Hall, Upper Saddle River

Kotler P, Keller K (2006) Marketing management. Prentice Hall, Upper Saddle River

Kotler P, Lee N (2005) Best of Breed: When it comes to gaining a market edge while supporting a social cause, corporate social marketing. Soc Mark Q 11(3,4):91–103

Kotler P, Levy S (1969) Broadening the concept of marketing. J Mark 33(1):10–15

Kotler P, Kartajaya H, Setiawan I (2010) Marketing 3: From products to customers to the human spirit. Wiley, Hoboken

Kozinets RV (2002) The field behind the screen: Using ethnography for marketing research in online communities. J Mark Res 39(1):61–72

Kozinets RV (2010) Netnography: Doing ethnographic research online. Sage publications, London

Kozinets RV (2015) Netnography: Redefined. Sage, London

Kozinets RV, de Valck Wojnicki AC, Wilner SJS (2010) Networked narratives: Understanding word-of-mouth marketing in online communities. J Mark 74(2):71–89

Kretz G, de Valck K (2010) Pixelize me! digital storytelling and the creation of archetypal myths through explicit and implicit self-brand association in fashion and luxury blogs. In: Belk RW (ed) Research in consumer behaviour, vol 12. Emerald Group Publishing Ltd, Bingley, pp 313–329

Lastovicka JL, Murry JP, Joachimsthaler EA (1990) Evaluating the measurement validity of life-style typologies with qualitative measures and multiplicative factoring. J Mark Res 27(1):11–23

Lemon KN, Verhoef VC (2016) Understanding customer experience throughout the customer journey. J Mark 80(6):69–96

Maignan I, Ferrell OC (2004) Corporate social responsibility and marketing: An integrative framework. J Acad Mark Sci 32(1):19–23

Maignan I, Ferrell OC, Ferrell L (2005) A stakeholder model for implementing social responsibility in marketing. Eur J Mark 39(9,10):956–977

Mathwick C, Malhotra N, Rigdon E (2002) The effect of dynamic retail experiences on experiential perceptions of value: An internet and catalog comparison. J Retail 78(1):51–61

McCracken G (1988) The long interview: Á four-step method of qualitative inquiry. SAGE, Newbury Park

McGrath MA, Sherry JF, Levy SJ (1993) Giving voice to the gift: The use of projective techniques to recover lost meaning. J Consum Psychol 2(2):171–192

McLaren K (2013) The art of empathy: A complete guide to life's most essential skill. Sounds True Publishing, Buchanan

Mossberg L (2007) A marketing approach to the tourist experience. Scand J Hosp Tour 11:59–74

Narver JC, Slater SF (1990) The effects of market orientation on business profitability. J Mark 54:20–35

Okonkwo U (2009) Sustaining the luxury brand on the internet. J Brand Manag 16(5,6):302–310

Okonkwo U (2010) Luxury online – styles, systems, strategies. Routledge, London

Orlitzky M, Schmidt FL, Rynes SL (2003) Corporate social and financial performance: A meta-analysis. Organ Stud 24(3):403–441

Osterwalder A, Pigneur Y (2011) Business model nouvelle génération. In: Un guide pour vision-naires, révolutionnaires et challengers. Pearson, Paris

Ozanne JL, Saatcioglu B (2008) Participatory action research. J Consum Res 35(3):423–439

Patterson A (2005) Processes, relationships, settings, products and consumers: The case for quali-tative diary research. Qual Mark Res Int J 8(2):142–156

Phillips W (2015) This is why we cant have nice things: Mapping the relationship between online trolling and mainstream culture. MIT Press, Cambridge

Pine BJ II, Gilmore JH (1998) Welcome to the experience economy. Harv Bus Rev 76(4):97–105

Pine BJ II, Gilmore JH (1999) The experience economy: Work is theatre and every business a stage. Harvard Business School Press, Boston

Preston LE, O'Bannon D (1997) The Corporate Social-Financial Performance Relationship. Bus Soc 36:419–429

Punj G (2012) Consumer decision making on the web: A theoretical analysis and research guide-lines. Psychol Mark 29(10):791–803

Rambo-Ronai C (1992) The reflexive self through narrative: A night in the life of an erotic dancer/researcher. In: Ellis C, Flaherty G (eds) Investigating subjectivity: Research on lived experi-ence. Sage, Newbury Park

Reed ES (1996) The necessity of experience. US: Yale University Press, New Haven

Rigby DK (2014) Digital-physical mashups. Harv Bus Rev 92(9):84–92

Rindova VP (1997) Part VII: Managing reputation: Pursuing everyday excellence: The image cascade and the formation of corporate reputations. Corp Reput Rev 1(2):188–194

Rodaway P (1994) Sensuous geographies: Body, sense, and place. Routledge, London, New York

Rogers C (1980) A way of being. Houghton Mifflin, Boston

Salzmann O, Ionescu-Somers A, Steger U (2005) The business case for corporate sustainability : Literature review and research options. Eur Manag J 23(1):27–36

Schmitt BH (1999) Experiential marketing. The Free Press, New York

Siltaoja ME (2006) Value priorities as combining core factors between CSR and reputation; a qualitative study. J Bus Ethics 68:91–111

Sleeswijk Visser F (2009) Let's put the knowledge in practice! Proceedings of IASDR, International Association of Societies of Design Research, Seoul

Smith NG, Drumwright ME, Gentile MC (2010) The new marketing myopia. J Public Policy Mark 29(1):4–11

Sobczak A, Berthoin Antal A (2010) Nouvelles perspectives sur l'engagement des parties prenantes: enjeux, acteurs, recherches. Revue Management et Avenir 33:117–126

Sorofman J (2014) Agenda overview for customer experience, 2015. Available at: https://www.gartner.com/imagesrv/digital-marketing/pdfs/agenda-overview-for-customer. Accessed 20 June 2017

Spar D, La Mure L (2003) The Power of activism assessing the impact of NGO on global business. Calif Manag Rev 45:78–101

Steinman RB (2009) Projective techniques in consumer research. Int Bull Bus Adm 5:37–45

Thomas MJ (1997) Consumer market research: Does it have validity? Some postmodern thoughts. Mark Intell Plan 15(2):54–59

Tran V, Voyer BG (2013) Teaching note: Chanel: Should the icon of timeless fashion catch up with its time and sell its clothes online? Case Centre 12, case:313–290-8

Varadarajan PR, Menon A (1988) Cause-related marketing: A coalignment of marketing strategy and corporate philanthropy. J Mark 52(3):58–74

Vargo SL, Lusch RF (2006) Service-dominant logic: What it is, what it is not, what it might be. In: Vargo SL, Lusch RF (eds) The service-dominant logic of marketing: Dialog, debate, and directions. Sharpe, Inc, Armonk, pp 43–56

Veblen T (1899) The theory of the leisure class. The Macmillan Company, New York

Venkatesh A, Sherry JF, Firat AF (1993) Postmodernism and the marketing imaginary. Int J Res Mark 10(3):215–223

Vigneron F, Johnson L (2004) Measuring perceptions of brand luxury. Brand Manag 2(6):484–506

Visconti L (2016) Stories are waiting, managers are not: Comprehensive guidance for brand story-making, working paper CCT Conference, Lille, July

Wallendorf M, Brucks M (1993) Introspection in consumer research: Implementation and implications. J Consum Res 20(3):339–359

Watkins R (2015) In: Diehl K, Yoon C (eds) Conceptualising the ontology of digital consumption objects, advances in consumer research, vol 43. Association for Consumer Research, Duluth, pp 275–276

Wohlfeil M, Whelan S (2012) Saved! by Jena Malone: An introspective study of a consumer's fan relationship with a film actress. J Bus Res 65(4):511–519

Woodall T (2003) Conceptualising value for the customer: An attributional, structural and dispositional analysis. Acad Mark Sci Rev 12(1):1–42

Index

© Springer Nature Switzerland AG 2019
W. Batat, *The New Luxury Experience*, Management for Professionals,
https://doi.org/10.1007/978-3-030-01671-5